THE

CHOICE TO

EXCEED OUR

CHRISTIAN

EDUCATION

Dr. Clara J. Ushman

The Choice to Exceed Our Christian Education
Copyright © 2025 by Dr Clara J Ushman

ISBN: 979-8-9945708-0-7 (Paperback)
        979-8-9945708-1-4 (Hardback)
        979-8-9945708-2-1 (E-book)

In loving memory of my spiritual guide, mentor, and lifelong friend: Katie M. Vogel.

CONTENTS

INTRODUCTION

Christian education is an extremely broad topic that has taken centuries to define. Throughout history and even so today, we are in a constant state of evolution. Evolution occurs not only in our society, but especially within the religious world. Today there are numerous world religions that can almost be found on every continent worldwide. Specifically, the purpose of this dissertation is going to be taking a closer look into the world of Christianity. Topics will include Christian history, Christ as the educator, culture, philosophies, global issues, denominational differences, education in the home, community, schools, and also a glimpse into the future.

Chapter 1 will be an overview into what exactly constitutes "Christian education." As with explaining almost anything, there must be an established definition to explain in termed words what is being discussed. The definition of Christian education is rather complex considering it is a two-word phrase that will need to be separated out. What is Christian? How is someone defined as being Christian? A basic answer may be that a Christian is someone who follows Christ. What does this mean to someone who knows about Christ or Christianity in general? Here is where the education part would come in. How is one educated? What tools, ideas, tests, measurements, and methodologies are used to "educate"? Various factors, structures, and developments have occurred over time in which education has grown and evolved, but one important detail remains the same—the learning. Each individual learns at their own pace. Some may be visual learners, meaning education may be easier for them as they are able to visualize or see the material being taught. On the other hand, some people can be audio learners, meaning they learn material stronger by hearing it. These are two of the most obvious examples; but others might include hands-on training, modeling, or shadowing.

In any case, the phrase "Christian education" is going to be explored throughout this book in different chapters that will each explore deeper into a realm under the Christian education umbrella. The thought questions asked in the previous paragraph hopefully sparked some thoughts and curiosity about what will be coming up next. Chapter 1 is again an overview addressing the introduction and definitions of what makes up Christian education, which will include looking at the various factors, changes, and developments that have continued on for over two thousand years now. Needless to say, education has certainly evolved over the past two thousand years and still continues to do so. The education evolution is what guarantees that the teaching/learning process will continue to be available for future generations as well.

Chapter 2 is an in-depth look at the history of Christian education. The history will break apart "Christian" and "education" dating back to various known origins or where and how each began. For example, what is the difference between education and Christian education? One might easily argue that education by itself would date back way before Christian education even became known. People have had to learn basic survival, family life, and working skills simply to get by; but people also knew of the Christian promise even centuries before Christ was on earth. Taking up when Christ was on earth, noted as AD 0, AD 0–1600 will be the first half or era discussed in terms of education and Christian education. Naturally, the remainder of the chapter will be looking into AD 1600 through our present day. The past two thousand plus years certainly will cover many historical events, and it would be nearly impossible to list all of them, but pinpointing what specifically led to the greatest educational and Christian educational occurrences is the goal.

Chapter 3 is exploring Christian education as philosophy. The history lesson from chapter 2 opens up more questions to be asked regarding how Christian education continues to be as prevalent as it is. Many times philosophical questions are more answered by personal belief as opposed to cold hard facts, but does that make it any less logical? Throughout history, there have been several various philosophers who openly asked the deeper questions, which many people were not and may still not be eager to address. Such is true with Christian education.

The goal of chapter 3 is not to ask the challenging and somewhat annoying questions such as "Could God make a rock so big that He could not move it?" No, the purpose here is seeing what various tests, measurements, factors, and results have come up. What have we learned from these results? How have tests and measurements been used or perhaps not used? What factors have been included with the development or cessation of Christian education? The most significant factor of this chapter is discovering the use of technology. Today our world is every day changing with technological advances that it is oftentimes rather difficult to keep up with. However, technology was not always an influence on the education system as it is now. Long before computers, phones, and iPads, most of education was simply done by word of mouth. Listening. Sometimes, especially here in America, we easily forget that other places within our world still learn best by word of mouth. Technology is not available for educational purposes in third-world countries and sometimes at our own back door. Different circumstances, either with or without technology, do not necessarily hinder the learning process. Despite worldwide-reaching technology, Christian education may not even be known in all parts of the world yet. What can and should be done about this? Who is responsible for making sure that Christian education is where it needs to be?

Chapter 4 is probably the most intense chapter yet. Christ as the educator. Christianity, defined as "followers of Christ," is referred back to Jesus Christ of the New Testament in the Bible. The Bible is also known as the Sacred Scriptures. Christianity believes the Scriptures to be divinely inspired by God as the absolute truth. Since Christians are the followers of Christ, Jesus would be the absolute educator. Christian education strives to model Jesus and follow His example to the best of our abilities. Needless to say, no one living today was present two thousand years ago while Jesus walked the earth, so Christians rely and believe firmly in the words of the Scripture as resource, guide, and reassurance for the human mission.

The first four books of the New Testament—Matthew, Mark, Luke, and John—are called the gospels. The gospels contain the stories and truth of Jesus's life while He was on earth. During this time, His ministry and the Christian mission began. Jesus is the educator! Jesus gave His life to the people, His followers. Therefore, Christians always view Jesus as the model of leadership. Clergy today strive to follow Jesus's example of leading people to and through their faith. Being a leader requires having followers who are open and willing to follow. Giving a follower's life to the leader is being a disciple just as Jesus's followers were in His time. Discipleship takes on an earthly job in itself by making Jesus's mission, the Christian mission goal known as Scripture instructs.

Chapter 4 will finish with another aspect of Jesus as the perfect model in terms of human morality. The education of morality inside and outside of the Christian umbrella is not always an easy topic to cover. The morality of heavier topics such as abortion, capital punishment, euthanasia, and homosexuality is vastly viewed in complete opposites by people, especially today. Yet the Scripture and Jesus do address these topics. Granted these topics were not as prevalent as they are today, which easily allows the context to be construed. Regardless, the truth of what is right and what is wrong has been and will always be an ongoing debate.

Chapter 5 is a look over the various denominational faiths included within the Christianity realm and their educational emphasis. The biggest and most recognized Christian faith is Catholicism. Catholicism is known as the universal church because in every Catholic church across the world, the exact same service or Mass will be celebrated. Catholicism does have its own separations too, such as traditional, Greek Orthodox, and the New American, just to name a few. Although the Mass liturgy may be the same, the faith practices could differ greatly.

The next major Christian faith realm is Protestantism. The Protestant Christians include many different faiths, again all the same core beliefs but very different worship styles. Some of these include Lutheran, Baptist, Methodist, Episcopal, and Presbyterian. These branches of Christianity are known as transplanted Protestant faiths or more American based. As opposed to the transplanted Protestant faiths are the Native American faiths or outside American based. Native American includes Latter-Day Saints, Seventh-Day Adventists, Pentecostal, and the newer faith of Scientology.

Chapter 5's exploration of the Christian denominations' emphasis on education will conclude (and as will the first half of this dissertation) by a brief look at the remaining faiths within Christianity that are nondenominational or not under a specific title heading. Nondenominational Christians take the gospel scriptures extremely literal, desperately trying to live their lives to the near perfection as Jesus did.

Chapter 6 is Christian education in culture. Culture is another vast spectrum that extends all over the globe. For starters, this chapter is going to begin locally looking into the American culture and even closer in the Midwest. It is rather surprising how different culture can be simply going into the next city without leaving the same state. Culturally differences within education are going to differ as well. Just as in the previous while discussing the denominational differences, culture can and does impact worship values too.

Extending Christian education globally is a really difficult task; however, a strong understanding of cultural differences can make the global outreach achievable. Global outreach should be a job for all Christians, but more often, Christian missionaries make taking Christian education their sole purpose. It is not difficult to find places in our world that have never even seen or heard anything related to Christianity! In various third-world countries, people are struggling for basic survival—by lacking food and clean water. When missionaries visit these locations, their mission has an even greater purpose—bringing hope.

Before leaving chapter 6, in culture, it is important to remember that educational roles can be vastly different but equally significant. For example, Catholicism especially places a huge emphasis on men being in clergy with the leadership role, while some Protestant churches welcome women clergy. Likewise, many school systems are dominated by women teachers rather than men. In the same manner, the age of educators can make a difference. Again for certain Protestant faiths, the older members of the church are the leaders and decision-makers. Other faiths encourage youth ministries for the goal of youth taking on leadership roles within the church. Is education influenced by men, women, young, or older teachers?

Chapter 7 is education within the home. Homelife plays a huge role in the education of individuals especially for children. Consider these questions. What kind of family background does this learner come from? Is there a religious base in the household? How important is a Christian education to all the members within the house? Do they know? Who decides? In some cases, a family may be very structured into attending church and school within a specific denomination that can date back for generations. Other families may be newer to Christian education perhaps learning through a new family member in marriage or a better school choice.

When a decision is made regarding what is best for the family, the most important element will be making a commitment. The commitment must be solid through both parents as well as for the child or children. Families of split religious choices can usually place a huge strain on what will happen with the children. Regardless of the circumstances, religious education must be reinforced. Positive reinforcement results in a happier and healthier relationship for the family's homelife. Children asking questions about wanting to learn more about their faith and other faiths should be addressed and welcomed. Perhaps this can become a learning experience for the entire community to evolve.

Homelife education may not always be the easiest choice to make. It is quite common for parents to defer their child's education not only within school but also within the religious community. Most often a family's religious choice is greatly influenced by the parents' upbringing or perhaps a new choice made by the marriage. It is rather common for a spouse to change denominations or faith practices to become the same as the new spouse, but again it can also be a joint decision for beginning their lives together. What happens when a child reaches an age to make their own decisions? The adult age is eighteen; but many times children, especially teenagers, find church to be boring or not "cool." When is he or she allowed to make another choice? Why is it so difficult for some families to comprehend?

Chapter 8 is discovering educational differences and similarities within schools. The main question is the difference between public and private schools. Religious education is certainly much more emphasized with private schools considering many of them are already affiliated with a religious denomination. Public schools are on restriction as to how much or little teachers are allowed to educate religiously, but this does not stop curious minds from wanting to know. In this case, several churches have available classes to accommodate students who want to learn more that are not taught in public school.

Relating back to chapter 7 briefly, homelife plays a huge role where education is concerned. How does this fit in with school education? Homeschooling. Many parents have decided and are deciding to homeschool their children. Education in the home is more private and personal to the child's learning ability. Along with regular education, parents will also be teaching religious education especially if the family is already committed to a religious affiliation. Does learning about Christian education in the home change the mission? Or does Christian education in the home enhance the mission more so than school learning?

Discussing education in schools by whether public, private, or homeschooling still required one more component: exploring the various age levels. In America, children are usually in school from age five to eighteen. Many psychologists have theorized and explained that a child's mind contains and grows with years of education. Each student is going to learn and mature at their own pace. For example, it does not make sense for a sixteen-year-old to be learning the alphabet, a system they have known for many years. Christian education is no different. Many simple Bible stories are told to children at young ages; but as they grow and mature within their faith, more questions will arise, causing curiosity and possibly some doubts. How much of a factor does age play?

Chapter 9 is analyzing Christian education as a community effort. Recapping from chapters 7 and 8, Christian education can be very strong within the home, church, and school life; but what about the everyday community? Consider asking another person, "Are your religious practices influenced by church, school, family, or community?" A person might look puzzled. Many communities are so vastly different in ages, races, and cultures that perhaps it is not as simple to identify. On the other hand, one may be shocked to know there is more in common within the community than there is awareness.

Some communities do regularly make an open effort to host gatherings, game nights, or dinners to welcome people and make the community closer. These events are necessary for community involvement to grow. Simply inviting a friend, neighbor, or family member to attend a frequent public event can really influence community. The same is especially true for a religious community. It is not uncommon to find a church smack in the middle of a residential neighborhood. Churches are to be welcoming of all people, so what better place for a community gathering to also be a religious education opportunity?

Perhaps the most tedious and even dangerous aspect of community involvement are moral issues. Christian education does include discussing morality just as Jesus did. Over the years, morality has become a major dilemma in church and state issues. In Christian education, such topics as abortion, euthanasia, capital punishment, and homosexuality may be taught as wrong; but the state and even society are fully supportive. Many debates, political campaigns, meetings, riots, and even smaller civil wars have been created by people expressing strong beliefs by either supporting or denying such issues. Humanity has a long way to go.

Finally, chapter 10 will detail what the future holds for Christian education. What does each denomination have set for future goals? What would families like to see happen? How are Christian educational goals being achieved? Mission statements and visions are wonderful to have in place wherever Christian education can be found, but are educators doing enough to make those statements real? What obstacles are hindering the learning process? Who is making the decisions and dedication to ensure Christian education for generations to come?

To answer the previous questions, Christians must take on dedication, participation, and faith. The dedication of Jesus's followers and the participation of the community together can make a huge difference. The increasing need for Christian education to be strengthened and reinforced is what keeps Christianity going. Focusing on not only the local needs, but also the needs of those across the world who desire to learn needs to be met. By striving to achieve the ultimate goal of extending Jesus's mission to all His followers, Christians ensure that the future will be the brightest and strongest it can possibly be. Keeping the Christian faith strong and burning within our hearts is all the encouragement needed to reach the mission goal. A long journey is said to begin with one step. Perhaps a first step could be self-examination.

CHAPTER 1

What Is Christian Education?

Factors and Structure

As mentioned in the introduction section, Christian education is a two-word phrase that covers a vast amount of knowledge. A basic definition would be "education that is taught about Christianity," but it is so much more than that. Education alone is a developmental occurrence. A person is always within a state of education; the process is continuous throughout an entire life. So is it true when discussing education in a religious realm such as Christianity. A person will be developing their own spiritual life while their forming self-awareness continues to bring them into God's image.[1] The spiritual life is grown and nurtured through Christian formation. Formation as a whole is ever changing and evolving to make whole. As described by Seymour and Miller, Christian and education together help all believers to accomplish these twelve important formational factors:

- Pray. Talking to God about the strengths and the weakness a person endures both communally and alone.
- Meditate. Connecting with all persons who center on God.

---

[1] Jack L. Seymour and Donald E. Miller, *Theological Approaches to Christian Education* (Nashville: Abingdon Press, 1990), 137.

- Practice solitude, silence, and simplicity. Creating space inwardly and outwardly where one will wait and listen for God's voice.
- Confess. Acknowledging a person's weaknesses and helplessness. Learning to be accepting of God's grace and gifts.
- Repent. Process wrong-doing. Not ignoring those most in need such as the poor, lost, forsaken, imprisoned, and other Christians worldwide.
- Proclaim. Exclaiming the Gospel message of Jesus. Taking the given mission to all Christians and to those thirsting to learn more.
- Praise. Showing God with gratitude and thankfulness for all He has done and continues to do for each of us.
- Communion. Openly celebrating the Lord's Supper at His table along with fellow Christians.
- Fasting. Remember those who suffer from hunger.
- Search for Scripture. Searching for answers from God's Truth. Asking questions, exploring faith, and educating others.
- Baptism. Celebrating the inheritance God has given us to be brought into and remain within the Christian faith.
- Service. Recognizing and remembering to be in constant service of those around us seeking their needs. Christians are to make sure that all the needs of others are met as Jesus Himself did.[2]

Each of these listed factors is essential to the Christian formation through education. A person will be continuously using and evolving in these factors to maintain their own spiritual growth and understanding. The maintaining is not always an easy element to do. For many Christians as with other faiths, discipline plays a huge role. An understanding of the factors needed in the Christian mis-

---

[2] List of twelve Christian education factors from Jack L. Seymour and Donald E. Miller, *Theological Approaches to Christian Education* (Nashville: Abingdon Press, 1990), 139–140.

sion requires discipline not only as a communal essential but especially for the individual. Discipline here is not to be looked at as a negative, but more as an important positive reinforcement. As the factors are continually reinforced, they are questioned, challenged, and sometimes even fully changed to further fit what the particular mission implies.

The factors are not strong enough alone with a person without proper discipline to maintain the structure. Christian structure, as with all structures, includes its own necessities. The first and most obvious necessity is the environment for which education is present. Is a classroom the only place where education can be found? Of course not. It is said that a person learns something new every day. That particular saying does not indicate a place, people, or purpose as to how or why the everyday learning occurs. Consider in the Old Testament while the children of Israel were in bondage, traveling, serving a king, and following the prophets, they were certainly not inside a classroom; but they learned more and more about God every day.

The Israelites learned throughout daily life by mere participation.[3] The tribal leaders were elderly who had been long educated from previous generations to continue what had been passed on to them. By the continuance of this education, the elderly and priests became the early teachers, which allowed them the respect of being in authority. Also, the children of Israel had been long promised by God that a Savior would be sent to save all His people. God's promise or covenant kept a partnership of participation going. Granted, Jesus Christ had not come to earth yet, so Christian education had not been formally established. However, the education of the pre-Christ people was just as strong and prevalent.

More often, much education about God and His promise would have been taught in the synagogues. The Jewish was and still is extremely loyal to that same Word of God. This is an example of another Christian education structure simply stated as existence. The existence of humanity, creation, Scripture, and even time is all proof

---

[3] Ibid., 141.

of education. Existence answers many questions such as the following: Where did God come from? How do we know? How did the Scripture writers know what to say? Why are the Scriptures still so important today two thousand years later? Christianity believes that God's very existence is the basis. God always has been and always will be present. Dating back to Genesis, the Scripture explains that God walked with Adam and Eve in the garden of Eden.

> Then the man and his wife heard the sound of
> God walking in the garden...[4]

God's physical existence is Him walking and calling for His people. Later on, God appears in a burning bush to Moses as well as speaks to others in dreams. Christianity firmly believes that God's Holy Spirit is the divine inspirer of the Scriptures, leading and guiding what exactly what was to be written for all generations to be educated from. Even today, through prayer and worship, God is very much in existence for all.

A person or learner has to make the commitment of making his or her own existence known especially where education is present.[5] A learner will often find that making their existence open will inspire others to do the same. Many people learn well simply by listening to each other. Seymour and Miller explain three key environmental structures: worship, instruction, and praxis.[6] In worship, there is usually a particular setting involved. Countless churches around the world vary in design, structures, and worship styles. More specifically, the difference in Christian denominations and world religions can also vary the worship style. Particularly in using worship as an educational setting, it is important to know that participation, motivation, and understanding are going to make the learning successful. The participation of the congregation can greatly influence a person

---

[4]   Genesis 3:8.

[5]   Jack L. Seymour, and Donald E. Miller, *Theological Approaches to Christian Education* (Nashville: Abingdon Press, 1990), 141.

[6]   Ibid., 143–44.

to become more motivated for worship. In turn, the motivation will lead to questioning and curiosity that creates the understanding. The desire of wanting to be educated further on how and why worship is done in a particular way will maintain the growth of Christian education to be continued.

The next key element is instruction. Classrooms especially usually have a set routine of daily classes along with lesson plans to follow. On the other hand, some educators find education can be done on a whim when questions arise. The blueprint of Christian educational instruction lies within skills and spiritual discipline.[7] Skills are developed over time; the more skills are practiced, the stronger they become. Spiritual discipline is the motivation behind taking those skills and using them to fulfill the Christian mission. By using the Scripture as the base, a learner's skills and spiritual guidance will further ensure that the element of instruction will be used properly and advanced as needed.

The third element is praxis. Praxis refers to the Christian attempt to faithful obedience.[8] In other words, Christians are to be constantly seeking out those who are in most need of Christ's mission. The challenging piece of the mission is the motivation and/or initiative to be searching out the hungry, naked, imprisoned, sick, and lonely. Jesus commands,

> As the church, we are actively called to search out strangers, not just stumble across them in a doorway.[9]

Jesus reminds Christians thoroughly that we have the power of protection for justice. Using the praxis taught through education and experience makes the mission more achievable.

The previous elements and structures are normally preformed within a group setting. It should also be noted that for some learners,

---

7   Ibid., 144.
8   Ibid., 145.
9   Matthew 25:31–46.

obtaining education can be best done on a personal and private level. Self-Christian education can be just as thorough. The Christian mission is not specified to be accomplished individually, as a group, at a particular time or place; it is simply told. God has given all humanity free will to choose on a personal basis. For some learners, that personal choice will help them become as fully educated for the mission as group learners do. In most cases, such personal experiences may not be openly discussed to keep the knowledge more personal. Each individual knows with his or her own heart and mind what is best. Perhaps God is leading them to another smaller mission while on the journey to the ultimate mission. God knows where He is leading each person. Likewise, Christians know how they will follow the instructions whether it is public or private.

Personal Growth

After exploring the factors and structures within Christian education, it is time to look at the development of the individual learner. The process of growth is continual for most human beings, being at birth, through adolescence, adulthood, and even the golden years. Ironically enough, most people especially children seem to learn best by association. Most famously, Erikson and Piaget would be attributed to intently studying human development. Jean Piaget describes the maturing of brain concepts he calls schemas. A schema is built up over time beginning at birth based on personal experiences. For infants, schemas are most effective by the assimilating and accommodating.[10] For example, a child may learn that the family dog is a pet; therefore, the child associates that every creature with four legs and a tail is a dog until they learn otherwise.[11] The ability to associate and identify creates the mental capacity to question and gain further knowledge. For adults, critical thinking can be based

---

[10] David G. Meyers, *Psychology*, 5th ed. (New York: Worth Publishers, 1998), 87.
[11] James C. Wilhoit and John M. Dettoni, *Nurture That Is Christian: Developmental Perspectives on Christian Education* (Wheaton: Victor Books Inc., 1995), 51.

on emotion and eagerness to know. Adults will engage more so with other adults and create more collaborating to develop knowledge. The psychologist Jean Piaget may be best known for his extensive research in the mechanics of cognition development from childhood through adult life. Cognitive development is described as "all the mental activities associated with thinking, knowing, remembering, and communicating."[12] By breaking down the ages within a person's life, it becomes easier and clearer for the one giving the education. A teacher would certainly not be explaining psychological cognitive development to a three-year-old.

Piaget breaks his cognitive research into four separate stages of human developmental growth. The first stage is called the sensorimotor stage or the infant stage primarily for the ages of zero to two. Infants learn mostly through the physical observation by using the senses: hearing, seeing, touching, smelling, and even tasting. At this age, a baby will lose interest rather quickly. For example, if a toy should be taken away from the baby's sight, it simply does not exist anymore. The exploring of that toy has ended. The exploration and use of language may begin to develop by the age that falls into the next stage.[13]

From ages two to seven, Piaget calls the preoperational stage. As mentioned, language use begins in the early part of this stage along with fantasy. Children who tend to daydream and play pretend are being creative by using their own thoughts and feelings together. Thinking and feeling are always tied together where learning is concerned. Children are very logical thinkers that perhaps often take parents and teachers by surprise. A child's logic is primarily based on his or her own understanding of the world at that particular time. For example, a five-year-old may be able to tell that quantity of milk is "too much" based on the size of a tall glass but not understand that same amount of milk is in a shorter wider glass. Piaget explains that

---

[12] David G. Meyers, *Psychology*, 5th ed. (New York: Worth Publishers, 1998), 87–88.

[13] James C. Wilhoit and John M. Dettoni, *Nurture That Is Christian: Developmental Perspectives on Christian Education* (Wheaton: Victor Books Inc., 1995), 53.

this is because the child is forming the operation of mentally pouring the milk but lacks the concept of quantity used.[14] Most importantly, even at this younger age, children can be less like adults in their thinking, but more like adults with their feelings.[15] For example, children may experience sadness or pain through feelings but possibly would not understand the sadness could be due to a loss. Likewise, pain could be an injury or illness, but the child only recognizes the uncomforting notion.

The third stage, Piaget describes as the concrete operational stage. This stage includes ages ranging from seven to eleven. Children here will learn facts more easily and begin to take their lessons quite literally. Children also will be learning about social issues and morality, which creates the separation of black and white with right and wrong. While learning more concretely about the world around them, children create competitions with each other based on learned values. The most obvious example is children's collections. It is common for a young boy to collect as many baseball cards as possible based on learning that baseball is a huge sport not only in the world, but also within his home. In the same manner, a young girl may wish to collect as many dolls and doll accessories again for the same reason. The collections have become an important value to the child, which will bring satisfaction and the desire to be recognized.

The final stage Piaget lists for cognitive development is the formal operations stage. Piaget includes ages twelve and up in this stage, also calling it the systematic reasoning.[16] Children are now becoming adolescents and beginning into adulthood. Adolescents are thinking more abstractly and solving hypotheticals in their education. Likewise, spirituality and faith are questioned more. Since adolescents are thinking in terms of abstract, they want to know the solid answers behind religious beliefs, mercy, and justice issues, to name a few. Just as with most questions, the complexity and desire for

---

[14] David G. Meyers, *Psychology*, 5th ed. (New York: Worth Publishers, 1998), 91.
[15] James C. Wilhoit and John M. Dettoni, *Nurture That Is Christian: Developmental Perspectives on Christian Education* (Wheaton: Victor Books Inc., 1995), 53.
[16] David G. Meyers, *Psychology*, 5th ed. (New York: Worth Publishers, 1998), 93.

answers fuels the motivation for these ages to learn. Piaget suggests that allowing young adults, ages twelve to eighteen, to struggle with their questions is better than simply giving an easy answer. For most, education is plentiful enough that struggling for answers should not be a roadblock. Instead, the motivation and interaction to reach such understanding should be monitored and supported as opposed to being hindered.[17]

Jean Piaget's research even today is still considered controversial. While Piaget does bring out many aspects included with cognitive development, there are other aspects left out. For example, the Russian psychologist Lev Vygotsky explained the importance of a parent-child relationship. According to Vygotsky, "Parents and teachers transmit to a child whatever skills, values, and perspectives that society needs." Further, Vygotsky commented that "the social context that surrounds us provides many of our thoughts, beliefs, and behaviors."[18] Basically, the importance of human contact and stability is the essential part that develops a child's ability to further their own cognition. The main difference, as opposed to Piaget, Vygotsky places most of his emphasis on the human contact rather than personal exploration.

One final area to consider in the development of the human cognition for learning is that of nature versus nurture. Is a person more influenced by their genes (nature) or their experiences (nurture)? How do these two interact, and/or what cause them to be the same? Genes, or the nature, are what make up the person such as body type, hair/eye color, and personality. The most research on nature has been done by studying twins. Researchers have wondered: are identical twins clones of each other? Considering that they share a great deal of the same genes as each other, would they be genetic clones? No. It is not physically possible to clone an entire human being. Being similar is not the same as total duplication.[19] In twin

---

[17] James C. Wilhoit and John M. Dettoni, *Nurture That Is Christian: Developmental Perspectives on Christian Education* (Wheaton: Victor Books Inc., 1995), 54.

[18] David G. Meyers, *Psychology*, 5th ed. (New York: Worth Publishers, 1998), 94.

[19] David G. Meyers, *Psychology*, 5th ed. (New York: Worth Publishers, 1998), 108.

studies, the answers of given questionnaires were usually more similar in identical twins as opposed to fraternal twins. When consulted with the results, the identical twins responded that they were treated most equally while fraternal twins, not looking quite the same, were more often treated as two separate people. So this begged the question: since fraternal twins were treated differently by others in their lives, would that be considered a nurture difference? Most psychologists agreed, no. The genes already within the twins are still the remaining basis for the questionnaire answers. The twins' own psychological cognition was always gene based.

In turn, personal experiences such as trauma, divorce, and success can affect the nurture side. Nearly all people will go through what are considered "hard times" at some point in their lives. These experiences can really influence a person's cognition as well as their physical appearance. Again, referring to the twin study. Some twins who had been split at birth and raised in separate locations with very different lifestyles are an example of nurture. The Hollywood movie *The Parent Trap* is actually a strong example of nurture. Two twins separated at birth, one to be raised by her father in the country while the other twin by the mother abroad. When the twin sisters meet, the differences are quite obvious, and the teaching of each other to live as the other sister becomes rather challenging. Regardless of using Piaget's stages of development or Vygotsky's social development, nature or nurture, all methods do strive to reach the goal of further detailing and understanding the human development and emphasizing how important the educational learning process really is.

Development

After exploring a few different methods of how mental cognition develops within children into adult age, now it is time to discover that cognitive development in Christian education. Another psychologist and theologian, David Elkind, took Piaget's research and expanded it with Christian development. Elkind was not so much interested in what children were taught with formal education, but he wondered what they asked on their own. What do children think when they are in church? What does prayer mean to them? Who do they think God is, and/or where is He? By asking these questions along with several others specifically based on age appropriateness, Elkind was able to discover that many of the answers were in fact common with Piaget's findings. The results were that younger children were unwavering in their thinking while the older children did answer with concrete and abstract thoughts. By using this discovery, Elkind educated many children with Piaget's research, finding it easier to relate. The growth of children's cognition with Christian education continues to develop with setting and the influences of the physical world around them.[20]

Piaget himself never made any reference to being a follower of Christ as Elkind and many other psychologists and educators did. However, Piaget's insights are used to remind the Christian educator of three basic biblical principles. The first principle is that Piaget helps educators to see that "the purpose of education is development." Considering that the ultimate goal of Christians is to develop to be more Christlike, educators need to focus on the development of people loving, knowing, and glorifying God. The danger of educating toward this goal is that too often educators may become too involved with expanding the programs or straying away from the necessary knowledge. Therefore, it is imperative that educators remember the goal, stay focused, and remain compatible with the educational level of their learners.[21]

The second principle that Piaget reminds educators is that learning is a social activity. Educators should always know that the knowledge is best fed by the body of believers or the church. People of almost all ages learn better when surrounded by other people specifically with the same beliefs. Strong lectures, journal writing, and solid preaching are also useful ways of learning; but Piaget's research

---

[20] James C. Wilhoit and John M. Dettoni, *Nurture That Is Christian: Developmental Perspectives on Christian Education* (Wheaton: Victor Books Inc., 1995), 58.
[21] James C. Wilhoit and John M. Dettoni, *Nurture That Is Christian: Developmental Perspectives on Christian Education* (Wheaton: Victor Books Inc., 1995), 59.

11

emphasizes that interaction with other people is a very positive method for growth. Likewise, learning should go beyond the familiar society by mingling with others from different societies, cultures, and lifestyles.

The third principle is that Piaget reminds educators that learning is a "disequilibrating and re-equilibrating process."[22] In other words, learning is not always a steady, simple process. Throughout life, a person is going to struggle with spiritual problems and be further frustrated and challenged while learning how to be Christlike. People are always going to be in a state of how we do live as opposed to how we should live. For Christian educators, the gospels are the best source for answers. The Bible is the tool for resolving and assisting with even the deepest human issues. By recognizing these three principles and the necessity of keeping them foremost in the educators' minds, the goal of Christian education will continually bring renewal for all followers of Christ.

One other important person to mention while exploring Christian educational development with the learner is James Fowler. Fowler was another psychologist who very much was solely interested in exploring faith development with learners of every age even beyond adolescence. Fowler openly stated that

> I see faith as a universal human phenomenon. When applied with Christian faith, God is the ultimate environment, while the relationship to Him and to others is transformed…Through the lens of the Gospels, God is in control of not only our ultimate destiny, but that of our current situations.[23]

Fowler presented his six stages of faith progress because he knew that mental and cognitive development is not the same for all stages of life.

---

[22] Ibid., 60.
[23] Ibid., 76.

Fowler begins with a stage infancy defined as less than one year of age. At this early age, a child is not yet aware of his or her faith or what faith even is. The baby is only aware of others who are responsible for taking care of it. A baby will feel separation anxiety when a parent is not present, creating distress, which is normal for this early stage. Fowler calls this a "pre-stage" considering the young age is not assessable for studying faith development.

Fowler's first stage is intuitive and projective faith occurring in early childhood. Like Piaget, Fowler emphasizes the imagination within children. Early ages are easily influenced by stories, images, symbols, and even dreams but not yet controlled by logical thinking. The real teachers here are the perceptions and feelings of the children. At this point, faith is merely shaped by the significant adults within the child's world. Needless to say, a child that is brought up within a religious home is going to be more influenced by the prayers, personal commitment, and symbols that the family provides. A child will most likely only think that this is his or her world but not fully understand the logical descriptions.[24]

Fowler's second stage is the mythic/literal faith for childhood and beyond. Again, relating to Piaget, the concrete operations of these stages coming out are allowing these ages to think logically in terms of categories, space, and time.[25] Fowler emphasizes faith as being mythic in the sense that the learners can now capture life meaning in stories, but literal in being limited with concrete thinking. Self-awareness and perspective are still developing in this stage, often making it difficult for learners to fully communicate with other learners. The mythic/literal faith is highly appropriate for educating at this stage and should be slowly set further aside as the development continues. Jesus's approval of childlike faith in Matthew 18:2–3 shows a child's humility, not regular childlike ways of thinking.[26] Many Christian denominations take the educating of children very

---

[24] Ibid., 77.
[25] James C. Wilhoit and John M. Dettoni, *Nurture That Is Christian: Developmental Perspectives on Christian Education* (Wheaton: Victor Books Inc., 1995), 77–78.
[26] Matthew 18:2–3.

seriously based on Jesus's words alone. One caution with the literal thinking in this stage is that some children very often find it rather difficult if not impossible to believe in a God who is invisible. In some cases as with Fowler, this may signal a serious struggle, and the educators, along with parents, should be present to assist this concern by explaining how the Scripture and experiences teach otherwise.

The third stage Fowler explains is the synthetic/conventional faith in adolescents and beyond ages. A strong relational component is present in this stage considering that many adolescents create identity with other adolescents. Stage 3 is considered synthetic because now the beliefs and values learned in the previous stages are becoming synthesized into perspectives. Fowler also explains that this stage is conventional in that a learner will adopt their beliefs and use them forming into a larger community.[27] The biggest development here is a huge emphasis is being placed on the self. A selfhood and self-identity are forming along with becoming a part of specific roles and relationships. With this in mind, people in this age are more involved with church and Christian learning because they see this as an extended family. Adolescents especially will learn that political activities and society issues are more rooted with religious beliefs than perhaps previously realized. A hesitation is that sometimes this creates dissonance and overwhelming dilemmas within the learners' minds. Such authorities of these various groups may become more challenging to understand or relate with. Along with this authority challenging, a person might also be overdependent on significant people within their own community. A person can easily become too much involved worrying about their status in the eyes of that particular authority person to which they look up to. The learner is thus allowing external control to become of utmost importance for learning dependency. Yet overall, Fowler believes that the growth in community awareness and personal relationship building is the essential piece of faith developing in this stage.

---

[27] James C. Wilhoit and John M. Dettoni, *Nurture That Is Christian: Developmental Perspectives on Christian Education* (Wheaton: Victor Books Inc., 1995), 78.

Fowler's stage 4 is the individual/reflective faith for young adulthood. Stage 4 is credited as a double development in the self and of religious thinking. The selfhood in this stage is in contrast to stage 3's self as now the person is developing more of a self-authority as opposed to a community self.[28] The self-authorization learned here is creating the need to make choices based on what is best for the self. A learner is not going to continually try to fit in with a particular group but more so with creating a self-identity and using personal reflections based on their own inner assumptions. An obstacle of this stage is the feeling of guilt or loss is more prevalent because the reliance of community is not as strong. In turn, now a person can rely on their own thinking without turning back to the community for help. Taking on too much personal responsibility and reflection can hinder the desire to further education, allowing negative judgments to be more present. Any person is going to be their worst critic and be harder on themselves than necessary. As with stage 3, educators need to be aware of these negative thoughts and be prepared to further educate with a positive attitude.

Stage 5 of Fowler's faith development is the conjunctive faith for midlife and beyond ages. Conjunctive faith becomes less aware of the self and is less sure of the judgments made with stage 4. The remaining self-awareness is deeper in a connection with God and has a much better grasp on the reality of their own perspectives. Stage 5 beliefs deepen in the divine and necessary theology needed to maintain being Christlike. A person will seek out their encounters, experiences, and already gained knowledge to share with others. Basically, stage 5 people are becoming educators because of the connection they made with the spiritual into their own life. Most learners who do become educators have done enough hard work in the earlier stages to reach this point. Yet some educators, such as the apostle Paul who did not have prior Christian education, can be transformed and spiritually filled enough to begin educational instruction. For those learners who do not wish to become educators, they should not think any less of being accomplished; again, the development process

---

[28] Ibid., 79.

affects each learner different at his or her own pace. Ultimately, at stage 5, people will be more comfortable reaching to those outside their own communities and be helpful in allowing others to learn truth and facts and not be limited by human perspectives.[29]

The final stage of Fowler's faith development is stage 6, the universalizing faith for the ages of midlife and beyond. Stage 6 is the final stage later in life where all of the other stages come together in cultivating personal faith. Here, a learner has a newer relationship with God, a full understanding of their own community both locally and globally. A newfound freedom is within this person who is more in tune with love and justice while putting divisions and oppressions aside. Fowler says,

> Universalization faith has a disciplined activist incarnation—making real and tangible—of the imperatives of absolute love and justice of which stage 5 has partial apprehensions.[30]

In other words, moving from stage 5 to stage 6, a person will prosper in their personal transformation of known reality into actuality. Stage 6 is the climax of Fowler's developmental faith stages.

By using these stages and growing with the best possible knowledge available, Christian education is sure to achieve Jesus's mission by continuing on through these stages, personal experiences, and self-desire.

Evolution

Christian education has certainly evolved vastly over the course of over two thousand years. Much of the evolution can be attributed to the many contributions that Christian education has given to

---

[29] James C. Wilhoit and John M. Dettoni, *Nurture That Is Christian: Developmental Perspectives on Christian Education* (Wheaton: Victor Books Inc., 1995), 81–82.
[30] Ibid., 82.

learners. One final time relating back to Piaget and Fowler, five specific contributions to Christian education have been identified based on their developmental research. The first contribution is that faith is a universal phenomenon. The theory behind this contribution is that there is a high view of humanity as a whole and every person has faith.[31] Some would argue against this by commenting that only religious people have faith. In terms of development, this is not true. All people will search for a deeper meaning life and question their existence, and others will search out a deity. The main difference between Christian and/or religious faith and secular faith is more of a faith versus fact. The basis of perspective, beliefs, and relationships will all work together to build up a person's faith. Is this basis the same or different for a nonreligious learner? Fowler asks, "Is the gospel a more adequate faith content than the stock market?" Many people put plenty of faith in both. Is one more influential than the other? The contribution is not meant to become a philosophical debate as opposed to understanding the intensity of what God has placed around us to explore.

The second contribution is the description of faith as being different from religion and belief. When discussing the evangelical church, Fowler places a critical distinction between faith and creed. Some denominations consider their creed to be a statement of faith in which the community recites and believes together.[32] Fowler reminds us that faith is dynamic and evolving by shaping our lives daily. Fowler argues against using a creed or profession of faith and use the individual's faith experience and expertise to demonstrate outside of the church walls. True nature comes from within the person's faith and belief. Education contributes with faith at the level of acceptance to which the learner is open. Ultimately, a person's faith will direct him or her into the involvement whether it be with a specific religion or personal belief.

---

[31] Ibid., 85.
[32] James C. Wilhoit and John M. Dettoni, *Nurture That Is Christian: Developmental Perspectives on Christian Education* (Wheaton: Victor Books Inc., 1995), 86.

The third contribution is a more complete faith view. As discussed, many psychologists' research has been looked at for the purpose of understanding the mind of the individual, thus making the educational piece easier; however, Fowler emphasizes this is not enough. The self-perspectives, relationships, and personal experiences are going to assist the development and educational growth of the learner far more than simply focusing on the measuring of the mind.[33] Fowler describes this as a "whole person" theory. The whole person is needed for the complete faith development to occur. Educators have to be able to understand that just as Piaget noted, not all learners are going to learn at the same levels and speed. When Christian educating is involved, the educator must always be sure not to limit the learner's mind to only spirituality questions. The whole view of faith is much bigger than that.

The fourth contribution is the sensitive listening to faith. Faith is not a concept that is black and white or open and shut. Faith affects people in various ways, and certain ways are not so obvious to see. Over time, evangelicals have paid close attention to teaching, theorizing, and explaining context but often overlook a structure to build upon. Fowler says,

> We have been so concerned with guarding *what* people believe that we have failed to listen to *how* they believe.[34]

At times, educators can become too intense on making sure all material is covered in a certain time or presented in a certain way but then do not make the time or effort to ask questions and gain insights in return from the learners. Faith matures just as the person's mind does. The caution with this contribution is not to categorize certain stages into specific developmental stages and then educationally leave that person there without nurturing their faith onward. The point of

---

[33] Ibid., 86.
[34] Ibid., 87.

faith development is to continuously be monitoring how people use and exercise their faith.

The fifth contribution listed is describing mature faith. The fourth contribution began to hint on this, but now the focus lies more on maturity as opposed to strength. The real question here is how is the maturity in faith determined? Is it possible for a young adult to be more developed in their faith as opposed to someone older? The life factors between ages can be greatly different. For example, a young person can lose someone special in their life and have to battle through the sorrow unexpectedly, while someone older may not have had that same experience yet. The faith in the young person can be greatly altered because of the tragedy. Likewise, teaching children about love and happiness will change as adults when life experiences come up. As mentioned in contribution 4, the context of teaching faith has to be accompanied with structure just as maturity has to be accompanied with strength.[35] Maturity is ever changing and evolving just as the human mind continues to do so, but maturity in faith needs to be ever present for the educator's goal to be achieved.

By remembering and recognizing faith context, global views, maturity, and the Christian mission, educators will be on as strong of a course as possible to further progression of all learners. Christian education has a complicated definition, a vast amount of history, and a great relation to the human mind and body. The development of the human mind is a continuous exploration that has been crossed with spiritual development. Each has similarities and differences. Each has its own factors and key elements that are ever present and in need of nurture to further the Christian mission. When educators use the lessons presented in Christian development and evolution, the future possibilities are endless.

---

[35] James C. Wilhoit and John M. Dettoni, *Nurture That Is Christian: Developmental Perspectives on Christian Education* (Wheaton: Victor Books Inc., 1995), 88.

CHAPTER 2

Christian Education in History

Christ as the Origin

Chapter 2 will take a quick overview at each of the Christian history that is being considered for the students' Christian formation. However, before diving straight into the historical background, is it important to consider and recognize what makes them "Christian"? To review, what is Christianity? Why is it important to know this? Put simply,

> The vast majority of Christians share a common worldview that explains the nature of God and God's relationship to humankind through the person of Jesus Christ.[36]

However, over the years, Christianity has branched off into numerous denominations all under the Christian umbrella heading. A great deal of this diversity occurs when various Christians come into contact with other Christians who share the same core belief but have different faith practices.[37] Although the current AD

---

[36] Jeffery B. Webb, *The Complete Idiot's Guide to Christianity* (Nashville: Penguin Group Inc., 2004), 1.

[37] John Thomas McNeill, Matthew Spinka, and Harold R. Willoughby, *Environmental Factors in Christian History* (London: Kennikat Press, 1939), 1.

timeline form was not in use yet, today Christianity in general dates back to AD 3–36 when Jesus Christ walked the earth. The word "Christians" was first used in the Antioch community of Syria to identify the non-Jewish followers of Jesus. Since this time and still today, Christianity includes a collaboration of history and a cosmic struggle between good and evil with Jesus ever being the central figure to follow.[38]

Jesus was indeed the origin of Christianity as He is the Christ, but it is important to note that even before Jesus, the Old Testament prophets had been teaching and foretelling of the Savior as promised to them by God. For many centuries, God's people believed in the promise or covenant made with God that a Messiah would be sent to them. The covenant came to fruition in the year 0 upon Jesus's birth. As this time came, John the Baptist was already proclaiming to the people that the Messiah was soon to arrive. The journey, preaching, and life of John the Baptist have greatly been accredited as the foremost herald of Jesus; but there is more to John's influence of early Christianity. Granted, because of the lack of resources from the time, greater knowledge of John's works outside of the Scripture is difficult to come by. The gospel writers even take a slightly different approach explaining John the Baptist. For example, Matthew 3:12 says,

> And in those days came John the Baptist preaching in the wilderness of Judea, saying, "Repent for the Kingdom of Heaven is at hand."[39]

Yet the Gospel of Mark proclaims John as the preparer for the Messiah, saying,

> The baptism of repentance unto the remission of sins.[40]

---

[38] Ibid., 1–3.
[39] Matthew 3:12.
[40] Mark 1:4.

Matthew and Luke portray John the Baptist as giving the warning of the upcoming judgment should people not heed his message while Mark portrays him more as someone who provides a hopeful instruction explaining about the remission of sin and believing in John's good news.[41] Is John the Baptist's mission the beginning of the Baptist branch within Christianity? Scholars have argued yes, considering that the gospel writers have gone on to specifically mention the importance of baptism to the people. Jesus Himself came to John the Baptist asking to be baptized. Jesus's baptism was one of the earliest outward signs for all the people to witness. Jesus made sure His baptism was marking the beginning of His mission on earth, which has made baptism become a pivotal moment for Christians ever since.

After Jesus's baptism, His true mission began with the calling of His disciples, performing miracles, and traveling to various cities. The Scripture is rather detailed especially within the gospels as to the traveling Jesus did on His time on earth. While traveling throughout the Galilee region, Jesus performed many miracles, taught thousands of people, and gathered numerous disciples in which Jesus commanded to continue on after His upcoming death.

After the time Jesus had walked the earth, His chosen apostles began to carry out the mission that had been into place for them. Jesus had commanded that Peter was the one whom the followers of Christ would later follow. Matthew 16:16–18 reads,

> Simon Peter said in reply, "You are the Messiah, the Son of the Living God." Jesus said to him in reply, "Blessed are you, Simon son of Jonah. For flesh and blood has not revealed this to you, but my heavenly Father. And so I say to you, you are Peter and upon this rock I will build my church, and the gates of the netherworld will not prevail against it."[42]

---

[41] John Thomas McNeill, Matthew Spinka, and Harold R. Willoughby, *Environmental Factors in Christian History* (London: Kennikat Press, 1939), 3.

[42] Matthew 16:16–18.

And as Peter had been told, he continued the mission along with the other remaining apostles to spread out even further throughout the regions to further what Jesus had begun. It is important to note here that in the branch of Catholicism, Peter is held as the first pope or chosen leader. Further, the remaining apostles may have been viewed as the initial College of Cardinals. The concept of a pope, cardinals, bishops, and priests would begin the early stages of the Catholic hierarchy. In the early centuries of Christianity and so even today, this hierarchy would become extremely problematic for the everyday people, royalty, and mostly between other involved countries.

While Peter was ordering the apostles out in pairs to visit the regions most in need of Jesus's message, his fellow apostle Paul, who had once been a Christian persecutor, was now one of the strongest voices for Christianity. Many times, Paul was criticized, threatened, and even arrested for his work; but that never stopped him from continuing onward. The Scripture contains several letters or epistle books within the New Testament that Paul had written to various people and specific regions were under terrible persecutions at that time. Some of the regions and even individual people, Paul never got the chance to actually visit himself due to his many arrests and long stretches in jail. Paul had many followers whom he sent out to try to reach as many of those persecuted as possible. Paul and his followers did indeed reach out the mission further than Jesus and even Peter had previously.

Jesus had promised His apostles that the Holy Spirit would be sent upon them so they could be spiritually filled to carry out their given mission. The Day of Pentecost was the first day in which the mission would be officially begun. On this day, Jesus's promise of the coming Holy Spirit was fulfilled. As each apostle was filled, each began preaching on various languages started by Peter. The strangeness of this occurrence was intensified by the fact that these apostles were also Jewish. They had just been following Jesus the past years and were now educating people about Him outside of the Jewish tradition.[43] The apostles and other New Testament writers did recognize a difference between teaching and preaching. Now, the apostles had learned what Jesus was doing by the teaching ministry presiding over the preaching ministry set up for the early Christians to follow. Some apostles such as Paul and Barnabas were more widespread in their ministry while others chose to remain within one area for a longer time preaching and teaching to individuals and smaller groups. Paul's sole purpose, while writing his epistles, was to teach. Paul emphasized the understanding and knowledge of the "absolute truths" that Jesus wanted all His people to know. Upon listening to apostles preach and read what the gospel writers and Paul had written/taught, many ideas and thinkers came about with the thirst to learn more, which is exactly what Jesus's mission was all about.[44] Paul himself took on a leadership role to expand the mission as greatly as he humanly could. Traveling over many regions and facing people of several different backgrounds never hindered Paul from journeying to where he was needed next.

Paul was ultimately journeying to Rome where the dictatorship rule and Christian persecutions were taking place. Paul certainly had a huge obstacle to handle considering that the early church as it was here was incredibly divided. Many places were still only beginning to learn about Jesus and what He had taught. Many people were divided as following the Jewish traditions that had already been ongoing for centuries; others were more apt to follow Peter as opposed to Paul, and for fear of persecutions, while many turned away from worship of all sorts.[45] Also, in regions around present-day Greece, people were still very active in following the worship of the Greek gods. For these individuals who had long worshipped multiple deities, it was extremely difficult to understand a newly found religion focusing on one God in three persons: the Holy Trinity. Likewise, many from the strong Jewish background could not fathom the Savior coming

---

[43] C. B. Eavey, *History of Christian Education* (Chicago: Moody Press, 1964), 82.

[44] Ibid., 83–83.

[45] Kenneth Scott Latourette, *A History of Christianity* (New York: Harper and Brothers Publishers, 1953), 114.

to earth in human form. The Old Testament covenant of a coming Messiah was a belief that God would come to earth as God and not as human flesh. Thus, the task of the apostles for decades to come would not be much easier to achieve.

While the early church during Paul's time was beginning to take form, not only were people divided among faith beliefs but also more divisions between a person's statuses was shaping. For example, since Jesus had come to earth as a poor human being, the people were more divided on social status between the rich and the poor. Questions regarding everyday life choices, morality, and education methods for teaching others also were causing divisions. Morality and education for the rich were not necessarily difficult choices considering many did not have to be concerned about such choices. However, those in the poor category were more likely to join with other neighbors and friends to become educated and pass on what they had learned to others.[46]

Those who were striving to teach the mission of Christ made it their everyday lifestyle to follow the morality and teachings that Jesus had provided. The main difficulty for all divisions wanting to learn more about Christianity was at this time, all of the education was word of mouth. The gospel writers as well as Paul had just begun writing the life of Jesus down in what would eventually become the completed Bible. Obviously, there were no printing presses, distribution methods, and usually not any writing materials available. With this having been said, just as today, it is still easy for ideas and lessons to be confused and/or lost within translations. People making the effort to reach out to the apostles, who followed Jesus personally, were the best sources of education. However, a handful of preachers could not possibly cover the entire population that was needed. Writing down all the details of Jesus's life and mission was essential not only to be passed on in the future, but at that time, Paul's letters that later became part of the Scripture were the only way some specific people and countries were communicated with.

---

[46] Ibid., 115.

Related to this, further divisions of hierarchy were becoming more prevalent considering leadership within the government was mostly persecuting people for fear of takeovers; and at the same time, people had to wonder if the apostles were really chosen by Jesus. Did they become powerful in leadership roles? Needless to say, many questions such as this one were being asked all over the region and beyond as Paul and the other remaining apostles branched out. Further on in the first century, church leadership was greatly taking form as officials, successors, and deacons were becoming promoted and/or named. While the New Testament mentions Pharisees, Sadducees, and priests, the diaconate is not mentioned. Deacons were selected based the Greek word meaning "a servant or minister." Likewise, the terms "elders" and "bishops" were being used interchangeably, which was already an early sign of denominational divisions as to what and whom should be in leadership.[47] Qualifications, skills, and experience would all become factors for leadership while very quick to evolve.

Within the first century at least, specific denominations had not taken place or given names yet; patterns of worship, leadership, and even celebrations were all taking various forms. Usually a wedding, funeral, baptism, and even the Eucharist could not be performed without someone within church leadership there to perform the ritual. However, some on the not-as-wealthy side found it more difficult for a church leader to always be present. Some allowed elders and even deacons of lower leadership status to fill in. The church of Rome was greatly disturbed by this to the point of writing declarations to the people reminding them of the importance of church leadership and that society should not be allowed to take it upon themselves to perform worship celebrations without church leadership. Rome even suggested that such acts done without church officials would be invalid. With many early Christians not agreeing with the Roman proclamations, further divisions of Christianity were now forming.

---

[47] John Thomas McNeill, Matthew Spinka, and Harold R. Willoughby, *Environmental Factors in Christian History* (London: Kennikat Press, 1939), 116.

AD 0–1400

Now that the Christian mission was beginning to take off and form up, the spread of the mission was not as easy. For the next several centuries, the conversion of the Mediterranean region was shifting toward Christianity. Geographically, the spread of Christianity was made easier by the adjoining territories and simple water routes.[48] In AD 330, the formation of Constantinople was already taking shape and in many ways foreshadowing what was coming for the Christian mission. As the Christian world was expanding, there were several bumps in the road, to say the least. One problem was the internal threat of heresy. For example, some who were still very solid within their Jewish traditions were trying to persuade the early Christians to fall back on their roots, reminding them of where they originated. Many of these heresies opposed the idea of Jesus as the Christ or that he had divinity as God the Father. During the fourth century, there were two major heresy groups that created much of the stir: the Donatism and the Manichaeism. Donatism originated as an African product of dispute over clergy assignments and organizational differences. Oftentimes, the confrontations here could become brutal to the point of smaller-scale wars questioning morality and sacramental issues to the extreme. Related to this, several orthodox views generated and became more prevalent based on these debates alone.[49]

By the year AD 313, Saint Augustine had begun challenging many of the Donatism theories. However, Augustine found it easier to challenge the Manichaeism heresies because as a young man, he himself had been a follower of Mani beliefs. Manichaeism originated from a Persian teacher who encountered Buddhism while taking on the soul struggles of Zoroastrianism. Mostly, Mani focuses a great deal on the light of goodness and darkness of evil. How do these struggle with each other? How can good and evil be compatible?[50]

---

[48] Donald W. Treadgold, *A History of Christianity* (New York: Athens Printing Company, 1979), 65.

[49] Ibid., 66.

[50] Ibid., 67–68.

While rejected nearly all of the Bible at that time, Mani only believed that the incarnation (Jesus as divine and human) and death were the only "pure" images that gave appearance to what Christianity was offering. Such disputes continued, while others like Augustine also continued to study into the deeper Christian mission.

Another challenge emerged for the Christian mission by the year AD 629 when a man named Muhammad from the Mecca region began his personal pilgrimage. Muhammad even at a young age enjoyed discussing with what he called men of the book, meaning those who dedicated their lives to religious study. By questioning those of the Jewish background and the Christian formation, Muhammad went on to take the teachings of both and create his own "book," the Koran. The Koran, while denying that Jesus was the Son of God, focused more on earlier Old Testament stories when God or "Allah" spoke directly to His chosen people. Muhammad had questioned and created enough debated theories that early Islam had begun. Islam did not contain much doctrine; rather, Islam followers focused on their five pivotal rituals that Muhammad had established. The five rituals included the credo, divine worship, almsgiving, fasting of Ramadan, and pilgrimage to Mecca, where it all began.[51]

Despite the Koran being against acts of violence, upon Muhammad's death, many of the Arab followers led armies to conquer the Byzantine and Persian Empires, along with Damascus and Alexandria, to even Constantinople. One Byzantine theologian, Saint John of Damascus, thought Islam to be a heresy upon Christianity, thus causing an expansion inconvenience. The Byzantine Empire had much degraded after it had been conquered. Issues of morality, sex within churches, and mutilation as punishment were all causing concern, especially when executions were becoming more prevalent often without reason.

On the flip side, religious achievements were also taking place. Lavish churches were being built with expensive array and glorious statues of the Virgin Mary and early apostles. Again, Saint John of Damascus along with Theodore of Studios argued and defended the

---

[51] Ibid., 78.

importance of the lavish churches, detailed statues, and necessity of such icons. After Saint John of Damascus had died dedicating over thirty years of his life to such work, Theodore of Studios continued stressing the need for icons to be found as many places as possible. Theodore took an early educational approach noting that many of poorer families could not yet read or write but still had a desire to learn more about Christianity. The statues, paintings, and iconic pictures were more than symbolic; they presented a message along with personal hope. Hope here being the visibility of such icons available for all society to admire, question, and be taught.

One such Christian theologian, Nicolas Zernov, who was a Russian educating toward an Eastern Orthodox view though very strongly advocating the importance of learning from icons, wrote perhaps one of the most truly inspirational messages of icons at that time.

> Icons are not merely paintings. They are dynamic manifestations of men's spiritual power to redeem creation through beauty and art. The colors and lines of the icons were not meant to imitate nature; the artists aimed at demonstrating that man, animals, and the whole cosmos could be rescued form present state of degradation and restored to their proper "image"...the artistic perfection of an icon was not only a reflection of the celestial glory-it was a concrete example of matter restored to its original harmony and beauty, and serving as a vehicle of the Spirit.[52]

By these paintings, art, and various icons being realized throughout the ages, Christian education continued to be visible for all people wanting to learn despite being undereducated.

---

[52] Donald W. Treadgold, *A History of Christianity* (New York: Athens Printing Company, 1979), 80.

By the year AD 1035, the entire Byzantine Empire along with other surrounding regions were beginning to crumble. To keep the empire from falling apart completely, the emperors of the time reached out for assistance against the Turks who were known for their fierceness in battle, thirst for blood, and eagerness to be aligned with a ruling nation. Considering the main goal of the Byzantine Empire was to expand their kingdom as widely as possible, having the Turks as allies became a promising challenge. Christianity at this time also became an ally for the Byzantine Empire as many were following the religion and openly journeying westward to continue the mission. Needless to say, the farther the expansion was moving, the more conflicts began to arise. Various battles were being fought more and more over the regions especially where Christianity was not welcomed.[53]

The Roman Empire, however, was especially being problematic considering the changes in successors and major declines in their economy. Long ongoing droughts and overpopulation generated the notion of moving eastward to seek help. Certain people with more ambitious natures viewed this as an opportunity for adventure, fame, and power over the conquered. By 1096, Pope Urban II was charged with the task of bringing the Western and Eastern wings of the Catholic churches together. The pope did not approve of the separations that were taking place and was hoping to compromise to avoid a full division. Matters became worse in the 1054 Schism, when Pope Urban II went on to answer a plea from the Eastern emperor to assist in the fight against the Turks. Many believed the pope was only allowing such fighting for a conquering of the Western church to be fully under the Eastern church. More specifically under a close watch and location to Rome.[54]

In 1144, the second wave of Crusades began when Jerusalem and a great portion of Europe fell to Islam. As mentioned earlier, the influence of Islam was greatly expanding even onto the Crusades against Christianity. The Muslims would maintain their leadership

---

[53] Kenneth Scott Latourette, *A History of Christianity* (New York: Harper and Brothers Publishers, 1953), 408–409.
[54] Ibid., 410.

over Jerusalem off and on for several centuries to come. By 1244, the third wave of Crusades came about because of three influential monarchs: Frederick Barbarossa, French king Philip Augustus, and King Richard I of England. King Richard reached out to the Muslim community and explained the importance of Jerusalem to the Christians. Surprisingly, without much fighting, the Muslims agreed to share the city of Jerusalem for worship practices only.[55]

A fourth wave of Crusades began when Pope Innocent II adventured into northern France against the Venetian fleets. Innocent II wanted to attack Constantinople that had originally been responsible for convincing the Western church to stop the Eastern church from allowing the Muslims to share Jerusalem rather than driving them out. Furthermore, Innocent II tried to start a fifth Crusade, which only took place in Egypt. The Crusade only resulted in the holy cross being returned to Rome. Likewise, the sixth Crusade was an attack of northern and southern regions. The territories that are now modern Germany were gathering allies to be defended against the Roman rule and spread of Christianity. The northern region was primarily in the Islamic hands as well. Pope Innocent IV went on to explore a seventh and even eighth Crusade wave. Egypt and France were battling not only over religious differences but also for wealth. France was eager to have the wealth and treasures within Egypt.[56] Mostly importantly, France did open a theological college that became a pivotal place of education and learning.

By 1291, the Crusades were finally coming to a close after many years of fighting and hardships to the empires and their people. Overall, the results were the Christian differences and split between the Eastern and Western sides. Specific differences of beliefs in the Holy Spirit, relics, use of leavened and unleavened bread, clergy roles, and ending destinations all factored into many of the battles that occurred over the century.[57] Throughout this time, the Christian

---

[55] Donald W. Treadgold, *A History of Christianity* (New York: Athens Printing Company, 1979–98).

[56] Ibid., 98.

[57] John Thomas McNeill, Matthew Spinka, and Harold R. Willoughby, *Environmental Factors in Christian History* (London: Kennikat Press, 1939), 272.

church has originated and evolved through several different transformations and changes. These changes and transformations led to American Christianity practices as seen today.

The various councils listed created the divisions seen here that were mostly battled against during the Crusades. Early Christianity had certainly faced a number of challenges from leadership, mission instruction, political hierarchies, societal changes, and geographical changes. Yet the most important and influential changes within Christianity were about to begin: the Reformation. The debates on the Reformation were ongoing, even so today, that challenged major ideas of Catholicism. Later these various Protestant faiths completely split off from Catholicism to begin their own sects. These various sects and denominations will be discussed in further chapters.

AD 1401–1700 Reformations

After the Crusades had subsided, denominational divisions were taking off, seemingly splitting more and more. For those who did remain loyal to the Catholic faith, they came more from the higher classes of society and those continuing the Latin culture as well as the Roman rule. Yet even those who did remain loyal to Catholicism of the time faced certain difficult challenges. Such challenges included the leadership qualifications of clergy, the morality of higher society members especially those in royalty, the existence of purgatory, and also the selling of indulgences.[58] From this point forward, as mentioned, people began questioning religious integrity as well as what was best for their own families.

The person who began a major series of events and probably the most well-known of the Reformation was Martin Luther. Luther had studied for many years and was a rather influential Augustine monk. Early on, he was assigned to further study and teach at the newly established University of Wittenberg. During his time at the

---

[58] Donald W. Treadgold, *A History of Christianity* (New York: Athens Printing Company, 1979), 130.

university, Luther often questioned himself wanting to know when it was enough for him to be cleansed of sin. He would very frequently be attending the church confessional, but he would not feel fully forgiven. Luther hit a turning point while studying a passage from Romans quoting Habakkuk: "the righteous shall live by faith…," to which Luther added the word "alone."[59] The phrase "by faith alone" became a huge slogan for impacting much of the Reformation practices. Luther preached that good conduct alone and repeatedly visiting a confessional was not enough for a person to be accepted by God. All people have wrongdoings and a person's faith in his or her heart was what God really looks at and treasures in His people.

Luther also went on to challenge many other issues that he and other Protestants were struggling with. One huge struggle was proving the efficacy of the indulgences. Were people really able to buy their forgiveness? Could the Catholic Church effectively forgive people with a piece of paper explaining their sin? Luther was much involved with these struggles that in 1517, he compiled a list of what became known as his ninety-five theses that were nailed to the church door of Wittenberg for scholarly debate.[60] Considering the theses were written in Latin, only the church scholars were able to read and question. The theses created such a debate that many of the Catholic groups including Dominicans and Augustinians rallied in protest. The protest reached Rome, causing the pope to summon Luther to council, charging him with heresy against the church. Pope Leo X reclaimed the importance of the indulgences and existence of purgatory to which Luther was ordered to remain silent. Luther's silence did not last long.

By 1520, Luther wrote his address to the German nobility that greatly attacked the walls and providers of all clergy. Again, the pope was angered and called Luther to Rome. Ultimately, Luther was condemned from the Catholic Church as well as opposing regions. However, Luther continued what he had begun preaching

---

[59] Ibid., 130; Ephesians 2:8–9.
[60] Donald W. Treadgold, *A History of Christianity* (New York: Athens Printing Company, 1979), 130.

more and stressing the importance of faith rather than works. Martin Luther's song "A Mighty Fortress Is Our God" explained what Luther believed to be his key points: the Scripture, not tradition, and the roles of laity and not clergy. In 1546, Martin Luther died from a complicated physical illness. Luther's points triggered the beginning of Lutheranism, especially within much of the German territories. Luther's followers continued to study and preach even more then what Martin Luther had started. Since many Catholics of the time began rejected certain scriptures as well, they turned to the growing Lutheranism/Protestant influence.[61]

The second major branch of Protestantism was began by Huldrych Zwingli and John Calvin. Zwingli paralleled Luther in many ways. Basically anything that was not sanctioned by the Bible was denounced. While Luther focused on indulgences and faith, not by works, Zwingli was a main advocate against the Eucharist. He taught that the Eucharist was merely a symbolic action, that the actual body and blood of Christ could not be present; they were only represented through bread and wine as a symbolic reenactment only.[62] In 1517, the German Switzerland territories were split on this particular theory with followers and opposers. Alongside Catholic cantons, during this battle, Zwingli was killed, and his "reforming" was picked up by John Calvin.

John Calvin was raised and educated within the church by his father. During his time at the University of Paris, Calvin greatly stressed the importance of morality and criticized all who did not take their own morality seriously. He was also influenced by the writings of Erasmus and Martin Luther. By age twenty-five, Calvin had already surrendered his Catholic background, been imprisoned, freed, found seclusion, and began writing his greatest publication. Calvin's book *Institutes of the Christian Religion* was arguably the most influential writing of the Reformation next to Luther's nine-

---

[61] Kenneth Scott Latourette, *A History of Christianity* (New York: Harper and Brothers Publishers, 1953), 729.

[62] Donald W. Treadgold, *A History of Christianity* (New York: Athens Printing Company, 1979), 135.

ty-five theses. One major area within Calvin's book was explaining the order and words of the Apostles' Creed. Calvin wanted to address God in three persons by recognizing the Holy Trinity. He wanted to begin with God the Father as the creator of heaven and earth; followed by God the Son, Jesus coming to earth conquering death; and finally the importance of the Holy Spirit. Finally, Calvin wanted to include the relationship of the people with their own world and society outwardly proclaiming their own mission.[63] By doing these changes, Calvin was not so much wanting to point out the wrongdoing of the Catholic Church or even the disagreements he was having with the current Protestants; rather, Calvin was merely giving positive influence to what believed about God, Christ, and humanity.

Another point that Calvin was often preaching was the sovereignty of God and our submission to His will. Likewise, Calvin believed that the essence of God transcends all human thoughts and knowledge.[64] Calvin professed that God focuses on the individual watching each person and how they live, what they think, and how much they strive to follow God. God is responsible for all the evil throughout the world including the plagues of the Old Testament and even the crucifixion of His own son. All of the good and evil in the world as well as the individual are willed by God to happen. Since God is the source of willing men to do evil deeds, each person should be equally responsible since God Himself is free from all injustice and wrong.

John Calvin argued that original sin originated from Adam back at creation as a revolt against the authority of God. Since this revolt took place, all descendants are automatically going to live with the same desire to revolt against God too. All of the good works that humanity has done or is striving to do are only acceptable to God

---

[63] Kenneth Scott Latourette, *A History of Christianity* (New York: Harper and Brothers Publishers, 1953), 753.

[64] Donald W. Treadgold, *A History of Christianity* (New York: Athens Printing Company, 1979), 753.

by grace: a special grace only given to those God has chosen for it. Calvin wrote,

> Apart from grace every man is under the deserved wrath of God. Man's salvation is entirely from the initiative of God. To effect man's redemption, God of His love and mercy gave the law to keep alive the hope of salvation until Christ should come.[65]

Further, God had a plan for the world from the beginning, and even though God hates sin, God chose humanity for His love.

One final note regarding John Calvin. Calvin, like Luther, also believed in the divine calling. Calvin preached that God appointed people at His choosing to perform and be assigned particular duties throughout their lives. A people must go above the law and beyond their own to follow the obedience of God's will. In doing so, a person will be freed from all external obligation through prayer and constant conversation with God.[66] A chosen person is most worthy to commune with God since the heavenly Father had given Christ as the advocate and mediator to all.

During all of this Protestant "reforming" times and transitions, the Catholic Church was not sitting back with no responses to be had. The response from Rome was often called a "counterreformation." Even before Luther's theses came out, the Catholic Church through their Council of Trent was on a revival mission of spreading Catholic doctrines out for more than clergy to read. Also, the previously mentioned abuses and accused clergy engaging in moral misconduct were being addressed and determined in what would be the proper way to discourage or punish for such actions. Catholicism still maintained connecting with certain backgrounds of the Jewish descent since the Old Testament was about the Jewish tradition. Many theologians of

---

[65] Kenneth Scott Latourette, *A History of Christianity* (New York: Harper and Brothers Publishers, 1953), 754.

[66] Ibid., 755.

this time believed the Catholic Church reaching out to Jewish tradition was only a grasp to keep one up on the Islamic people who were still growing and causing more separations.[67] However, the Islamic community had suggested their faith beliefs to be more vastly different than the basic Christian beliefs, especially Catholicism. Most likely the counterreformation was an overall plea for people to follow the original faith community that Jesus Himself had started. Rome found a great ally with the Church of England and Spain. The Spanish army had conquered and currently controlled areas within South America and had sent Christopher Columbus out to expand the ownership across the ocean.

One great leader of the counterreformation was Saint Ignatius Loyola. From an early age, Ignatius had suffered a terrible wound that led him partially crippled for his life. His crippled body did not stop him from wanting to study theology. Ignatius felt that his injury may have caused him a spiritual crisis as well as physical. Therefore, he produced his own manual or self-help book full of meditations and prayers. One distinguishing phrase he often used was "study yourself." After several visits to Rome and through Jerusalem, Ignatius also went to the University of Paris to further his study. While in the university, he met and worked closely with Francis Xavier to found the Society of Jesus or Jesuits.[68] In 1534, seven young men took the vows of poverty, chastity, and obedience similar to the monks and thus were the first class of Jesuits. Pope Paul III officially declared the Jesuits as an order within Catholicism. One major important vow that all Jesuits make is taking on the responsibility to perform any and all missionary work. Because of this missionary promise, the Jesuit community became one of the most educational teachers throughout all of Europe, which even today is a huge asset.

Along with the educational bursts, the morality within the Catholic clergy had greatly changed for the better, mostly because of Pope Pius V who ordered a stricter watch over all the clergy that

---

[67] Donald W. Treadgold, *A History of Christianity* (New York: Athens Printing Company, 1979), 149.

[68] Ibid., 150.

remained in place for the next two centuries.[69] As a way of renewing the church once again, Michelangelo spent many years painting the ceiling and walls of the Roman Sistine Chapel. Several of the paintings depict the darker side of where the church had begun, resorted, and continued out from. Related to this, the church's history was also visualized along tragic and darker stories from the Bible. The most inspirational painting of Michelangelo that covers the entire back wall of the Sistine Chapel is called *The Last Judgment*, beautifully expressing those reaching upward to Jesus at His judgment day.

The vast education from the Jesuits, the incredible artwork of Michelangelo's paintings, and the better availability of the Bible now being translated in more languages for everyday people to read were certainly causing a much stronger change for the Catholic Church, bringing many followers back. Geographically, the Catholic Church with the Jesuits were reaching out further west than ever before. Now the Jesuits were preaching their missions and educating people through Ukraine, Poland, Ethiopia, India, and China and eventually to Japan.[70] India and China were not as easy to educate in Catholicism considering the Hindu community was already present there. To avoid another Crusade of religions, the Jesuits remained more discreet and actually took some interest in learning from the Hindu culture and also early sign language. Japan was fuller of already established social organizations and several political units. Yet the mission and education of the Jesuits still continued in other places where the Christian boost was needed most, even so today.

AD 1700–Present Day

While moving into the mid to late 1700s, many of the English and German settlers were journeying eastward to the land the Spanish (Columbus) had been exploring. Once in the newly form-

---

[69] Ibid., 152.

[70] Donald W. Treadgold, *A History of Christianity* (New York: Athens Printing Company, 1979), 155.

ing America, settlers wished to establish their religion with people of similar beliefs. The Massachusetts colony state was primarily English Puritans, Pennsylvania was British Quakers, and Virginia became the English Anglicans, while the area of Maryland remained loyal to Catholicism.[71] It can be argued that many of the settlers chose to leave because of the ongoing disputes within hierarchies and the unbalanced economies, but mainly because of religious turmoil. The overwhelming curiosity for people to take the long dangerous journey across the Atlantic Ocean openly showed that people were almost willing to risk their own lives and safety for a chance at a new beginning.

Upon arriving in what was called the new world at that time, people soon discovered that the land was extremely large and wealthy for farming. However, as the settlers continued moving east, the Native American tribes that had been living there for centuries before did not welcome the newcomers. Coming from an English background, it was not uncommon that the settlers would easily wish to fight and conquer the Indians for this newly forming land. Some chose to cause disputes while others reached out seeking help from the Native Americans using their knowledge of the land for development. Alongside learning how to properly farm the land, store water, build structures, and discover newer areas, some possible early religious leaders took an interest in learning the already present practices of religious beliefs the natives were using. Since the Native American people were so closely engaged with the earth, sky, water, winds, and basically all elements, settlers learned that "spirits" of the earth are necessary for survival. The richness of the soil, regular need for rain and climate changes, and the significance of day and night all explained time. Native Americans had studied the seasons and the phases of the moon and created their own calendars based on planting and harvest.[72] Despite several valuable lessons that the

---

[71] Kevin M. Schultz and Paul Harvey, "Everywhere and Nowhere: Recent Trends in American Religious History and Historiography," *Journal of the American Academy of Religion* 78, no. 1 (March 2010): 129.

[72] Ibid., 131.

natives had taught, that conquest desire still prevailed, pushing the Indians farther away, even restricting them to only allowed territories the British set.

Just as in Europe, each state wanted different laws while others desired a more unified country. In 1776, when the colonies officially signed the Declaration of Independence claiming their freedom from all English rule, the first amendment clearly stated,

> Congress shall make no law respecting an establishment of religion, or prohibiting the free exercise thereof; or abridging the freedom of speech, or of the press; or the right of the people peaceably to assemble, and to petition the Government for a redress of grievances.[73]

Early government leaders agreed that religion would never be determined by any state. Each individual free American would have the choice of establishing and openly practicing whichever religion they desired.

Over the next century, America continued to grow and thrive on their self-proclaimed religious freedom. The idea of being able to choose a person's own religious practice created the desire for more education. Economically, America continued to move westward, especially during the great gold rush; but by the civil war, the country had literally torn itself apart. Many states still remained loyal to the religions usually of their upbringing and local community. As the social status of the early states was becoming really separated, religion and human rights took on a whole new concern. Several wealthy plantation owners of the Southern states were kidnapping and selling black slaves to work on their fields completely against their will. The slaves were treated very harshly, no pay, long hours, and terrible housing conditions. These people were not even allowed

---

[73] Kevin M. Schultz, and Paul Harvey, "Everywhere and Nowhere: Recent Trends in American Religious History and Historiography," *Journal of the American Academy of Religion* 78, no. 1 (March 2010): 132.

to be human; they were property of whoever had bought them. The Northern states began greatly rebelling against the Southern way of life.

Many protesters including the early Quakers stood extremely strong for human rights. The Southern states opposed to let their "property" go so much that the civil war broke out and lasted four years with both parts of the country experiencing horrific losses through human life, property, and religious value. During this dark time in American history, President Abraham Lincoln had the awful duty of trying to reunite the country as one nation again, but Jefferson Davis leading the South refused all offers of peace settlement. The most pivotal changing moment within the civil war was Lincoln freeing the slaves. It was now law that no person could keep another in slavery or be handled as property. Lincoln stated,

> All men are created equal in the eyes of God. Each side reads the same Bible and prayers to the same God, but the Almighty has His own purposes.[74]

In the end, the South finally surrendered to the North to stop further bloodshed. For many years to come, the country had to rebuild their lives, strive to change with the newer laws, and secure a future.

As the 1900s came about, America was dealing with outside countries once again fighting among each other. World Wars I and II had American soldiers fighting as allies with other countries, some of whom they had separated originally. By the stock market crash during the Great Depression of 1920, many people were striving merely to survive. The country had been so deprived of money, food, and resources in order to support the war effort that the importance of safety was more important than everyday human survival. Eventually, the outcome of World War II did begin to slowly rebuild American life. In the meantime, churches of nearly all denominations were trying to support their people as much as possible, but

---

[74] Ibid., 159.

the lack of resources was too great. Religion was turned to by many people who had nowhere else to receive support. In some cases, even people who did not belong to a specific religious denomination were simply attending the closest church merely to find encouragement, find hope, and offer prayers.

Here again was an opportunity for church leaders to see what exactly people were looking for within the church. Since the depression had been such a horrible time, religious communities had learned a valuable lesson on how to reach out to people in most need. What has to be changed? What can be done to keep these people support one church as opposed to others? More Protestant faiths had blossomed out from these various questions. Likewise, by the 1950s and 1960s, the issue of segregation had propelled once again the importance of human rights and value of equality. The Baptists especially reached out, making the black communities extremely welcomed, which did create some tensions with other denominations for a time. In a small way, there are people from that time who still harbor such feelings.

In the present time, specifically over the past twenty years until now, society has continued the push on equal rights. The segregation of skin color still has some areas concerned as does the homosexual community. Again, this is referring back to human rights and equality. The Catholic Church along a few others still maintain that certain issues such as homosexuality, abortion, capital punishment, and euthanasia are morally wrong. The argument is not so much based on an issue of human rights, but more so what the Scripture had originally instructed. The notion of ending a human life under any circumstance and/or judgment of others' decisions is not the will of the Christian mission.

In conclusion, chapter 2 has journeyed from Jesus's time all the way 2,014 years to our present day. Many battles, discoveries, challenges, and adjustments have been looked at. On a sidenote, this would be considered a small overview; the vast details of Christian history are still being explored even now. Throughout our look in this chapter of Christian education history, there have been several high and low points of rich commitment and poor fighting. For whatever reason, religious organizations continue to stand the test of time and strive to keep the Christian mission going. The mission has never become any easier to teach or express. As society continues to evolve, it does become difficult for people to always keep the much-needed importance of achieving Jesus's set mission. The constant changes within the religious communities are always going to be in need of more efficient methods and resources to remind their followers of why the religious community has survived the test of time and will hopefully continue to do so.

CHAPTER 3

Christian Education as a Philosophy

Chapter 3 explains the theological, philosophical perspectives for how various dialogues and conflicts promote Christian education and formation. This analysis will include several examples of how and why philosophical divisions occur all throughout the Scripture and even today. Many different Scripture references are going to be quoted and then related to philosophical examples that people may encounter that are very similar to those within the biblical stories. Philosophical theories, tests, measurements, results, and advances in technology all have played factors in the continuance of Christian education seen now.

The chapter will continue with two more subcategories explaining examples of current Christian perspectives. This will explain and teach other methods that assist with those previously listed conflicts. Remaining positive and keeping a healthy lifestyle will ensure that conflicts do not have to be all that terrible to deal with. Jesus set some wonderful and powerful examples in the New Testament as models for humanity to follow. The ministry program is a great place to watch learners become models to each other.

Biblical-Theological-Philosophical Perspectives

The first subcategory of this chapter will be concentrating on biblical examples of reasoning together, constructive disagreements while reaching a resolution, and overcoming divisions by lifting up Christ. All three of these categories will cover many details in describing what a new worshipper can be expecting by becoming a part of the Christian educational setting. There will be several instances of disagreements, conflicts, and divisions for members to encounter. All of these may occur at any time with any person. Family, friends, teachers, and especially other learners (peers) will at some point cause one of these instances to happen. Depending on the person's personality, situation, and faith, these factors will determine what type of solution can be expected. However, knowing that current everyday situations are not that different from biblical situations can be a huge comfort. Christians need to remember that relating back to Jesus's examples is the best way for all solutions to be met.

Reasoning

Philosophy bases several of its theories on those of reason deriving from the human mind. Various theories, questions, and discoveries all come from a person's reason in discovering an idea of value. The Hebrew and Greek Bible versions have several examples of people trying to use their own reasoning to solve problems and create understanding. The first biblical example mentioned is reasoning together. The Scripture gives several examples of reasoning together for a bright and solid solution. In the Old Testament, while the Israelites were experiencing much confusion and disagreements, the prophet Isaiah wrote,

> Come now, let us reason together, says the LORD. Though your sins are like scarlet, they shall be as white as snow; though they are red as crimson, they shall be like wool. If you are willing

and obedient, you will eat the best from the land;
but if you resist and rebel, you will be devoured
by the sword. For the mouth of the LORD has
spoken.[75]

Another Bible translation uses the wording of "settle the matter" as opposed to "reason together." Do reason and settle mean the same? The Lord commands "come" as speaking to all people. Coming to the Lord and trusting His decision will solve any matter. This was a huge reminder that the Israelites needed at the time to remember that God was on their side and wanted them to be unified together and to avoid the consequences of divisions and more conflict. Biblical commentary for this passage reminds the readers that the invitation "Come now, let us reason together" shows more of a call for negotiations between the people and God. The word "reason" originates from a law term used for arguing, convincing, or deciding a case in court. The people were to be convinced by their argumentation with God that He was right, and they were wrong about their condition.[76]

In the same manner within the New Testament, the people still had much to learn. Jesus tried to teach the people how He wanted them to live, but they still did not understand. The concept of reasoning or knowing of the human reason did not reassure the importance of what was being spoken. In Mark 12:24, Jesus says,

Is this not the reason you are wrong, because you
know neither the Scriptures nor the power of
God?[77]

Thus, it is a statement also reminding a Christian learner that they may or may not understand the reasoning behind the Scripture as much as they may think. Not having full understanding is not

---

[75] Isaiah 1:18.
[76] John Walvoord and Roy B. Zuck, *The Bible Knowledge Commentary: An Exposition of the Scriptures* (Wheaton: Victor Books, 1993), 1.
[77] Mark 12:24.

always a bad notion. The thirst for knowledge and desire to learn can be a huge motivator for any learner to keep going. So more education is needed while discernment is being made.

Needless to say, there are plenty of times when an educational learner will have disagreements or learning opportunities of their own, especially while in early learning stages. A newer wonderer will encounter disagreements with various people since this is a new atmosphere. For example, disagreement could occur with ministers, teachers, advisors, parents, and with decisions regarding worship. In reality, dialect or dialogue discussions with family can take some rather ugly turns, but there is always the solution of doing what is best personally. In respect to teachers and advisors, it is important to realize that the educational process may be that long. Differences can easily be put aside for the sake of success, or if not, someone can retake the course with another teacher. In any case, these disagreements can be resolved.

Conflicts

Conflicts do arise when there can be struggle when deciding what worship style or places within the church atmosphere especially if this is a new location for the learner. There are certainly a variety of new experiences waiting for the student to find, but often, religious practice may be one of the experiences that are avoided. Yet it is important to realize that another important factor that comes into play while searching for that comfortable religious atmosphere is new personal relationships. This could be a time in which the learner will potentially meet their future spouse. Personal relationships may very well be one of the biggest examples there is for reasoning together on so many different levels specifically when the relationship becomes a possible marriage. In the New Testament, Jesus makes special note of conflict within marriage relationships. Consider this, in Matthew 19:9, Jesus is being tested by the Pharisees on how divorce in marriage should be handled.

> I tell you that anyone who divorces his wife, except for marital unfaithfulness, and marries another woman commits adultery.[78]

The people had already been given laws on marriage from Moses, but Jesus was there to teach what God wants in marriage. Marriage is a huge life-changing commitment to another person that some people will be discovering while others may not. Again, a huge discernment is being made. Is this a proper time for marriage, or should marriage wait until a better time? Thus, it is important to consider the conflicts of marriage that can lead to divorce from the beginning to lessen the reality of a negative outcome.

Mission for Truth

Related to this, God sets examples and commands for knowing His truth and establishing His mission. Paul explains that the knowing of truth is a privilege that God wants humanity to strive for but often not quite accomplished. Paul writes in 2 Timothy 3:7,

> Always learning and never able to arrive at a *knowledge of the truth*.[79] (Emphasis added)

Once again, the biblical commentary explains that learning what truth Jesus gave humanity is a constant in life, but the ultimate knowledge of knowing His truth is a glory to be discovered with Him in the next life. This may be a disagreement for humanity now, but it can also be a comfort to know what wonders of God will someday be related to His people.[80] Likewise, an interested learner may not see their whole picture now, but the future surprise and wonder is

---

[78] Matthew 19:9.

[79] 2 Timothy 3:7.

[80] John Walvoord and Roy B. Zuck, *The Bible Knowledge Commentary: An Exposition of the Scriptures* (Wheaton: Victor Books, 1993), 24.

certainly worth the wait just as the wonder of fully knowing God's truth.

In the same manner, it is important to remember that while the learner is discovering their "whole picture" and enduring everyday tasks, Jesus commanded His great commission to be within the goal of humanity. The goal of the Christian education is continuing the mission that Jesus commanded to His disciples. All people were to be brought into His mission and to carry that mission throughout life. Matthew 28:18–20 reads,

> Then Jesus came to them and said, "All authority in heaven and on earth has been given to me. Therefore go and make disciples of all nations, baptizing them in the name of the Father and of the Son and of the Holy Spirit, and teaching them to obey everything I have commanded you. And surely I am with you always, to the very end of the age."[81]

The mission of humanity is to carry out and bring God's people into the one understanding of Christ.[82] Many Christians will encounter this mission while they discover their own faith beliefs. The hope being that these learners will use their education to carry and teach the mission throughout their lives. Jesus made it clear that His people are to be filled with His authority and to take His mission onto every person throughout life's journey. This is a true comfort and challenge for all people, especially those still finding purpose.

Further into the New Testament, the apostle Paul wrote numerous letters to various people and countries in hopes of bringing them a solution to the many problems each person and country was facing. Paul explains an example of disagreements in a letter to the Hebrews,

---

[81] Matthew 28:18–20.

[82] John Walvoord and Roy B. Zuck, *The Bible Knowledge Commentary: An Exposition of the Scriptures* (Wheaton: Victor Books, 1993), 25–26.

in which he teaches how the blood of Christ is what brings all of God's people together despite divisions. Hebrews 9:15 states,

> For this reason Christ is the mediator of a new covenant, that those who are called may receive the promised eternal inheritance—now that he has died as a ransom to set them free from the sins committed under the first covenant.[83]

Paul reminds the Hebrews that Jesus paid the ultimate price for humanity so that the conflicts and disagreements would no longer be in the way of receiving a place at God's right hand. These words are truly a comfort to find peace in. However, a new learner might wonder if he or she is supposed to be willing to sacrifice their life to following Jesus's mission. From the philosophical perspective, this is almost making a life-and-death question for the greater good.

Perhaps exploring what other people in biblical times were experiencing could bring some more clarity into light. In the same manner, Paul again offers words of encouragement to the Corinthians while they continue to struggle in conflict. Paul explains to the Corinthians that resolving conflict must be based on how they communicate with one another. Communication is a key component for resolving many issues or at least creating reasoning. Paul writes,

> For this reason anyone who speaks in a tongue should pray that he may interpret what he says. For if I pray in a tongue, my spirit prays, but my mind is unfruitful. So what shall I do? I will pray with my spirit, but I will also pray with my mind; I will sing with my spirit, but I will also sing with my mind. If you are praising God with your spirit, how can one who finds himself among those who do not understand say "Amen" to your thanksgiving, since he does not know

---

[83] Hebrews 9:15.

what you are saying? You may be giving thanks well enough, but the other man is not edified. I thank God that I speak in tongues more than all of you. But in the church I would rather speak five intelligible words to instruct others than ten thousand words in a tongue.[84]

Continuing the mission for truth, communication plays a huge role in the New Testament era as it does today. In many cases, communication is the only way any resolution is going to come about. Paul writes many other examples to various countries that are all on the brink of destruction because they have lost faith and not taken the time to communicate with each other and especially with God.[85] This message of reasoning should hit right at the heart of certain learners who may be feeling the pressures of doubting their Christian formation. Paul's letter is words of comfort that all conflicts will pass and matter little while on earth. If only more people took the proper amount of time to consider this point, then just imagine what the world would be like.

Paul often speaks with the distinction between the words "justification" and "reconciliation." These words are attributed to God's forgiveness of His people. Forgiveness has everything to be gained for the believer. By remembering this, people are prompted to ignore the obvious importance and often overlook the justice and mercy factors.[86] Some scholars have argued that by Paul making these distinctions within forgiveness, he tragically made a huge flaw in the study of Christian education. Justice and mercy are indeed present for forgiveness. However, they are there together for a reason and should not be separated. In a way of thinking about this clearer, justice makes the mercy merciful while the mercy makes the justice justified. Paul almost creates a division of explaining how God uses forgiveness. God as the

---

[84] 1 Corinthians 14:14.

[85] John Walvoord and Roy B. Zuck, *The Bible Knowledge Commentary: An Exposition of the Scriptures* (Wheaton: Victor Books, 1993), 29.

[86] W. R. Farmer, C. F. D. Moule, and R. R. Niebuhr, *Christian History and Interpretation: Studies Presented to John Knox* (Cambridge: University Press, 1967), 363.

father makes all final judgments. Without God's mercy being present within His judgment, all humanity would fall short to sin. Likewise, how can there be any sort of reconciliation for a person to learn from without the grace and mercy of God? Jesus's teachings about the importance of forgiving one another were more than clear. While Paul certainly took Jesus's journey forward, some historians and theologians wonder if Paul was still trying to grasp forgiveness for himself. The Scripture explains Paul's earlier life as Saul who persecuted Christians by the hundreds for believing in Jesus, following Him, and preaching about Him. After Saul's conversion to Paul, his life changed forever, but was there a lingering doubt regarding his own forgiveness?[87]

Disagreements Reaching Resolution

Philosophy has been based on disagreements, questions, and evidence for centuries. People want to know more about all sorts of topics. Theories can most effectively be argued from two different sides wanting to resolve an issue or by simply making their own opinion or discovery known. Even so in biblical times, the early Israelites disputed with God. The second example mentioned is constructive disagreements while reaching a resolution. Within the Old Testament, there are numerous examples of people having disagreements with God. Then by His miracles and intervention, they find faith again. However, in the story of Jonah after he is sent out on his mission, he becomes furious with God for not following through on a threat to destroy the city of Nineveh, in which Jonah had been sent to preach. Jonah had to be reminded of God's power and to test Jonah within his anger toward God. Jonah 4:4–5 reads,

> Now, O LORD, take away my life, for it is better for me to die than to live. But the LORD replied, "Have you any right to be angry."[88]

---

[87] Ibid., 364.
[88] Jonah 4:4–5.

Anger and frustration can be seen in Christian minds today as they face many of these same situations between peers, families, careers, and God. Yet it is essentially important to take a step back and remember why the disagreement is taking place. Should the disagreement be taking place?

Just as God taught Jonah a lesson in anger control, Christians know that a solution can be found too.[89] Without conflict and challenges, the learning can become too easy or even boring. The disputes can create the need for defending ideas or question personal intentions behind certain beliefs. The entire basis of theories and philosophical measurements are fueled by the very questions asked of theologians and curious minds of today.

In terms of finding solutions, philosopher and theologian John Knox had experienced several disagreements of his theories. Knox had three important elements that are specifically attributed to him. First, Knox believed in a very dynamic ever-changing history that follows the progression view of the world order. Knox's biggest example to this theory is his interpretation of Jesus as an act of God in human history. In Knox's book *Jesus Lord and Christ*, Knox wrote,

> The utmost and inmost, it is given us to know of God's "substance" is that he is love…and love is not a metaphysical essence but personal moral will and action…What we are trying to say is that [Jesus's] supreme importance is best seen when he is viewed as the living creative center of the supremely important event of human history, and also that the "nature" of Christ is most truly known under the same category: God's action is the divine nature of Christ.[90]

---

[89] John Walvoord and Roy B. Zuck, *The Bible Knowledge Commentary: An Exposition of the Scriptures* (Wheaton: Victor Books, 1993), 55–58.

[90] W. R. Farmer, C. F. D. Moule, and R. R. Niebuhr, *Christian History and Interpretation: Studies Presented to John Knox*. Cambridge: University Press, 1967), 4–5.

Knox continues this theory by explaining that the church's Christological development speaks only of the events of Christ and is nothing less than divine. Christ cannot be explained in a definition but only as a story of action.[91]

Second, events do not happen based on time and/or location; rather, events occur as a result of previous planning and afterward reception. Knox is keen on the awareness of particular events. Do certain events have the significance enough to become necessary for commitment? What are the preconditions that factor into how a particular event takes place? For the philosophical side, these questions are tremendous. By asking about significance, the door has been opened for debate and need for evidence. From the theological viewpoint, the significance can be attributed with faith, especially believing the validity of the Bible. Therefore, the extra questioning and evidence is not necessary. Knox argues both cases in that the biblical insights concerning God's purpose and the dynamic quality of His image created order. The very basic nature of humanity is described as a "ground of being," and Christians follow their "sovereign ruler." For Knox, this theory alone is a guarantee to the basic Christian insights.[92]

Third, an event in life only comes to life based on how a person accepts the event. Does the person respond with commitment, doubt, or nothing? Relating with his second theory, a great deal can be determined from one particular event. For Knox personally, the challenges, questions, and debates that arose from his theories were enough to teach him whether or not a person can rise to the occasion disregarding what the occasion maybe will make the impression within one's mind for future reference. Will the person learn from this experience? What can be taken away by this one particular event happening at this very moment? Knox again was not too concerned with the time and/location, but rather the circumstances around the occasion. For Christian education, this understanding places a whole

---

[91] Ibid., 5.
[92] Ibid., 13.

new outlook on the facts building up theological reconstruction as needed.[93]

In the same manner, Saint Augustine shared as well as contrasted some philosophical ideas with John Knox. Augustine further examined what was known as the procrustean treatment of evidence. Put simply, philosophy, theology, and historical studies are three studies that are best described as three divisions: pure, applied, and apologetically. A "pure" scientist will follow his beliefs in faith interpreting any evidence finding using morals, society, and human intelligence to explain. More often, this pure method will keep a tentative outcome in promise that after further testing and exploring, the data can change. The negative criticism here is that usually the outcome will change at a time that only seems appropriate to the discoverer pending another finding to compromise his.[94] Closely related to this, the "applied" scientist will accept the findings of the "pure" scientist perhaps less intently but will apply the finding to a society setting as fairly and to the benefit of people as possible.

The third division of the apologist may be more grayish than the black and white of the pure and applied. Usually the apologist may follow the pure but not so much the applied methods. The apologist may wish to deeply test ideas and place as much emphasis on the human intellect as opposed to making a conclusion and/or applying the result.[95] The apologetic approach will make more hypotheses and want to test every aspect as to what makes the finding plausible for use. Again, there is a negative here. While wanting to test every hypothesis may be beneficial, it can become too easy for the scientist to place more of his or her own beliefs into the process wishing more to found correct rather than gathering unnecessary criticism.

Saint Augustine was certainly an apologetic scientist. He studied the fruit being the downfall of creation in Christian history, giving

---

[93] W. R. Farmer, C. F. D. Moule, and R. R. Niebuhr, *Christian History and Interpretation: Studies Presented to John Knox*. Cambridge: University Press, 1967), 16.

[94] G. L. Keyes, *Christian Faith and the Interpretation of History* (Lincoln: University of Nebraska Press, 1966), 83–84.

[95] Ibid., 83–84.

him a personal control over the study in his theological profession. Likewise, Augustine studied the Christian creed wanting to fully understand the truth behind every line so as to be able to continue his own Christian education.[96] Augustine placed a firm belief in the need for church doctrines to be fully explained to be compared with the truth of the Scripture. Indeed, the explanations researched within church doctrines was truly an undertaking; but even like so many scholars today, not every hypothesis is deemed correct.

One major difficulty that Saint Augustine came across while studying church doctrines was the amount of secular studies that had already been in place. Augustine was certainly thorough on explaining the historical facts especially where the Scripture was concerned, but much of history is scientifically based as opposed to biblical. For Augustine's research, scientific fact always leaves room for error where the Scripture as the divine truth does not. Therefore, Augustine classified his research as true history as opposed to false history. This was not to say that all scientific history was incorrect, but it was to admit that true historical research was in full agreement with the Scripture to further the Christian faith understanding.[97]

Saint Augustine was challenged often by other secular theories. Considering his deep Christian faith, he was regularly asked about the evolution theory. On the surface level, Augustine admitted the theory to be false history considering the overall evidence supporting evolution was still weak and that the Genesis creation explicitly states God created man. The biggest argument made in this debate was how can man be created in God's own image if humans originated from primates? The Scripture does explain that God created animals first and then placed man in the garden over the animals, but that does not explain man coming from animals. Augustine's need for logic always to be found within the Scripture made it difficult for him to debate with. The sense of wanting to one-up his debaters with a certain closed-mindedness to the secular realm still makes him explained as impractical by some educators.

---

[96] Ibid., 85.
[97] Ibid., 86.

Earlier within this chapter, there was a brief look at reasoning and decision-making. Augustine uses reason as a main instrument for explaining his own treatments of philosophy. Augustine firmly believed that the Scripture was the only true testament of what salvation is and how to receive it. The most intriguing idea relating to salvation that Augustine suggested was that God may only reveal His true nature to select persons. Would these persons be the most intelligent? Knowledgeable? How and why these particular people? Was there a pattern that God had planned out even within the Old Testament of chosen prophets used for Christians today? Could these hypotheses be limited to the Christian faith and not the nonbelievers? God's divine revelation would always be the first true knowledge, whereas philosophical questions would come in second. In other words, for Augustine, faith must take precedence over reason. Before anyone can apply reasoning to an idea, that person must believe in the idea itself without question to ensure the idea's explanation of existence. However, Augustine does not ever deny human ignorance, doubt, and failures to withhold any discovery. The main cause for these downfalls concerns those not giving the proper instruction to either completely deny or affirm what has truly been discovered. Augustine himself commented that

> the Christian faith, as traditional taught by the Church, must always be taken as true. Historical evidence, secular sciences, intellectual disciplines, philosophical speculation, and the Canonical Scriptures themselves are used never really to test, but only to illustrate, the plausibility of a hypotheses.[98]

Related to the philosophy of existence, our Christian beginning alone had a rough start with the fall of man through sin. Sin has been an ongoing philosophical debate for many centuries. Why did God

---

[98] G. L. Keyes, *Christian Faith and the Interpretation of History* (Lincoln: University of Nebraska Press, 1966), 123.

allow sin? Why is Satan so powerful? Was sin being a part of the human world a test that all humanity would be subject to pass? For humanity, even man fell short of God's obedience. His love was always present to pick up the pieces. God knew what was going to happen and allowed the events to occur for our benefit to learn from and to know that God would always be there for us even today. In essence, when man took to sin, humanity was dethroning God and minimizing His importance in our lives. Yet God's plan was to be the center of our lives, and in return, we are the center of God's life. By being created in the image of God, we cannot even be parted from Him or His heart.[99] But sin coming into the lives of man, humanity became subject to sin and death for all times. Sin was never an element that would leave people alone. Only by the grace of God would people have hope of being freed from sin. Satan has made God's people bonded to himself by proving that his temptations are enough to further us from God. Yet if we are bonded to sin, what can be done to save us? Was this question meant to be asked and explored even with Adam and Eve?

God's lesson of redemption is more important than ever to understand. God's plan achieved two major lessons: seeing man's insufficiency and seeing God's abundant sufficiency. Man has to learn there are consequences behind every wrong choice that includes sin. People are given free will to make decisions on their own, but human weakness is a need for strength. When a desperate need for change is fully recognized, the possibility of one accomplishing their own redemption breaks through.[100] The moral question of good versus evil comes up here by being darkened by sin, as well as their spiritual understanding. A clouding of judgment. Perhaps a reverse in logic occurs. A person may see an evil as a greater good or a good act creating a bad atmosphere. As long as the person's belief is still strong, the true nature of redemption cannot be found. The sin has not been recognized. There is no set time for sin to remain or be forgiven; each person's perception will differ. For humanity, God's purpose of educating His people becomes clear.

---

[99] C. B. Eavey, *History of Christian Education* (Chicago: Moody Press, 1964), 22–23.

[100] C. B. Eavey, *History of Christian Education* (Chicago: Moody Press, 1964), 23.

For years, people have been discovering their own weaknesses and helplessness, education from the Scripture, and other people have greatly picked up some pieces. God tests people with the chance to choose obedience over temptation. Education can assist in recognizing what these specific tests may be and how to overcome them. Each person will undergo many challenges throughout life. Based on education and experience, an educated person will be more likely to step back from the bad and turn to God as the ultimate good. Again, recognizing the weakness and need for support, reaching out to God is always a right choice. For example, a film made a few years ago depicted Morgan Freeman playing the role of God in a movie called *Evan Almighty*. In one scene, Morgan Freeman, "God," is speaking with Evan's wife, Joan, who has just left Evan, taking their children away somewhere. While she is sitting at the diner lost and confused, "God" comes up to her as a waiter and explains to her patience. He asks, "When a person prays for patience, do you think God gives them patience or the opportunity to be patient?" This line directly portrays the recognition of forgiveness and the need for it. People often believe that God does not hear their prayers or will never answer their needs, but usually the prayers have been answered but not recognized.[101]

Failure is truly written all over history as well as Christian history. The old saying "History repeats itself" seems to be more true now than ever. Many people through all of the Scripture fell short on various tasks God commanded of them. Such people as Noah, Abraham, Joseph, Jonah, David, Daniel, and even Jesus's own apostles. Regardless of their falling short on God's missions, they never ceased to continue to be the best they humanly could. Education often tells the stories of great prophets and kings through the Old Testament, but someone as heroic as Moses even disobeyed God's command. Paul writes to the Corinthians,

> He has chosen the foolish things of the world to confound the wise."[102]

---

[101] Ibid., 24.
[102] 1 Corinthians 1:27–29.

Perhaps this passage may be construed in different ways, but it should bring a sense of hope that every though foolishness will occur, the wise are not always going to thrive.

One of the greatest gifts humanity ever received from God was free will. God allowed people to make their own decisions and choices of how to live life. In a sense, God allowed each person to be the architect of their own destiny.[103] Throughout time, education has grown, technology has changed, and human society has certainly created its own entity. Satan uses every opportunity within human life to tempt a person into making a wrong decision. A longtime theory suggested that Satan was once an angel of God who fell away in refusal to serve Him. God allowed the falling away for Satan to choose as he would. Some humans have chosen to fall away from God for whatever reason, while many remain faithful and often thank God through prayer, worship, and service. Perhaps these select persons learned from personal experiences or perhaps from solid Christian education. Either way, the reward of God's kingdom will certainly be within their reach while they continue God's mission.

Christian Worldview

One final point to mention with the biblical examples of reasoning together, constructive disagreements while reaching a resolution, and overcoming divisions by lifting up Christ can be seen in various views through the Christian worldview lens. This will be how other religions will look at Christianity, while comparing and contrasting specific techniques. Surrounded by other religions and political influence, Christianity will not change or solve anything through isolation. The nurturing of church development has originated from several years of conflict that may have been nurtured in the wrong way and are just now getting to be resolved. This conflict and noneffective nurturing can be pointed to the lack of formal education in the past. Only recently has Christian worldview really

---

[103] C. B. Eavey, *History of Christian Education* (Chicago: Moody Press, 1964), 26.

taken a stand within formal education due to the vast amounts of research and technology that are evolving every day. Christianity has its own education with theology that other religions do not or are still finding.[104] In any case, the core Christian belief that has affected its worldview the most is salvation. Salvation is the liberation from all conflicts, political issues, social differences, and basic human weakness. Differences in view of good/moral versus bad/immoral issues stems from all of the areas that salvation will free humanity from. The Christian worldview will be and should be ever evolving with the times, but the theology itself remains constant. Only when a worldwide peace can be found will the Christian worldview become simply a worldview.

Testing Theories

For Christian education, as with many theories and philosophies, the best place to begin explanation is from the beginning. While Christians as well as the Jewish community both believe in the Scripture as God is the creator of all, philosophy does not always agree. Many scientists believe strongly in the big bang theory. The big bang theory explains the earth's existence over billions of years, stressing that the universe is in a constant state of expansion. Based on the cosmos and stars, creation began out in space by the mixing and rearranging of particles, atoms, and molecules, creating much of nature seen today.

While scientists have for centuries further detailed the big bang theory by including radiation experiences, geology information, botany, and various other resources, Christian education does recognize this as a popular and rather detailed explanation. In question of philosophy, this has more detailed and scientific evidence behind it, which does make this theory more plausible to some as the true beginning existence. Usually, those most challenging Christianity on

---

[104] Jack L. Seymour, and Donald E. Miller, *Theological Approaches to Christian Education* (Nashville: Abingdon Press, 1990), 168–169.

this theory might be atheist stressing the facts over the Bible creation story.

The other major theory in creation is evolution. Charles Darwin is most attributed to this theory based on his life work of exploring nature. Darwin argued that nature caused natural selection for evolution to occur while humanity forced artificial selection including selective breeding, thus creating the outcome by choice as opposed to natural. By collecting various fossils and artifacts from around the world, Darwin continued to theorize that the natural sciences were a basis for the difference in the diversity of life. Primarily, Darwin focused on the diversity between animals and humans. Charles Darwin was indeed quite familiar with the biblical story of creation, but like many scientists before him, Darwin questioned the validity of creation being done in seven days by God. Although Darwin did question the creation story, he did not assume it to be completely wrong or without some promise. Yet as Darwin furthered his research, he saw that there was more in common with primates and humans. He began drawing depictions of primates strictly as animals and creating images of the primates evolving into fully grown human beings.

Along with creation, one major debate that philosophers have been debating for centuries is the concept of time. How is time measured? Just as in the beginning with debating on where and how the earth began, the same questions are asked for the end. The measuring of time usually includes time and space based on earthly artifacts, the views of history, and the ongoing search of new evidence. Many scientists have referred back to mathematical formulas and measuring science against physical energy uses while others have argued that physical energy creates its own laws within science with the generations of psychology.[105] More often, scientists have studied the differences of naturalism and materialism. What is the major difference between these two ideas? Elements of earth that are natural originate from the earth and have managed to remain, appearing through the test of time. On the other hand, materialism elements have been

---

[105] Jack L. Seymour, and Donald E. Miller, *Theological Approaches to Christian Education* (Nashville: Abingdon Press, 1990), 182.

created from those natural elements, and some have even managed to last longer. Does this existence make one more relevant than the other? A question of survival comes up.

Related with naturalism and materialism is the question of microevolution and macroevolution. Microevolution explains changes in frequency that occur over time within a populated area.[106] These changes are attributed to four major areas, namely, mutation, selection (natural and artificial), gene flow, and genetic drift. Mutation recalls changes of DNA and cell structure over time. The natural selection processes are selected by nature itself while the artificial selections are processed by humanity. Gene flow is monitoring the exchange of genes against other populations outside of their own origins. The genetic drift occurs when random sampling happens within nature, causing an unforeseen outcome.[107] Usually these microevolution changes are seen on a smaller scale later, resulting in bigger changes.

On the other hand, scientists explore the study regarding macroevolution. Macroevolution explains the changes at or above the level of a particular species.[108] Macroevolution will still look at the four areas—mutation, selections, gene flow, and genetic drift—only on a bigger scale and usually within one particular species. Also, called speciation, the macroevolution process will determine where a species may eventually end up depending on where the studied changes may force the species into. Using both micro and macroevolution studies, scientists still continue to connect the truth behind all natural existence together.

One mathematician and scientist named Butterfield once commented,

> The eliciting of general truths or of propositions
> claiming universal validity is the one kind of con-

---

[106] Douglas Futuyma, *Evolutionary Biology* (Boston: Beacon Press, 1996), 47.

[107] Ibid., 47.

[108] Nicholas J. Matzke and Paul R. Gross, *Analyzing Critical Analysis: The Fallback Antievolutionist Strategy* (Boston: Beacon Press, 2006), 1.

sumption which it is beyond the competence of history to achieve.[109]

Considering many are still questioning and testing our existence, this quote may not be entirely wrong. Yet what constitutes these truths to be valid? Another scientist who did always agree with Butterfield made his comment, explaining,

> Historical experience is a disclosure of inner nature of spiritual reality and that only on the acceptance of this philosophy can we maintain the distinctness and independence of history as a science.[110]

Related to this, history, combined with zoology, has shown several years of change. Specifically the change of evolution relates back to giving validity to Darwin's theory of humanity coming out of the animal world. But those in the Christian world fully believing in God creating the world, heavens, and entire universe may view Darwin's theory as an illusion. Interestingly enough, if Darwin's theory is viewed as an illusion, how is spirituality explained?[111] There may not be enough physical evidence to support a human with animal characteristics, but is there enough evidence or proof to show spirituality? Again, history comes into play. For spirituality, Christians relate back to the Scripture further explaining that the Holy Spirit being the third part of one God in the Trinity is the one who is responsible for our Christian interpretation and educational knowledge use. However, the Holy Spirit is taught through history. The Scripture is a huge detail of history including who/what the Holy Spirit is. Since this spirituality is originated as historical, does this mean that the logic is only based on history? Experience? Or personal faith?

---

[109] Ibid.

[110] Jack L. Seymour, and Donald E. Miller, *Theological Approaches to Christian Education* (Nashville: Abingdon Press, 1990), 184–185.

[111] Ibid., 185.

In the same manner, relating back to questioning the beginning and ending of time, what is the scientific or philosophical theory on end-time or, as the Christian faith calls this, eternity? If creation began as total darkness into light, will that light eventually return to darkness? Current science is slowly showing that the earth is falling apart. Evolution has taken huge leaps and bounds, but when will this be ended? Science cannot fully ignore that some occurrences fall into a realm of unseen eternity, such as death.[112] No one in history has come back from death to explain if there is a total darkness of nothingness or the light of God. Here is a prime example of where philosophy and Christianity can differ greatly. Not only Christianity, but many other world religions believe in an afterlife either in a paradise of some sort or perhaps coming back to earth in reincarnation. The belief in reincarnation has some philosophers especially thrilled that their belief can be key in explaining or even proving that human/animal evolution will continue. For those not believing in the afterlife and fully expecting death to be the complete end, why would living life in a certain way even matter? Christian education has battled this question against nonbelievers for centuries. Explaining that God transcends time as the Alpha and Omega can be really difficult for many to understand. Jesus was the only known human to overcome death and return to earth, which is more than enough evidence for the Christian realm; but for those of other faiths or no faith, this is nothing relevant.

To answer the various questions above just as with any questions where an answer is sought or perhaps even the unknown occurs, a test is often used to see what the resulting finds will be. One such test is that of asking about the authenticity of Jesus as His teachings. Did Jesus's teaching really correlate to the teaching attributed to Him?[113] Scholars have most often created parallels in the story of Jesus's life through the gospels searching for relationships that cross another gospel for similarities and differences. To illustrate these parallels that

---

[112] Herbert G. Wood, *Christianity and the Nature of History* (Cambridge: University Press, 1934), 206.

[113] W. R. Farmer, C. F. D. Moule, and R. R. Niebuhr, *Christian History and Interpretation: Studies Presented to John Knox* (Cambridge: University Press, 1967), 171.

have been used for testing purposes, Farmer, Moule, and Niebuhr broke their findings down into twelve specifics that primarily cross-check the Gospel of Matthew with Luke.

- Matthew 20:1–16 Parable of the Laborers in the Vineyard. Jesus rebukes the attitudes of those who are self-righteous while criticizing those who resent God's mercy toward sinners. / Luke 15:1–32.
- Matthew 13:24–30 Parable of the Weeds. Jesus commands that no effort be made to separate sinners from the righteous. God will choose at Judgment Day. / Luke 5:27–32.
- Matthew 21:28–32 Parable of the Two Sons. A man must follow his father's will. Obedience is rooted in faith and prepares for the coming kingdom. / Luke 18:9–14.
- Matthew 22:1–10. Parable of the Marriage Feast. God is offended by the disregard of obligation and thus opens His kingdom to those who claim Him. / Luke 5:27–32.
- Matthew 6:1–6 Almsgiving, Prayer, and Fasting. People are not to do good works seen by men; do not seek recognition, rather gratitude from God's forgiveness. / Luke 7:41–43.
- Matthew 18:21–33 Reconciliation and the Parable of the Unmerciful Servant. We are obligated to forgive our brother because we have been forgiven by God. People are never to calculate the magnitude of sin. / Luke 15:1–32.
- Matthew 5:43–48 Love of One's Enemies. God loves all including His enemies therefore we are to love as God loves. / Luke 13:1–9.
- Matthew 25:1–12 Parable of the Ten Maidens. According to Jesus this is the danger of postponing repentance. / Luke 12:35–38.
- Matthew 25:14–30 Parable of the Talents. If God is untrustworthy, we are to reject Him, but God is truly trustworthy and we often offend Him with our own mistrust. Notably, we have nothing to lose and everything to gain by trusting in God. Example related to another passage from Matthew. / Matthew 6:19–21.

- Matthew 13:44–46. Parable of the Hidden Treasure and the Pearl. When a person enters into the kingdom of God, everything he processes is joyfully disposed. Luke 19:1–10.
- Matthew 7:7–11 God answering prayers. We are always to keep completely trust in God. Honoring our earthly father is greatly important too, but how incredible is our father in heaven to answer all prayers. / Luke 11: 5–8.
- Matthew 13:31–33 Parable of the Mustard Seed. God's purpose may have begun rather small in the beginning, but His purpose is much larger than one person will ever fathom. We cannot discern the future by only trusting faith. / Luke 17:20.[114]

While concluding these twelve examples, the authors verified four specifics. First, the parables that are found only in Luke, researched individually, do indeed represent a relationship with the early writing of Matthew. Second, the early Matthew tradition is mainly parables including the words spoken in the Sermon on the Mount. Third, the teachings represented in these gospels are highly integrated and deep in character. Finally, the parables and correlations previously listed are seen to be central as a nucleus of teaching.[115]

Technology Influenced

A physical scientist named Blaise Pascal, who was greatly interested in scientific versus religious theories, once said,

> Physical science will not console me for the ignorance of morality in the time of affliction.[116]

---

[114] W. R. Farmer, C. F. D. Moule, and R. R. Niebuhr, *Christian History and Interpretation: Studies Presented to John Knox* (Cambridge: University Press, 1967), 121–123.

[115] Ibid., 124.

[116] John T. McNeill, Matthew Spinka, and Harold R. Willoughby, *Environmental Factors in Christian History* (London: Kennikat Press, 1939), 361.

Pascal was stating the problem of ordinary man with morality, while having an ignorance of religion. Many of the uses of technology had been based on scientific notions. The astrology of the stars is used in the number system, many inventions had come from a Greek background, and even Saint Francis of Assisi took an interest in how nature is used. The conflicts of various doctrines and early Christian education without much records made the basis of learning shaky for some. How are we using this early technology?

The early Greek interest in natural process through creation caused the Romans to challenge their original concern as to how and why the earth began. Perhaps the first cause of man being created in perfection, then allowing the fall of man to happen was a paradox in establishing a relationship with God. Likewise, the thirst to achieve the knowledge of God created a major dependency on divine grace. The divine grace moved into the human soul was carried out through discipline and obedience and overall happiness of humanity. By taking this discipline forward, modern science was born.[117] God had already implanted the idea of curiosity and creation into the human mind. From this point on, humanity was in a constant state of exploration and discovery.

By the nineteenth century, there was a major struggle between the worlds of science against philosophy. What made a discovery scientific as opposed to a philosophical theory? Several scientists including Isaac Newton continued deeper into their search of newer discoveries hoping to clarify differences in science and philosophy. Helmholtz, who was an assistant to Newton, once commented,

> The philosophers accused the scientific men of narrowness; the scientific men retorted that the philosophers were crazy. And so it came about that men of science began to lay some stress on the banishment of all philosophical influences from their work;...no regard was paid to the rightful claims of philosophy that is, the criticism

---

[117] Ibid., 362–363.

of the sources of cognition, and the definition of
the functions of the intellect.[118]

These scientists were not admitting there are no philosophical questions involved with their science but rather that the criticisms used made it more difficult for philosophical theories not to
be recognized. In terms of religion, philosophy was really difficult
to ignore. After years of civil wars, divisions, and the Crusades, it
was apparent that religious followers were all debating on their own
search for truth. Was this truth philosophically based? Or had the
basis of these religious debates been scientifically proven?

The Scripture had provided many details and thorough descriptions of events that had taken place. One major area that scientists
and philosophers questioned was the logic or truth behind the miracles Jesus performed in the New Testament. Where was the scientific proof of these miracles occurring outside of what the Scripture
writers had written? The scientist Kant who took an especially closer
look at the theological science questioned: Is there a separation of
abstract religion and scientific verifications? Were religious experiences the same as scientific data? Is religion built out of materials
only furnished by the sciences?[119] The definition of spirituality or
how an incident is considered spiritual has been an ongoing paradox
for Christianity against scientific reasoning. For Kierkegaard, there is
a distinction between a judgment of facts and a judgment of value. If
theology is built up by personal experiences that create the values in
which people share, does this challenge scientific fact?

Perhaps scientific fact is best explained with technology. The
technology of today seems to be even more out of control than even
in control. People are constantly being pulled in different directions
by several large companies always trying to outdo each other in the
need to win the battle of what is the best product to make human
life easier. Does technology really make education easier? Some older
generations who are constantly struggling trying to keep on today's

---

[118] Ibid., 364.
[119] Ibid., 368.

trends would quickly argue no. Technology has the tendency to make life more difficult for the people who choose not to partake in it. The younger generations especially in schools now are nearly all required to have a computer with them as part of regular classroom learning. Children at younger ages already know how to tap into various internet usage more so than their parents. Many schools and libraries have Wi-Fi access available to all users free of cost. When the costs of such technology is taken into consideration especially for a major school supply, many parents discourage the idea because it may take away from basic handwriting. People in lower-class communities are not privy to the technology of today. Does this mean that their children's education should suffer?

Perhaps in some educational settings, technology can be easier to start up, explain, and finish; but for others, it may just get in way. Whatever happened to hands-on training? There are still many jobs in our world that do not require any technology uses. For example, many people have learned to be farmers from previous generations simply by family learning. It can be rather unlikely for a farmer to be using a computer in a tractor or tending to cattle. For Christians, the missionaries who travel to several third-world countries may only be making the journey with nothing but their own motivation. Teaching God's Word to other people who cannot read and/or write defeats the purpose of bringing technology into the picture. Several people in the world want to be reached but do not have the sufficient sources to do so. Are these people choosing not to be educated considering they have no technology, or are the missionaries forcing their work upon them? If the learning desire is present, technology, fear, or poverty will not stop the mission.

Even though technology may be somewhat scarce in some areas of the world that missionaries are reaching out to, it does not mean other alternatives cannot be used. Today our social media has overtaken many forms of everyday communication. Facebook, Twitter, and even email are used to spread information faster than most missionaries can travel. Again, the libraries allowing free Wi-Fi access can keep people closely connected with each other regardless of how far in distance they may be. Likewise, social media can keep groups of people informed of changes, prayer requests, and ideas to share with all the group members at one time without physically meeting. While social media to some may be rather impersonal, for others it can be an educational lifesaver. For those who are greatly involved with social media, a feeling of security is usually present knowing that they are being heard along with other people who share the same beliefs.

In terms of Christian education, many preachers and teachers simply use the Scripture alone without any technology. At one time, the mere idea of having a paper copy for anyone to access outside of clergy was unheard of. Today the idea of translation and printing is taken for granted. Again, relating back to personal experience and stories has often been a leading point for many preachers. Teachers find that using group discussions can be more effective than simply reading or researching a specific topic. Surprisingly, people openly admit that they have learned more from other people than by any other forms of education. For those who are efficient with technology, their awareness of knowing that some posted information can be completely false and deceiving discourages them from wanting to be educated in that manner. Good educators recognize the need for learning adaptation regardless of the criticisms and costs. Also, recognizing that technology may be useful can be helpful but can also be a hindrance to any learning process.

In conclusion, we have explored several different people, places, and time frames in which philosophy has and still does come up. Many of the questions asked by philosophy may be simply ongoing headaches to other people, but God is pleased when people are questioning the Scripture, faith, and thirst for more faith answers. Jesus says, "When two or three are gathered in my name, I am always among you." These words alone should be comforting enough that regardless of who you are, where you may be, what sources are available to you, or how you will measure up in the learning process does not matter. God knows what is in the heart of all learners. As we all continue to ask, seek, find, and knock unopened doors for answers in whatever burning questions our hearts may have, Jesus promises that we will be given answers to our asked questions, find what we are seeking, and unopened doors will be opened.

CHAPTER 4

Christ as the Educator

Lifting Up Christ

Chapter 4 details overcoming divisions by lifting up Christ that leads to a few more connections. It should be well-known that new learners can learn so much from all the surroundings throughout their life, but not quite as much as they will encounter during their earlier years.[120] The importance of listening and visualizing becomes ever so crucial. The human body has two ears and eyes, so listening and visualizing should not a problem, right? Wrong! All learners need to know how to listen properly and what to deeply see. This will create a huge difference on the impact of personal communication. Communication is the key to reaching any sort of understanding or common goal. Lack of communication is how many divisions begin and usually end up remaining true. This is true for the learners evolving with their education.

Christian education begins with the teachings of Jesus Himself. Jesus used the Scripture as a basis for teaching. The challenge at that time, being that the Old Testament was the only Scripture known to the people, was Jesus had to perfectly connect the words of the Old Testament with the words He was preaching that were later

---

[120] Sean Covey, *The 7 Habits of Highly Effective Teens* (New York: Fireside Rockefeller Center, 1998), 165.

recorded as the New Testament. Considering that Jesus was the Son of God, His words came directly from His divine self. He would have no human source to reference while preaching to the people or performing miracles. Jesus taught the people as God, "as one having authority."[121]

The old cliché "Actions speak louder than words" comes up usually where education is being presented. The actions of a person can truly define if they have learned a certain material more so than any written test could achieve. More importantly, for the benefit of teaching the people then and even so Christian education now, Jesus exemplified His words directly into His actions. The New Testament writers, specifically the gospel writers, were writing about Jesus's life as direct followers. These writers even included stories of Jesus being challenged by Pharisees and Sadducees who were skeptical and reluctant to the words Jesus spoke. How could an ordinary person speak with such conviction and confidence? The Pharisees, Sadducees, priests, and other public officials did not recognize Jesus as God and therefore did not observe with proper reason. As with nearly education, the mere questioning of a teaching can be enough to learn from.

Related for education purposes, Jesus did not come to earth to reform (repent) the people, start wars, or even become a ruler; His sole purpose was to teach. Jesus wanted to be the perfect teacher example for all people to learn from, to shape attitudes and ideas, and mostly to follow God's will.[122] Jesus's disciples were key examples for students. Often, the Scripture teaches that Jesus spent alone time with His disciples, training them how to continue His ministry and follow through by His example. The goal was for people to finally come to the realization of whom Jesus was in their presence as well as ours. For the most part, Jesus's teaching about the kingdom of God, the laws, and Jesus's place within these was "taught by His Father to Him."[123]

---

[121] C. B. Eavey, *History of Christian Education* (Chicago: Moody Press, 1964), 77.
[122] Ibid., 78.
[123] John 8:28.

The disciples often called Jesus master, which in Greek translates as "teacher" or in Hebrew "rabbi." Rarely was Jesus referred to by any other titles within the Scripture. Even with His toughest critics, Jesus was still referred to as the teacher. The gospels describe Jesus as "walking" and "talking" among the people as to being completely comfortable.[124] Further, Jesus was described within many different settings. He was always apt to preaching/teaching in a variety of places. The gospels describe Jesus teaching in various settings including on a mountain, by the sea, at a well, at His home, at the temple, and even in the Jewish synagogues. Considering that Jesus was informal regarding His teaching, it made the listeners more comfortable with Jesus more approachable and relatable. For the audio learners, Jesus spoke many parables and preached to crowds of all different backgrounds. For the visual learners, Jesus performed outward hands-on miracles witnessed by many. The many parables, miracles, and other actions of Jesus were all methods of teaching that people were questioning. What could I be learning from this man? Obviously after years of struggling, Christian education has taken this perfect teacher example and applied to teaching today.

From the very beginning of Christianity, there was a rather turbulent background considering it took years for people to know and understand whom Jesus really was. Not only at His time, but references for later years. Many of the New Testament books and letters did not record anything regarding Jesus's life until after He had left earth. Overall, the gospels reflect several stories of Jesus's life, miracles, journeys, crucifixion, and resurrection. In fact, the gospels overlap stories with different details appealing to different audiences, although theologians for centuries have been wondering why so much of Jesus's life from childhood until adulthood is left out. There is little mention of Jesus's mother, Mary, and even less mention of Joseph. Did they have other children? How was Jesus taught? Did He behave as a child? Who were His friends? Was Jesus ever married? Many of these questions have been asked and speculated on by various curious minds of all different Christian faith backgrounds. Some answers

---

[124] C. B. Eavey, *History of Christian Education* (Chicago: Moody Press, 1964), 78.

are discussed to the point of seeming logical, while others are left to the imagination. Even still, more questions regarding the power of Jesus as God's son have to be taken on pure faith. Most importantly, without the stories, miracles, and life of Jesus, Christianity would not have its foundation.

Jesus's birth, boyhood, and youth are not too detailed. The Scripture tells us that Jesus was born in a manger in Bethlehem, a town associated with King David. Jesus and His family lived in Nazareth following all Jewish traditions as taught through the Old Testament. Considering that Mary was family to Elizabeth, the mother of John the Baptist, provided full disclosure that this family was completely dedicated to God.[125] Joseph and Mary outwardly had Jesus circumcised and presented Him in the temple to God as according to Jewish customs for male children. Scholars would assume that Jesus was given all proper instruction to the Jewish laws and customs during His upbringing considering Jesus often quotes the Old Testament while preaching to the people.

Little is known about this time of Jesus's life until about the age of thirty when His public career began. Some scholars have theorized that Jesus did not begin His adult career because of His obligation to his mother. The Scripture does not mention when or how Joseph died, but historians believe that Joseph had died at a younger age, leaving Jesus responsible for taking care of His mother, home, and family as the eldest son.[126] Was Jesus preparing for His mission during this time? Did He already know about His miraculous ability to heal? Did Jesus already have a plan of where He was going to go? Were His parables and miracles already planned?

Whatever the reason may be behind the delay in Jesus's mission beginning, it did and does matter. His mission began outwardly at His baptism. John the Baptist had already long been proclaiming the coming of Jesus. When the day finally arrived that Jesus came to John asking to be baptized, John was overwhelmingly hesitant.

---

[125] Kenneth Scott Latourette, *A History of Christianity* (New York: Harper and Brothers Publishers, 1953), 35.
[126] Ibid., 36.

Again, scholars have debated why Jesus needed to be baptized at all. The most common theory is that Jesus had John baptize Him to officially begin His mission on earth and for people to witness the event for future generations. The most important element of the baptism of Jesus was also that this is the only occurrence in all of the Scripture where the entire Trinity is present. God the Father spoke from heaven in a cloud, Jesus the son in the water, and the Holy Spirit represented as a dove sitting on Jesus. What indeed a remarkable way to outwardly show all the people that their long-awaited Messiah had finally come. Jesus was He.

One reoccurring message that Jesus spoke about was the kingdom of God. Jesus explained that many people had been living in darkness for so long that He had come to be their light. The kingdom of God was so incredibly important that all people were to give up their food, clothing, and families to "seek first the kingdom."[127] As Jesus explained further, the kingdom was to evangelize and use the gospel message more commonly known as the good news. Jesus preached many stories and details about how and who was to receive the kingdom. For most people, the message of giving up basically all they had was not the joyful message it promised to be. The focus of being comfortable in the earthly life seemed more of a priority as opposed to the promise of the heavenly kingdom.

As Jesus continued to describe the mission and purpose of seeking the kingdom of heaven, the focus became an individual level. The societal structure, institutions, and customs of that time created much effect on how individuals chose to live. For example, the respect for the Sabbath day did not stop Jesus from healing the sick or giving food to the hungry. As Jesus said, "I have come to seek and to save that which was lost." In particular, He meant lost individuals. Many of the parables Jesus spoke were about seeking the lost: the lost sheep, the lost coin, even the prodigal son who had lost his way and returned home.

---

[127] Dale T. Irvin and Scott W. Sunquist, *History of the World Christian Movement* (Maryknoll: Orbis Books, 1970), 38.

Some people of that time and even today found Jesus's words about the kingdom and humanity to seem hopeless. Keeping the faith and trying to live maintaining the mission and believing in the promise of living with Jesus in paradise had to grow from an impossibility into a reality. Jesus had come to teach and heal in mind, body, and soul. Jesus fully believed that all people had the ability to achieve all possibilities as long as they continued to pursue and attain them.[128] Basically, Jesus already saw the kingdom of God on earth in which He had commanded His own disciples to carry out the mission in His name. The only true way for people to believe and keep the faith strong was to reach out, teach, baptize, and continue with complete faith.

Even Jesus's closest apostles struggled with Jesus's humanity. Was it really possible for this man to be completely human and completely God? As a human, Jesus ate, drank, talked, walked, slept, and even cried. He also preached for many hours a day to all people who would listen. Often when Pharisees, Sadducees, or temple priests were listening, they too questioned Jesus's message and by what authority He had to speak about God and the kingdom as He did. These church leaders found it very difficult to believe this man could possibly be the son of God. Yet as the son of God, Jesus performed many miracles including healing sickness, driving out demons, feeding multitudes of people, changing water into wine, and most importantly conquering death.

Under all the circumstances and disruptions that Jesus had caused among the people, it was no wonder at that time that He would be arrested and executed. Jesus knew this was all going to happen, so why did He not retreat away and let His disciples protect Him? The disciples knew that Jesus had foretelling of His death for some time, but why would it happen so soon? After all, Jesus had only been preaching His mission for three years. Yet Jesus never showed any resistance to arrest, mockery, abuse, or the crucifixion itself. Jesus was to take upon Himself all the sin of humanity and

---

[128] Kenneth Scott Latourette, *A History of Christianity* (New York: Harper and Brothers Publishers, 1953), 40.

offer Himself up to God as the ultimate sacrifice for all Christians to believe and be saved. In His last few moments on the cross, Jesus called out to God calling Him *Father*. Immediately upon His death, darkness overcame, an earthquake erupted, and the temple veil split, causing great fear. Had the people just made a terrible mistake that God was punishing them for? The Scripture does not mention that one person was hurt when this event took place, only that soldiers commented that Jesus was truly the son of God.[129]

The three-day event taking place here climaxes in Jesus's resurrection. Christians celebrate His resurrection as the first Easter. Jesus had not been defeated by death but had triumphed His sovereignty. The disciples were not expecting Jesus to rise from the dead, which surprised and awed them. Many of the disciples were hiding from the Jews for fear of their involvement with Jesus. After seeing the empty tomb, Jesus appeared to them several times so they would all come to believe. Jesus commented, "Blessed are those who have not seen and still believed." Was this the second coming of Christ that Jesus had spoken of?[130] Now that Jesus had come back from the grave, what was His next mission? Surprisingly enough, after Jesus's appearances, His final mission was to be taken into heaven and to remain there, leaving the disciples alone.

The Scripture tells us in the Acts of the Apostles that Jesus did not leave the disciples alone. Jesus has told them that the Holy Spirit was to come upon all of them so they would be completely filled to carry on the mission. Fifty days after Jesus's resurrection, the Feast of Pentecost brought the Holy Spirit down to the disciples as promised, so each went out preaching to those of whose languages they could now speak. Peter spoke out first, leading the way as Jesus had told him, "Upon you, Peter, I shall build my church." The church was now beginning. The mission was set for the disciples to move outward even farther than Jesus had to spread His message all over, performing miracles and continuing the great commission that had been placed upon them for all Christians then and now to continue.

---

129 Ibid., 56–57.
130 Ibid., 60.

For Christian education today, it can be rather difficult to imagine what it was like to experience these events of Jesus's life in person; we have the foundation laid out perfectly because of it. After previously reviewing the context in which Jesus was preaching, educators now are left asking questions like how can we be like Jesus in our teaching? In what areas of our lives should we strive to be like Jesus? How might we be more responsive to Christ's Spirit in our teaching and empowering to others?[131] Perhaps an easier answer would be in Colossians 2:3, which states,

> In whom are hidden all the treasures of wisdom and knowledge.[132]

Peter Hodgson, who is a recent researcher and author of Christian education theories himself, describes the truth of Jesus's earthly teachings in this way:

> Christian theology of education takes its orientation on the paradigmatic figure of Jesus of Nazareth, who incarnates God's Wisdom in His teaching and practice, his way of living and dying. The central image of His teaching was that of a new and radically open community of freedom in which God's Wisdom prevails as opposed to the foolishness and weakness of human wisdom. This divine Wisdom overthrows the dominant logic of the world (hierarchical, authorization, juridical, dualistic) in favor of a new logic, that of grace, love, freedom, of uncoerced and fully reciprocal communicative practices.[133]

---

[131] Robert W. Pazmino, *God Our Teacher: Theological Basics of Christian Education* (Grand Rapids: Baker Academic, 2001), 63.

[132] Colossians 2:3.

[133] Robert W. Pazmino, *God Our Teacher: Theological Basics of Christian Education* (Grand Rapids: Baker Academic, 2001), 61.

The quote above certainly gives a clear picture as to what exactly Jesus's teaching and wisdom should relate to, but it also raises questions in regard to including both the Christian aspect and general education. For us to understand the point, we recognize that Jesus as the Divine is the perfect example and model of the education process. The Christian portion is simply remembering that Christian education is the following of Christ. As long as the following of Christ's example and His educational model is being exercised, allow the Holy Spirit to come to rest.

Discipleship

The mission placed upon Christians then and now is based on the evangelizing discipleship necessary for education. Just as today, the concept of discipleship is not always easy to understand or follow. Jesus encountered many of those same doubts. Jesus explains the importance of being lifted up to His disciples in a couple of other ways although they may not understand it. In John 12:32–34, Jesus predicts His upcoming death. He explains,

> "But I, when I am lifted up from the earth, will draw all men to myself." He said this to show the kind of death he was going to die. The crowd spoke up, "We have heard from the Law that the Christ will remain forever, so how can you say, 'The Son of Man must be lifted up'? Who is this 'Son of Man'?"[134]

This created much debate among the disciples and all who heard Jesus speak, for they did not know what Jesus was telling them was about to happen. Asking questions and creating intersocial debates was the disciples' only way of possibly understanding what Jesus was

---

[134] John 12:32–34.

trying to teach them.[135] Questioning can often be imperative with Christian education. It will be very common for a learner not to fully understand what is being taught to them at the time whether it be a positive or a negative lesson. Just as the questioning can be extensive, finding the right answers must also be as important. Perhaps the right answer to one may not always equal that of another person; but simply sharing thoughts, ideas, and hopefully some powerful actions can be enough of a learning experience alone.

Most people who are followers or disciples can often lose their own way when trying to move forward or carry on the mission alone. Often, whenever a group setting occurs for educational purposes, there is a leader or leaders usually with many followers or learners. Hopefully, one of the ideal goals from this group setting would be to establish enough motivation and enthusiasm into all the group members that they will want to pursue the educational role by becoming leaders of other disciples. Jesus was/is the perfect example for all leaders and disciples to follow.

Leadership

Christian education depends a great deal on successful teachers who are most likely also very motivated leaders. Leaders often include several different qualities and characteristics. Not all leaders are going to share the same techniques and/or ideas, but that does not make them any less efficient. Rather, the differences can create more creativity to be known. Noel Tichy was an author who extensively researched what it means or requires for successful leaders. Everyone has leadership potential; it just simply needs to be found. Tichy explains that first and foremost, a person must begin with a teachable point of view.[136] By achieving an attainable point of view,

---

[135] John Walvoord and Roy B. Zuck, *The Bible Knowledge Commentary: An Exposition of the Scriptures* (Wheaton: Victor Books, 1993), 1–3.

[136] Noel M. Tichy, *The Cycle of Leadership: How Great Leaders Teach Their Companies to Win* (New York: HarperCollins Publishers, 2002), 73.

the leader must also be making their knowledge known and available to the learners. This can be done by sorting through the ideas and beliefs of what is already known or unknown and developing ways to communicate the education as clearly as possible.[137]

The most productive way for this type of learning to be achieved is through what Tichy calls the four elements. The first element is idea; the ideas are the plan for success alone. The second element is values; the values are the ones that support the achieving of success. The third element is emotional energy; leaders must generate excitement about the ideas and values for motivation and interest. The fourth element is simply called the edge; the edge is making those difficult decisions and teaching through them. Most often emotional energy and edge often coincide with each other. Without the emotional connection to the learning material, there would be no need for the edge decisions to be present.[138]

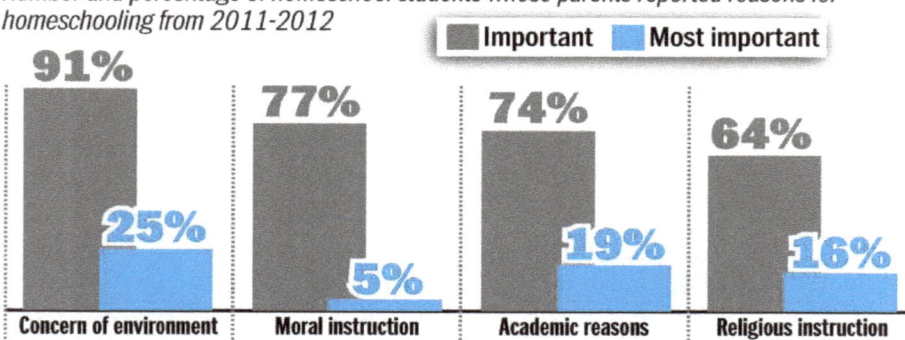

Reasons for homeschooling in the United States

Number and percentage of homeschool students whose parents reported reasons for homeschooling from 2011-2012

■ Important   ■ Most important

91% — 25% — Concern of environment
77% — 5% — Moral instruction
74% — 19% — Academic reasons
64% — 16% — Religious instruction

Tichy reiterates again that by using these elements for any type of educator, a solid and successful leader can emerge. Remember that

---

[137] Ibid., 73.
[138] Ibid., 76.

idea, values, emotional energy, edge, and even a little fun can go a long way. Christian education educators, as with any and all educators, have to remain motivated and loyal to the beginning teachable point regardless of what the outcome may be. Room for changes and improvements cannot be overlooked.

In the Old Testament, leadership took on many various forms—from prophets and kings to even judges. As with nearly all who are in a leadership role, challenges of power and/or authority are bound to happen. Consider this, the Israelites have a debate between God and the god Baal. When the prophet Elijah hears this, he offers a challenge to the prophets of Baal by asking them to build up an altar and ask Baal to set fire to the offerings. Elijah will do the same for God. After several days of the prophets and people praying to Baal, no fire came to the altar. After seeing this, at the time of sacrifice, the prophet Elijah stepped forward and prayed:

> O LORD, God of Abraham, Isaac and Israel, let it be known today that you are God in Israel and that I am your servant and have done all these things at your command. Answer me, O LORD; answer me, so these people will know that you, O LORD, are God, and that you are turning their hearts back again. Then the fire of the LORD fell and burned up the sacrifice, the wood, the stones and the soil, and also licked up the water in the trench. When all the people saw this, they fell prostrate and cried, The LORD—he is God! The LORD—he is God![139]

This story reminds the readers that God is all-powerful and is always present. The people with Elijah had lost faith in God, but after seeing His power prevail over the god Baal's nothingness, the people were again reminded that God is God. As the passage ends, the people are praising God and lifting His name high. God's power

---

[139] 1 Kings 13:38.

even today reminds us with a slap in the face that all humanity needs God from time to time. Consider that without the slap-in-the-face reminder, personal learning will become more and more difficult because once it is forgotten or ignored that God is always present, humanity will falter and thus needs to be put back on track.[140] So from time to time, those newly interested in being educated through a specific religion will still be searching for the answers to "Who am I?" or "Where am I meant to be or go?" and will slowly find the answer.

In the same manner, consider this passage from the Scripture where Paul begins emphasizing how quarrels from not listening create a disastrous outcome. First Corinthians 1:10–17 reads,

> "I appeal to you, brothers, in the name of our Lord Jesus Christ, that all of you agree with one another so that there may be no divisions among you and that you may be perfectly united in mind and thought...I follow Christ." Is Christ divided? Was Paul crucified for you? Were you baptized into the name of Paul? For Christ did not send me to baptize, but to preach the gospel—not with words of human wisdom, lest the cross of Christ be emptied of its power.[141]

The passage here blatantly explains in the opening verse that without the divisions of people, "all may be perfectly united in mind and thought." Biblical commentary points out that the church belongs to God, not man, period. Perfection cannot be a task ignored. Human nature will always be sinful, but humans have free will and the choice to strive for perfection in order that a perfect unity can be accomplished. God knows that His people are going to

---

[140] John Walvoord and Roy B. Zuck, *The Bible Knowledge Commentary: An Exposition of the Scriptures* (Wheaton: Victor Books, 1993), 1.
[141] 1 Corinthians 1:10–17.

fall short because of sin, but that is not a reason to give up![142] Had the Corinthians recognized this, their problem of division might not have existed.[143] Consider what the vast differences in the Christian educational worldview would be now if this passage was taken seriously and fully understood.

However, the example stated "overcoming divisions." There are certainly more than enough divisions that anyone new to religion will face. It may be divisions of age, race, program majors, ethnicity, and personality types. All divisions will coincide with one another at some point. Divisions are more important to Christian formation than most realize. Even Jesus explains that there are divisions in life that must be overcome. In Luke 12:49–53, Jesus says,

> Do you think I came to bring peace on earth? No, I tell you, but division. From now on there will be five in one family divided against each other, three against two and two against three. They will be divided, father against son and son against father, mother against daughter and daughter against mother, mother-in-law against daughter-in-law and daughter-in-law against mother-in-law.[144]

In the same regard, Paul wrote about the differences within the church communities at that time that are not all that different in their differences as today especially, within our modern-American atmosphere where the interdenominational aspects are going to come together. In 1 Corinthians 11:18–19, Paul explains,

> In the first place, I hear that when you come together as a church, there are divisions among

---

[142] John Walvoord and Roy B. Zuck, *The Bible Knowledge Commentary: An Exposition of the Scriptures* (Wheaton: Victor Books, 1993), 1–2.

[143] Ibid., 1–2.

[144] Luke 12:49–53.

you, and to some extent I believe it. No doubt there have to be differences among you to show which of you have God's approval.[145]

This message can be rather reassuring for any doubtful learners that may be feeling left out because of religious background differences. God wants acknowledgement of our differences, but also the coming together for the greater good.

Finally, on a personal level, it is important to remember that the human body does not have perfection and will encounter suffering throughout life during trials, challenges, and woes. No one person is exactly like another, and that is what keeps humanity's uniqueness special. It is even more special for a younger person who is just starting out in the world. In 1 Corinthians 12:25–26, Paul reminds the readers,

So that there should be no division in the body, but that its parts should have equal concern for each other. If one part suffers, every part suffers with it; if one part is honored, every part rejoices with it.[146]

Youth Ministry

Another example of leadership for many Christian educators is youth ministry. Youth ministry is charged with teaching and relating to the relationships of younger people. It is known that younger people need relationships to guide them against false misconceptions regarding the church.[147] Younger people are drawn to what is understood. God is the ultimate relationship within the Trinity by express-

---

[145] 1 Corinthians 11:18–19.
[146] 1 Corinthians 12:25–26.
[147] Kenda Dean and Ron Foster, *The Godbearing Life: The Art of Soul Tending for Youth Ministry* (Nashville: Upper Room Books, 1998), 27.

ing Himself as Father, Son, and Holy Spirit. Christians thrive off on the love given from God in this form, which in turn is why Christian educators will use this lesson to relate God with youth ministry. The Christian educators' goal as leaders is to make sure that their youth students understand, explore, question, and act upon how God's love has made, is making, and will make an impact on the student's Christian development.[148]

Morality Education

While studying Jesus as the perfect educator and model, one major area must be addressed, the same area that many educators tend to shy away from: morality. Moral debates on various subjects have been an ongoing battle for centuries. As humanity has evolved, many of those same issues are still coming up. The Old Testament describes various examples of how the Hebrew people were to live, which today's Jewish customs still take extremely seriously. However, as with all of humanity, many of the Old Testament people fell short of their moral choices too. For example:

- Adam and Eve chose to eat fruit from the tree of knowledge, strictly going against what God had commanded of them.
- Cain chose to commit the first murder by killing his brother, Abel.
- Moses chose to disobey God's instructions of tapping the rock once for the Israelites to have water.
- King David chose adultery with the married woman Bathsheba. David also had Bathsheba's husband killed in war so he could have her to himself.
- Jonah chose to ignore God's order of traveling to Nineveh to spread the message of repentance for the people to be saved.

---

[148] Ibid., 27–28.

In the gospels, Jesus is tested many times on various subjects, but the most important test or challenge Jesus faces is that with Satan—the true epitome of true good against true evil. Matthew 12:23–32 is Jesus giving a perfect answer on the distinction of who He is and who Satan is.

> All the crowds were astounded and said, "Could this perhaps be the Son of David?" But when the Pharisees heard this, they said, "This man drives out demons only by the power of Satan, the prince of demons." But He knew what they were thinking and said to them, "Every kingdom divided against itself will be laid to waste, and no house or town divided against itself will stand. And if Satan drives out Satan, he is divided against himself, how, then, will his kingdom stand? And if I drive out demons by Satan, by whom do your people drive them out? Therefore, they will be your judges. But if it is by the Spirit of God that I drive out demons, then the kingdom of God has come to you…Whoever is not with me is against me and whoever does not gather with me scatters. Therefore, I say to you, every sin and blasphemy will be forgiven people, but blasphemy against the Spirit will not be forgiven. And whoever speaks a word against the Son of Man will be forgiven, but whoever speaks against the Holy Spirit will not be forgiven, either in this age or the age to come."[149]

Jesus is explicitly describing the vast differences between believing in Him and believing in Satan. Jesus explains that the divisions created by Satan are not going to stand. Satan will not prevail. Jesus says that those who are not with Him are against Him, as in taking

---

[149] Matthew 12:23–32.

the side of Satan. Further, Jesus explains that those who do not gather (assuming Christian followers) will be scattered. In other words, without acknowledging Jesus...people are lost. Period. Likewise, Jesus firmly says that blasphemy speech against the Holy Spirit will not be forgiven in the present time or in the future. Basically, the end of time will hold no forgiveness as well. Even the Pharisees and some of the crowd gathered during this speech thought Jesus to be embracing the power of Satan to speak out and perform evil. Little did they or we know that Jesus would teach this lesson regarding the power of evil for all to be educated.

The passage above, Matthew 12:23–32, is not strictly all horrible thoughts and promising of no hope. Granted Jesus is making a very strong point in His explanation of His power against the power of Satan, but the lesson here for believers is most comforting. When Jesus says that "it is by the Spirit of God, then the kingdom of God has come to you," He means exactly that. Jesus did not know when the kingdom of God comes or will be coming. He says "has come," as in now. The kingdom of God has come to those who believe and Jesus is that kingdom sent by God for us. Some scholars would argue this to be a true test of personal belief choices. Was Jesus trying to teach us that we are to make the choice of Him (good) against Satan (evil)? Jesus knew then and knows now how easy it can be for humanity to suffer while making more difficult choices, but Jesus also reminds us that the Holy Spirit is always to guide us to avoid our "scattering" away.

Jesus also reaches out to teach us more regarding moral lessons and choices by calling us to our own conversion. The Gospel of Mark explains that Jesus had come to Galilee preaching about the good news and reign of God.

> The time has come...and the reign of God is at hand. Be converted and believe in the good news.[150]

---

[150] Mark 1:15

Conversion can take on several different feelings, actions, and emotions for many people; so it can be rather difficult to fully explain how a true conversion experience would happen. The conversion that Jesus asks of us has been best explained by three separate points. First, one must recognize that a call to conversion is the joyful proclamation of God's own love calling to you for a change of heart.[151] Matthew 7:17–20 reminds Christians that "the good tree will bring forth good fruit and the evil tree will bring forth evil fruit."[152] When answering the call of conversion, a Christian will strive to become the good tree not only to produce their own fruit, but also to nurture and educate others to become good trees and bear good fruit too. The nurturing and educating here are the outward actions made that are proving that the person has chosen to answer the call by yearning for the kingdom of God's presence. Likewise, the outward participation of the sacraments of baptism and penance is a conversion as well. Baptism and penance are a receiving of the Holy Spirit through conversion while receiving forgiveness to begin anew from a broken relationship with God. Regardless of who or what a person may do while answering their call to conversion, it illustrates much for their Christian future.[153]

The second point considers God's role in the conversion. The relationship between God and His people has been an ongoing discussion by theologians for centuries. The question of sin coming into the world—did God allow this? Why has God given us free will? What does He expect us to do? Does a person get saved simply through doing good works? Is salvation only a reward that we cannot fully possess? For conversion, the purpose of theology is to explain the relationship and roles of God, humanity, faith, love, gospel truths, law, etc. For Christians, we know that it is God who saves. God through Christ has transformed humanity from dark into light, which is God's ultimate gift in our lives. The spirituality strength-

---

[151] Charles E. Curran, *A New Look at Christian Morality* (Notre Dame: Fides Publishers Inc., 1968), 25.

[152] Matthew 7:17–20.

[153] Charles E. Curran, *A New Look at Christian Morality* (Notre Dame: Fides Publishers Inc., 1968), 29–30.

ening through the Scripture explains how God has converted many people before this time and also gives detailed instructions of what being open to the conversion calling in point 1 refers to. The gospels of Matthew and Luke each have their own section recalling the Sermon on the Mount. When Jesus delivers the Beatitudes, He is recognizing that even the poor, the hungry, the mourning, and the suffering are all going to be satisfied. Jesus also reaches to children and women and dines with sinners. God's role for conversion includes all His people. By keeping the heart open to the Holy Spirit, God will ever be maintaining His role.[154]

In relation to the second point, the third point discusses a person's response to the conversion process. Consider again the questions asked in point 2: The question of sin coming into the world—did God allow this? Why has God given us free will? What does He expect us to do? Does a person get saved simply through doing good works? Is salvation only a reward that we cannot fully possess? After learning God's role in the conversion process, have these questions changed? Point 3 considers how a person's response to the conversion can be seen, nurtured, or hindered. God works in His own mysterious, independent way, but humanity has to be very much dependent on God and others. A person will be in need of help during some times within life; the same is true from a Christian conversion standpoint. Relating back to point 1, answering the call of conversion will rely a great deal upon how much openness the person is going to have in moving forward. God will always be there doing His part; but again the free will may cause confusion, doubt, or even a complete shutdown. Here is where Jesus reminds us to be open to the Holy Spirit allowing such doubts to be handled. Reaching out for forgiveness, expanding the prayer life, and being further educated as with many other examples are all actions that are proclaiming a conversion response. Most importantly, if all else can be doubted, know this: the Christian response to conversion is our gift back to God.[155]

---

[154] Ibid., 39.

[155] Charles E. Curran, *A New Look at Christian Morality* (Notre Dame: Fides Publishers Inc., 1968), 46.

Christians are commanded by God to make a conversion, and by doing so allows the Holy Spirit to take over. Christians are more motivated, ready, and charged to move forward. Moral issues are forever going to remain with human life, but by accepting the conversion with and through Christ, the good and right moral choice will be much easier to achieve.

The teaching of moral issues continues to evolve and somewhat become more complicated to define as our social movements wave on. Is there a connection between what society dictates and what education may teach? Children who appear to grow up in happy homes with solid education, church, community helpers, and overall good habits seem to respond better with social issues.[156] Yet can these reactions be based on a strong childhood upbringing, or are these teachings going to become worthless once a child grows into adulthood and might consider thinking the exact opposite? Perhaps those coming from other backgrounds have more inside information and further are open to learning about such issues. Many of these same questions were asked and researched by Robert Owen. Owen was an educator in the early 1800s providing education to not only children, but several wealthier class adults. Owen's particular interest in how a child's mind grows in terms of making moral choices was based on the parents, family background, economic status, and overall social interaction with other adults and children. Owen believed that all of these factors were involved and could easily be introduced in schools as activities for development. In 1819, Robert Owen said,

> In the education of the children, the thing that is the most remarkable is the general spirit of kindliness and affection which shown towards them, and the entire absence of everything that is likely to give them bad habits, with the presence of what whatever is calculated to inspire them with good ones; the consequence is that they appear

---

[156] E. B. Castle, *Moral Education in Christian Times* (London: Unwin Brothers Limited, 1958), 266.

> like one well-regulated family, united together
> by the ties of the closest affection…we could not
> avoid the expression of a wish that the orphan
> children in our workhouses had the same advan-
> tage of moral and religious instruction.[157]

Needless to say, Owen explicitly believes that a well-rounded family and close affection play a huge role in moral judgment. However, Owen also acknowledges that even the working children who have lacked formal education and perhaps are rather sheltered from the outside world shared the same advantages. So relating back to the earlier questions, perhaps the family background and/or every-day was not a factor as previously thought.[158] Owen's final point by the end of his life was simply that moral education is all about the "doing." By training the self in morality despite background and prior education, the "doing" and taking action in moral issues creates an unbroken belief that the person will continue to evolve and usually stand fast in their desire to learn more and make the best moral decisions that are important to that particular person.

The following smaller sections are going to explain briefly the bolder moral issues that are most common in today's world. Each topic has been and still is being debated against church and state as moral issues. Since these topics are extremely broad, a brief overview will include a basic description of what the area includes and various arguments whether good or bad on how this topic should be improved, changed, stopped, or maybe ignored.

Four major concerns are currently ongoing and/or have happened within the recent time. Americans have been suffering and dealing with anxiety, dilemma, and frustrations regarding several moral issues. The first concern is the religious backing of issues that are believed to threaten the family life including abortion, homo-

---

[157] Ibid., 269.

[158] E. B. Castle, *Moral Education in Christian Times* (London: Unwin Brothers Limited, 1958), 270.

sexuality, pornography, and the liberation of women.[159] The second concern focuses on human rights or "secular humanism." This is the clash of religions against secular in such areas as peace, justice, reconciliations, and other national involvements. The third concern is a striving for power within America. The United States has been one of the largest countries in the world in terms of population and economy, but does this make it necessary to continually challenge other countries? Is America too greedy while other nations are starving? Related to the third concern is the fourth, a constant frustration over the American economy. The powerful big government and political leaders strive to make the best decisions for America, but why are the rich getting richer and the poor getting poorer? Capitalism within the economy continues to be an emotional and extremely important commitment that takes precedence more than needed. All of these concerns are labeled as the "moral majority."[160]

Disclaimer: I am not placing my views within these sensitive areas; just detailing.

Homosexuality

History has shown that homosexuality has been occurring for many years, but not until rather recently has the voice of the homosexual community been as loud demanding equal rights as now. Same-sex couples are demanding equal marriage rights throughout nearly all of the United States. In terms of political law, only some states have granted these marriages while others are still only performing civil unions. Marriage is a key importance for homosexual couples just as it is for heterosexual couples. Even before Christianity beliefs came about, early Greek mythology and even some Native American cultures told stories and artwork of same-sex couples being

[159] Paul T. Jersild and Dale A. Johnson, *Moral Issues and Christian Response* (New York: Holt, Rinehart, and Winston Inc., 1988), 31.
[160] Ibid., 33.

together and the importance of maintaining a healthy sex life for fertility of the earth.

Again, there is a difference within the Christian denominations as to whether or not this lifestyle is allowed. Many denominations are performing same-sex marriages within their churches, which are completely supported by the belief that love between two people is not to be questioned or challenged. The most common arguments may include the Genesis creation story of one man and one woman becoming one flesh and also the Code of Leviticus explaining that a man is not to use another man in place of a woman.[161] Man and woman are to be joined together for the purpose of becoming one and for purposes of procreation. Most notably, the Catholic Church stresses this strongly that homosexual marriage is not allowed because it is physically impossible for procreation to occur. Likewise, open homosexuals are not to participate in the sacraments because of the sin they are choosing to live in. However, the newer American Catholic Church is welcoming of the homosexual community performing their marriages and allowing them to partake in all sacraments. For many people, the basic argument is love. When a person is in love with someone of the same sex and happy, what and who should stop them?

Abortion and Stem Cell Research

Abortion is the removing of an unborn fetus during pregnancy. The common arguments that arise from abortion are as follows: Is an abortion the correct choice when rape or incest is involved? What happens when the woman's life is in danger because of a complicated pregnancy? What if the fetus's stem cells can help determine other health issues? Perhaps the DNA within a developing fetus can help in cancer research. Abortion clinics continue to pop up all over the United States. In some states, a parent permission is required for

---

[161] Paul T. Jersild and Dale A. Johnson, *Moral Issues and Christian Response* (New York: Holt, Rinehart, and Winston Inc., 1988), 154.

an abortion to take place, while in others, a minor can simply walk without any family knowing the situation. Likewise, pharmacies and health care are covering abortion contraceptives or making it easier for these to be acquired. Many people are in the fight to stop all abortions and actively seek help for those women who have experienced an abortion. In some cases, men who did not know about pending fatherhood are in great need of comforting.

For Christians, again the morality choice is should a woman be allowed to do with her body what she believes best, or is a woman ending another life not her decision? The Catholic Church holds a very strong stance against abortion. The Roman Catholic church's Declaration on Religious Liberty chapter 2 entitled "Religious Freedom in the Light of Revelation" states,

> The Declaration of this Vatican Council on man's right to religious freedom is based on the dignity of the human person, the demand of which have become fully known to human reason through centuries of experience.[162]

So proclaiming the dignity of the human person makes the argument strong in that even an unborn child is still a human being. Likewise, when is a child considered a person? Many say at the time of conception while others defend the early pregnant stages as mere grouping of cells. Christians are to respect and protect all life.

Euthanasia and Suicide

Many people are not as familiar with euthanasia. This term is questioning a person in a serious medical condition as on life support. When is a person's life to be terminated? Who gets to make the decision? Catholic hospitals will not allow a person to be taken off life support. Again, this relates to the declaration quote previously

---

[162] Ibid., 357.

mentioned. A person's life is being ended. A doctor may explain that all organs have failed leaving only the breathing tube as supporting air. Is a person still living? Or is he or she simply existing? What constitutes life and death for this situation? No brain activity? Paralysis? Or has the person already put in writing that he or she does not wish to remain alive on a breathing tube? The morality here can be a question of respecting life or a person's wish.

A fine line along with euthanasia can be suicide. Sometimes a person may wish to end their own life while still conscious enough to make the decision. Perhaps the pain and discomfort has become so great, death would be a pleasant welcome. Or maybe the person does not wish for loved ones to watch them suffer. In other cases outside of the medical realm, a person who commits suicide has already performed an irreversible act. For Christians, God's mercy and forgiveness are always present, but those left behind are never going to understand why a person would end their own life. Suicide is best described as a permanent solution to a temporary problem. Being able to catch the warning signs, reaching out, and doing whatever possible to prevent such a horrific action from taking place can never be taken seriously enough. God knows when the time for all human life to end will be. Should we ever be allowed to decide that for ourselves?

Racism

Racism within American has certainly taken some huge turns throughout the past two hundred years. When African Americans were first brought to America, they were beaten, tortured, and sold as property to rich white landowners, forced to work extreme hardships against their will. The lowest point in American history greatly stemmed from the debate over racism, the slavery of blacks leading to the Civil War. Although there were certainly other differences that caused the Civil War, the keeping of blacks as slaves was foremost on the battlefield. President Lincoln during the war even declared the Emancipation Proclamation into law, stating that no man was to own another and all slaves were to be freed. Eventually, the Southern portion of the country surrendered, allowing the North to win; but it was a terrible price for both sides.

Years after the Civil War, the rights of African Americans did not get much better. Throughout many places in America, segregation was still holding strong. Black people were only allowed in certain areas, not allowed to vote, usually working for unfair wages, and very much treated as completely unequal and less superior to the white race. By the 1960s, a huge movement for African American rights finally took headway with leaders such as Dr. Martin Luther King Jr. Black people were allowed to be in the same areas as whites especially in the workplace and colleges. Granted, many people today experienced this movement and still have hesitations regarding the direction racism could take. The riots of Ferguson, Missouri, were based on seeking retaliation for the murder of a black teenager. America in some ways has come full circle to now the white race being challenged. So what about racism within Christian education?[163] We are all made in the image of God. Racism should never replace our faith or mission. The belief of superiority because of skin color is a repression to our Christian goal. Church unity and global outreach are to welcoming of all types of people just as Jesus did.

Women's Movement and Rights

As previously mentioned, one of the moral majority concerns was that of women's rights. Not too different from racism, a woman was for centuries merely property to a man and the bearer of children. For these women, there was not much else allowed outside of servitude. The Genesis creation story explains that God took the rib of Adam to create the woman Eve. Women were made from man for companionship. God certainly did not command the man to own the woman. Even in Jesus's time, women were still considered

---

[163] Paul T. Jersild and Dale A. Johnson, *Moral Issues and Christian Response* (New York: Holt, Rinehart, and Winston Inc., 1988), 96–97.

property along with being the keepers of the home, bearing children, and being available to serve the man as the head of household. Again, it was not until later in American history that a woman was allowed to vote or hold down employment outside of the home. Many older generations today still see a woman's place as being in the home cooking, cleaning, and attending to the children while the man goes out into the workforce. Women are the nurturers who are best used within the home to keep the place proper. Now, women are rapidly overtaking the workforce and, in some cases, outperforming the men.

For Christianity, women's roles have evolved greatly too. Many of the Christian educators especially within private schools are women. Getting back to the Scripture, women played some rather major roles that are often overlooked. In the Old Testament, Eve was the first woman, the mother of earth and the first children. In the gospels, Mary was chosen by God to be the earthly mother of Jesus. Jesus reached out to women of His time, preaching, healing, and teaching them just as his apostles. Sexism was an issue of Jesus's time as it was many years later, but even then, women were still property and easily shamed. Jesus made no distinction.[164] Later, Saint Paul had many women disciples who bravely preached the Christian mission. Today in various Christian denominations, women are the ministers, pastors, and even elders making major church decisions. However, on the flip side, there are some denominations not as welcoming to women in church hierarchy. The Catholic Church does not allow women to become priests or bishops, stating that Jesus came to earth as a man; therefore, men are to be the leaders. In a rather similar way, America has never had a woman president. Perhaps the country has not been ready for this type of change or perhaps we are? Maybe someday traditional Catholicism will change this too.

---

[164] Paul T. Jersild and Dale A. Johnson, *Moral Issues and Christian Response* (New York: Holt, Rinehart, and Winston Inc., 1988), 134.

Capital Punishment

Capital punishment includes the death penalty because of a crime committed. The moral dilemma here contains the question of whether a crime is bad enough for death to be the proper punishment. How are crimes determined in terms of severity? What if the person is fully repentant and has done everything possible to make amends? Who ultimately decides that a person's life should end? Best spoken by a member of the French chamber of deputies in 1830, Lafayette said,

> I shall ask for the abolition of the punishment
> of death until I have the infallibility of human
> judgment demonstrated to me.[165]

What a loaded statement. Even today not many of the states in America carry out capital punishment, but when it does happen, the earlier questions are asked. Once capital punishment has happened, the life is gone. The decision cannot be reversed. So in a case where a person may be found innocent after death, what can be done? For Christians, God forgives all sins. Christianity teaching forgiveness strives to know that there is nothing so great that forgiveness cannot be sought. The value of human life is such a precious gift, and people can be deserving of mercy and second chances.

Capitalism, Socialism, War

The moral majority including capitalism, socialism, and war is a blending over into a category of different concerns. Capitalism has become such a huge part of the American way of life that many people are frustrated with the economy.[166] The price of inflation continues to rise while everyday workers' pay either remains the same

---

[165] Ibid., 202.
[166] Ibid., 289.

or becomes lower. The national average minimum wage is not near enough to support an average person's basic life expenses. Each year, Americans are concerned with what the government will decide in terms of taxes, insurance, and the cost of living. Most Americans argue the rich (usually politicians) get richer and the poor (everyday workers) get poorer. America thrives on being a wealthy nation to the remainder of the world, but are the people thriving?

Socially, people are suffering. The poor and homeless in some communities are overwhelming. These people have no place to turn to and even little possessions. Some of these people are victims of violence, unemployment, economic pressure, and loss of property. The social economy has not been all that sturdy to lean on when prices continue to rise and volunteers become less. Some Christian organizations reach out to these needy people on a regular basis, but sadly others only reach out at holiday times. Jesus reached to everyone despite social status. The parable of the Good Samaritan still remains a famous example of helping out a stranger. Also, the Beatitudes mention the rewards of helping those in need. America may certainly have its share of needs, but many missionaries travel to third-world countries helping those with even less.

On a final note, America has certainly been in various wars over the years. World Wars I and II were fought over problematic moral issues. These wars tried desperately to save the innocent people that Hitler was immorally massacring. How many of those wars could have been avoided? How many innocent people were sacrificed? Does creating a war for our protection justify the killing and attacking of innocent people in other countries? These moral questions continue to be raised year after year. Those who do serve in wars come back telling stories or horror and may suffer the effects for the remainder of their lives. How many more lives are going to be placed in jeopardy because of our lack of moral judgment?

In conclusion, Christ as the educator is a huge obligation to measure up with. Christians have a clear blueprint set up by Jesus at how, what, where, and why Christ had to educate us. Although the Bible has few examples of religious versus economical differences, the importance of following Jesus's examples for the mission and making correct moral choices has never been clearer.[167] Everyone has their choices to make, but remembering that Jesus is our educator and the Holy Spirit is our guide, Christian education will not weaken. Recognizing people who are educated are an influence to those seeking the same. Christian educators who continuously follow Christ as the educator will certainly keep the mission going.

---

[167] Paul T. Jersild and Dale A. Johnson, *Moral Issues and Christian Response* (New York: Holt, Rinehart, and Winston Inc., 1988), 6.

CHAPTER 5

Christian Education Denominational Emphasis

Christian education has been and continues to be split up into several ongoing and developing denominations. Each denomination, whether Catholic, Protestant, Orthodox, or nondenominational, contains its own educational values including worship styles, community practices, and personal growth. The following is a breakdown further detailing an overview of what each denominational focal point is. It is important to note each of the educational values listed is essential for the specific denomination to function.

Globally, Christians can be found all over the world. In fact, current statistics show that nearly one-third of the entire world population is Christian! Yet within the United States, these Christian diversities are the most prevalent and easily magnified. It has been easier for Christianity to change and evolve with the United States considering there is freedom of religion to practice as one believes fit.[168] This indeed creates a difficult atmosphere to monitor. Currently this is not a known test that can prove a person's Christianity per se other than self-proclamation, although some of the different denominations within Christianity do have specific requirements for their

---

[168] Jeffery B. Webb, *The Complete Idiot's Guide to Christianity* (Nashville: Penguin Group Inc., 2004), 13.

faith practices that would qualify them for such a test. Yet once again, since the United States has the freedom of religion, this testing is not essential to the identification of Americans; it is merely a statistic. Considering that there have been and continue to be ever-changing statistics within the American culture concerning religious denominations and choices, a consistency can be difficult to locate.

Catholicism

Chapter 2 explained the history of Christianity primarily beginning with the Catholic faith as began by Peter selected by Jesus. While looking at the statics of Christianity as a whole, the Protestant population has the greatest number of followers due to the many sub-denominations under the Protestant heading. However, Catholicism is largely number one, although the number of practicing Catholic followers has been shown to be immediately followed by the non-practicing Catholic followers within Christianity. One of the biggest claims within Catholicism is that because of its being the biggest area of Christianity, it is the one and only true church. This claim is based on Jesus commanding His disciple Peter. Matthew 16:16–18 reads,

> Simon Peter said in reply, "You are the Messiah, the Son of the Living God." Jesus said to him in reply, "Blessed are you, Simon son of Jonah. For flesh and blood has not revealed this to you, but my heavenly Father. And so I say to you, you are Peter and upon this rock I will build my church, and the gates of the netherworld will not prevail against it."[169]

After Jesus's ascension to heaven, at the time of Pentecost, Peter became the leader and shepherd of the people. He later traveled to Rome and remained there until he was martyred. Thus began

---

[169] Matthew 16:16–18.

the popes and hierarchy of the Catholic Church as the successors of Peter.[170] Related to this, the Catholic Church expresses that the church's hierarchy is the only persons who have received authority in an unbroken manner directly from the time of Jesus. This also partially explains how the church received its name. The word "catholic" means universal. It is the universal church of all God's people. This indeed makes the Catholic Church a huge power not only in the religious world, but in the secular world as well.

The greatest difference between the Catholic Church and all of the other denominations within Christianity is the belief and faith practice of Holy Communion. Catholicism believes in seven sacred practices called sacraments. The most practiced sacrament is that of Holy Communion or Holy Eucharist, as it is called within the Catholic Mass. Catholics believe that during Holy Communion, the bread and wine used will be consecrated into the divine body and blood of Christ. Jesus becomes present within the bread and wine; thus, they are consuming and carrying Christ within their own bodies. This practice is vastly different from what most other Christian churches believe. Holy Communion stand as a symbolic act of sharing bread and wine and/or grape juice as Jesus once did with His disciples, although Jesus Himself is not in the bread and wine while they are being consumed, hence the major difference. For the Catholic faith, this major belief difference is known as the transubstantiation. The bread and wine are consecrated into the body and blood of Jesus Himself. The placement of Holy Communion/Eucharist in the Catholic Mass is given the utmost importance as it is the symbolic point of the liturgy. This does not undermine any other parts of the liturgy, especially the Word, but to show the extreme importance and regard this sacrament needs to be given.[171]

Another major difference between Catholicism and most Protestant faiths is their strong reverence for Mary. The Scripture explains that Mary was chosen by God to become pregnant by the

---

[170] Milton V. Backman, *Christian Churches of America: Origins and Beliefs* (Provo: Brigham Young University Press, 1976), 3–4.

[171] Ibid., 17–18.

power of the Holy Spirit to give birth to the Son of God as a human. Catholicism honors Mary as a pure, holy virgin who said yes to what God asked of her despite the terrible consequences that could have come upon her within her social community as a pregnant unwed woman. The Bible does mention what happened to Mary after seeing her at the foot of the cross during Jesus's crucifixion. Catholicism believes she was taken up to heaven in body and soul since no remains of her have ever been found. Since the angel expressed that Mary had found favor with God, Catholicism continues to honor her as the eternal mother.

A final major point when speaking of Catholicism needs to recognize that their religious truth is based on the Scripture and tradition. The church itself is the only true interpreter of the Scripture and thus the true teacher of it too. Also, the writing and words of the Scripture are known to be truly inspired by God. Likewise, tradition is disclosed and created through the forefathers, councils, and popes of the early Catholic Church. These important men and decision have set up the ways that future generations are to follow. Therefore, the Scripture and tradition will always be present within any sort of Catholic ceremony because these two areas make up their religious truth that distinguishes them from Protestant faiths.[172] All Catholic Masses are celebrated in two parts: the liturgy of the Word (Scripture) and the liturgy of the Eucharist (Scripture and tradition based).

What can be expected from the Catholic community? There are many different Catholic churches within the United States that have a huge support simply because of the denominational following. A Catholic Church today is going to be more formal and attentive to detail throughout the liturgy service normally. However, in some more conservative parishes, setting this formalness is not taken that seriously. The dress code can be more casual, and usually the older parishioners might be more welcoming to newer people, wanting the experience to be a positive one for more to join. This may or may not always work, simply because the Catholic Church is very traditional

---

[172] Milton V. Backman, *Christian Churches of America: Origins and Beliefs* (Provo: Brigham Young University Press, 1976), 17–19.

on how a service should be conducted, and many worshippers will feel this is not to be terribly different from the norm.

For non-Catholics, it is essential to remember that only those of the Catholic are allowed to take Holy Communion. This practice does not exclude anyone but rather to uphold the church theology.[173] By maintaining this practice, the Catholic faithful practice a closed communion as in not open to any and all not sharing the same belief. Because of this, many practicing Catholics are turning toward the newly founded American Catholic Church that stresses the importance of welcoming all people. Traditional Catholicism does not allow Eucharist to those divorced, non-Catholic, homosexual, or who are in the midst of what is considered a sin. The American Catholic Church allows all people of any background, lifestyle, or such to be fully part of the entire liturgy. After all, Jesus was welcoming of all people too, so why should the church be any different today? Considering how much the times in our society are changing, this newer Catholicism has been growing rather quickly and continues to do so.

Episcopal

Not too distant from Catholicism is the Episcopal denomination. In the practice of baptism, the Episcopal Church does practice the infant sprinkling and dedication; they also encourage the sponsors or godparents to be directly related to the child to ensure the religious nurturing. Later in the child's life, the Episcopalian church will instruct the child to receive the sacrament of confirmation. This practice is different from the later-discussed denominations by not believing this to be a sacrament, but a laying on of hands in which the child will renew the promises of the godparents and sponsors made on their behalf at baptism. Likewise, the community considers the Lord's Supper as a memorial and living experience to all com-

---

[173] Carmen Renee Berry, *The Unauthorized Guide to Choosing a Church* (Grand Rapids: Brazos Press, 2003), 144–145.

municants while sharing the bread and grape juice used. Episcopal churches use wine instead of the grape juice. This is a comfort and blessing to all who share within it.[174]

In the authority of an Episcopalian church, it is believed to be apostolic successions. In their tradition, every man is seen to be his own priest. In other words, all believers make up priesthood under one leadership to live closer to God. In this denomination, a sacrament should not be administered to people without being ordained or specially recognized within the church, a call from God to be a preacher. Within the Episcopalian church, a bishop is not an order, but an elder set apart for particular tasks. Also, a bishop is not ordained but consecrated into that position. In Episcopalian churches, local congregations do not elect ministers; they are directed by bishops to lead and must be appointed by the bishop to do so. The overall governing bodies within these churches consist of clerical and some laypeople.[175]

What can be expected from the Episcopalian church community? Again, being similar to Catholicism, a conservative structure can be expected. Liturgical programs and prayer books are available all around to again actively participate in the worship. Worship is best expressed and learned through participation first by the individuals and ultimately the entire congregation. One important detail to remember in the Episcopalian church is that no one will ever expect a person to do anything against their own beliefs. They are to encourage that a spiritual experience is delivered fully.[176] People are then encouraged to take this spiritual fullness out with them into the world.

---

[174] Milton V. Backman, *Christian Churches of America: Origins and Beliefs* (Provo: Brigham Young University Press, 1976), 113.

[175] Ibid., 114.

[176] Carmen Renee Berry, *The Unauthorized Guide to Choosing a Church* (Grand Rapids: Brazos Press, 2003), 172–173.

Lutheran

Lutheranism is the next Protestant branch to be examined. To recap slightly from chapter 2, this branch of Protestantism was not originally intended to become a religion of its own. Martin Luther who was a Catholic monk during his time made various discoveries throughout his early life that turned his beliefs away from the Catholic practices in the late 1400s to early 1500s. For example, in Luther's visit to Rome during 1510–1511, he quickly became more aware of the lives of clergymen and was not too pleased with what he had discovered. In the same manner, the excessive use of indulgences as a way of offering forgiveness to the people caused Luther further doubt.

With further study, Luther concluded that salvation did not come from the sacraments, as was the prime teaching of the Catholic Church. Luther firmly believed in Ephesians 2:8–9, which states,

> For by grace you have been saved by faith, and this is not from you; it is the gift of God; it is not from works, so no one may boast.[177]

He also concluded that salvation did not come from the works of man or from the church itself. For Luther, salvation is a direct gift from God that comes from hearing and studying the word of God. Grace becomes manifested through faith, which justifies the person to God.

Ultimately, these discoveries and beliefs came out publicly when Luther nailed his ninety-five theses to the massive church doors on October 31, 1517, without considering the clarifications, interruptions, or extreme repercussions. Despite having high backing patrons, Luther was ordered several times to recant what he posted against the church, but he refused continuously. He refused enough and even went a step further to be the first person to translate the entire New Testament from the Greek language into German for more people

---

[177] Ephesians 2:8–9.

to be able to read. It was a personal goal for Luther to make the Bible accessible to all believers who wished to study but did not have the educational skill and had language barriers. In doing so, Luther began to reorganize the Catholic Mass and thus prepared a new religious ceremony. It was not Luther's intent for this new system to become a whole new liturgy, but as the Reformation evolved and Luther's new small and large catechism took more and more notice, the denomination of Lutheranism was already up and running. At his death in 1546, Martin Luther declared once more that he did not want to form a new denomination to be named after him, but despite his efforts, the German community had already adapted to his teaching.[178]

Like the Baptist faith, Lutheranism has its own noticeable beliefs. Lutherans also believe that baptism is necessary for salvation, although this should be done in early infant stages as opposed to waiting until adulthood. Next, in Luther's understanding, the celebration of Holy Communion is the resurrected Christ and not the transubstantiation (changing of elements) that the Catholic Church believes. Not regularly taking communion can be seen as sinful and a lack of spirituality. Holy Communion is also an absolution from one's sinful nature to be done in a private or public setting, although not all groups of Lutheranism follow this tradition. In traditional practice, a youth around the age of fourteen (known as an age of reason) will participate in the confirmation ritual to become full members of the Lutheran church and join the community by partaking in Holy Communion for the first time. Today, the Lutheran church has evolved into many different groups called synods, yet each holds the same core beliefs. These divisions are growing more each day from differences in politics, society, geography, and simply traditional changes. Despite these divisions, the Lutheran church still remains one of the most powerfully followed Protestant churches. [179]

---

[178] Milton V. Backman, *Christian Churches of America: Origins and Beliefs* (Provo: Brigham Young University Press, 1976), 71–74.
[179] Ibid., 77.

What can be expected from visiting a Lutheran community? Most of the Lutheran educational institutions consist of grade schools, high schools, colleges, and many seminaries where people are training to become pastors and leaders within the church. There are not as many as the Catholic or Baptist following, but certainly enough not to be overlooked. Once again, the importance of community will be present. The Lutheran church emphasizes preaching a bit more than the other churches will. This ensures that the message of the gospel is proclaimed and taught the best that it can be. For a newcomer, the Lutheran community will be more involved with missionary works and lending more a hand with the community around them. Smaller groups participate in Bible studies and further questioning God's Word.[180]

Presbyterian

Another church denomination to mention and examine is the Presbyterian denomination. This particular denomination continues to be somewhat newer to the Protestant community especially within America as opposed to the previous denominations. Presbyterianism has not been in existence as near as long as the others. By the latter 1860s, there was a movement of reformed churches that continued to evolve. This was not at all surprising considering that the Civil War had recently ended and the entire country was on the mend. These reformed churches began stressing God's sovereignty and describing their personal relationships with God in a covenant manner. The Presbyterian Church was a particular way for congregations to be linked to each other for a network of church functions to arise. Because of this linking of churches together to build up mutual support, Presbyterianism was and still is believed to have derived from the Episcopal way of thinking. Both churches wanted to maintain that support of other churches to encourage each other by sharing in

---

[180] Carmen Renee Berry, *The Unauthorized Guide to Choosing a Church* (Grand Rapids: Brazos Press, 2003), 158–159.

other churches' joys and sorrows. This indeed proved to be a rather useful method of contact since the growth of both churches thrived greatly hereafter.[181]

Another major similarity between Presbyterianism and Episcopalian, besides both originating from the United Kingdom, is the use of an elders' team. (The Greek word for elder is "presbyter" in which the letter shows up in the New Testament during Paul's letters to Asia Minor on how churches were to be affiliated.) Each church has a session of elected representatives that will participate in a district meeting that came to be known as the presbytery. Once these presbyteries became bigger with more representatives, the body itself was called synods. Today that synod is known as the general assembly church within the United States in now one of the biggest known meetings for the Reformed churches. These national decisions filter down into policies for each of the individual churches to follow and maintain. If the policies need to be changed or altered, it will be presented during the next general assembly meeting.[182]

What can be expected from the Presbyterian Church community? An interested party can expect to find much movement and participation. A Sunday worship service will be more on the formal side but will include standing, clapping, and open singing. Once again, it will not be uncommon to find a Bible and hymnal directly in the pews or chairs to encourage participation. It will be important to notice here that the Lord's Supper will not be celebrated every Sunday but usually will be available throughout the month as needed. For Presbyterianism, membership is not required for participation. They openly welcome all who are within the Christian faith and simply want to be closer to God. If membership is desired, the decision is solely up to that person to make.[183]

---

[181] Jeffery B. Webb, *The Complete Idiot's Guide to Christianity* (Nashville: Penguin Group Inc., 2004), 143.

[182] Ibid., 144–145.

[183] Carmen Renee Berry, *The Unauthorized Guide to Choosing a Church* (Grand Rapids: Brazos Press, 2003), 218.

Methodists

Continuing on within the Protestant branches, the next would be the Methodist faith. Methodism is still one of the most energetic revivalists within the religious community. The Methodist faith was founded by John Wesley who was a respected leader. Wesley encouraged people to seek the light of Christ and to live according to that light. Growing up, Wesley had a great deal of Episcopal education and was even ordained a deacon by the bishop of Oxford in 1725. Wesley had learned that the Episcopal denomination was rather similar to Catholicism. Eventually, Wesley, wanting a more liberal direction, began gathering and leading smaller groups of men who would visit prisoners, engage in weekly Bible studies, and become actively involved in humanitarian activities. Since all of these activities were done methodically, the group called themselves Methodists. After being recognized for these works, Wesley was asked to become chaplain for an Indian community. While being chaplain, Wesley realized that he had a great purpose and love for missionary work, although he did find it rather difficult at times to teach people of other religious beliefs since they had already been taught in a different manner, usually Catholic.[184]

Wesley's teaching and practices slowly began spreading throughout the Americas especially during the time of the American Revolution because Americans were even further splitting off from the Church of England. Since there were few religious practices that had filtered into America at this time, it was easier for Wesley to appoint such leaders as Thomas Coke and Francis Asbury to delegate what was to be the first Methodist Church. To become an active preaching member of the Methodist faith, generally a person would be asked to fully answer four specific questions: (1) Are you converted? (2) Do you know and are you willing to abide by the rules of the society (Methodist society)? (3) Can you preach to others adequately? And (4) have you a horse to travel? Today, these questions have evolved

---

[184] Milton V. Backman, *Christian Churches of America: Origins and Beliefs* (Provo: Brigham Young University Press, 1976), 99–102.

into more serious beliefs based on the person. A Methodist accepts or rejects the gift of salvation as given by God and always remembers that signification is a doctrine that represents the historical traditions of faith. Methodists understand that baptism is the beginning of growth within the Christian faith, and being baptized as an infant is being dedicated as a child of God. It then becomes the full responsibility of the godparents and sponsors to be sure that the child will grow up in the understanding and knowledge of the Christian faith. However, in the Methodist teaching, a godparent or sponsor should not be directly related to the child to ensure that outside teaching of the Christian faith is being encouraged along with the family. [185]

What can be expected from a Methodist community? The Methodist service will be very structured, and usually ushers will be everywhere to instruct a person where to sit. Liturgical programs and prayer books are available all around to again actively participate in the worship. Worship is best expressed and learned through participation first by the individuals and ultimately the entire congregation. Again, the sermon is a huge importance for the service, and participation is a necessary requirement! If a worshipper is looking for a church community that requires participation to ensure faith development, the Methodist community would be a great place to begin.[186]

Baptists

The next Christian faith within the Protestant community, which also happens to be the largest denomination, is unquestionably the Baptists. Baptist followers should be best categorized by six distinguishing beliefs with the believer's baptism being first and the most prevalent.[187] A believer's baptism is a highly used practice and/

[185] Ibid., 110–111.

[186] Carmen Renee Berry, *The Unauthorized Guide to Choosing a Church* (Grand Rapids: Brazos Press, 2003), 295–296.

[187] Milton V. Backman, *Christian Churches of America: Origins and Beliefs* (Provo: Brigham Young University Press, 1976), 113.

or ritual in which an adult will complete after much preparation in self-reflection and personal dedication. Just as John the Baptist did for Jesus, a person will be immersed into a small pool of water, and when they come up from the water, they are now devoting their life to the Christian faith and Jesus's mission.

The second belief is that those who are converted will make up the regenerated church. This belief is that the Lord's Supper stands as a memorial for the Baptist faith in which this is a symbolic act of remembrance of the death of Jesus Christ. By living this faith out in their everyday lives, Baptists strive to bring more people into this shared stand for the regenerated church to expand as far and wide as possible. Considering John the Baptist was able to dedicate his entire life to baptizing people and preaching the coming of Christ, so should be continuously ongoing until Jesus's return.

The third belief relating to number 2 is that Jesus Christ will return to earth again as He promised in the New Testament. Humanity should always be prepared and eager for the Christ to return again and take all believers onto heaven with Him. Maintaining the importance of preparation for current Baptists, and by reaching out to non-Baptists and/or those desiring more education, keeps the Baptist third belief strong and ongoing.

Likewise, the Baptists also, as stated in the fourth belief, hold a strong belief in the independence of each congregation. In other words, each congregation is only subordinate to Jesus Christ and not to the rule of any other religious organization. The importance of working the given mission has too much value for other outside influence. It is not to say that the Baptists do not work with others; they simply keep their goal in the foremost of their worship, practices, and beliefs.[188]

Fifth, the absolute separation of church and state remains imperative. This belief has been slowly shifting in a different direction as some smaller Baptist branches are not as eager to maintain the full separation. Society creates a difficult choice where the separation of church and state is involved. Many of the state societal issues are

---

[188] Ibid., 116.

touchy topics that most religious organizations question in terms of morality, thus causing confusion on both sides.

Sixth, and the pillar of the denomination itself, the Baptist community maintains a huge advocate of religious liberty. All people are under God and have the choice to accept, change, or reject any sort of religious faith however they see fit to do so. Belief 6 is done with the greatest respect to the rights of others and the hope of others joining or at least wishing to be more educated.[189]

Historians of the Baptist faith relate their origin to the New Testament when Jesus Christ Himself was baptized as an adult by John the Baptist, thus beginning this greatly used model and ritual throughout the Baptist faith widely today. Although during the Middle Ages, while various religious groups were being further divided as were the Baptists, the principles taught within modern Baptists' beliefs were still being paralleled. This finding further promotes the idea that the Baptist faith is the fallback of all Protestant denominations.

Likewise, the Baptist faith relies very heavily on the teachings of the New Testament as the supreme authority for determining religious truths and understanding the inspired Word of God. In any case, Baptists have continuously gathered over four million members and growing each day. The Baptist community remains considered the most conservative body of American Christians today, which does shed light to the understanding of why this particular branch of Protestantism has such a strong following and continues to get stronger every day.

What can be expected from the Baptist faith community? Just as the Catholic Church, the Baptist Church has a strong following within the American church realm too. At any of these Baptist worship locations, great encouragement is always present! The Baptist community will be very welcoming and open on any level to invite new members and get them involved. Baptists have a general tendency to "tell it like it is" and should be a response from the congregation to ensure involvement. It can be easy to confuse this great

---

[189] Ibid.119.

enthusiasm for being informal; this is certainly not the case. Baptist members are very proper in dressing up and will go out of their way to welcome any newcomer into their family and encourage the congregation to partake in Holy Communion despite their religious background. As long as a "born again" feeling is present, the Baptist community would be a suitable fit. Consider too that in the welcoming process, a great deal of opportunities will come along such as small group Bible studies, choir ministries, and even mission work.[190]

Latter-Day Saints

As opposed to the transplanted Protestant faiths, these next churches fall under a different category known as the Native American religions, meaning that the religion is based on origins within America. The first church here is the Church of Jesus Christ and the Latter-Day Saints. This church originates back into the early 1800s when the founder, Joseph Smith, was exploring as many of the religious organizations that he possibly could trying to find one he was comfortable with and one that fit his beliefs. His family floated from Presbyterian to Methodist, which he described as a "tumult of opinions." Smith prayed to God asking frequently what church to belong to, and God answered him through a dream vision. Smith explained that God told him not to join any of the current churches because they all followed a doctrine that was incorrect. God promised him a fullness of the gospel within his life that would be made known when the time was right. From this vision, Smith became even more determined to find the answers he was seeking. Smith came across an ancient record that he translated and brought into the public that became known as the Book of Mormon. This book was not to replace the Bible, but only to supplement the Scripture for further understanding and learning. In doing this, Joseph Smith had already established his own church that became known as the

---

[190] Carmen Renee Berry, *The Unauthorized Guide to Choosing a Church* (Grand Rapids: Brazos Press, 2003), 265–266.

Church of Jesus Christ of Latter-Day Saints. Even today, this name and the Book of Mormon are still practiced and taught to new members every day. Before his death, Smith wished one important aspect of his church, and that was the importance of missions. Smith knew that his church was never going to survive if the Word was not brought to other people in different locations. Smith's wish was indeed taken to heart and granted. The Church of Jesus Christ of Latter-Day Saints is more prevalent now with much of the credit to their outstanding efforts of placing missionaries all over the world, bringing people the gospel message of Jesus, just as Smith had been promised in his vision by God.[191]

What can be expected from the Church of Jesus Christ of Latter-Day Saints within a community? The Book of Mormon will be read from and taken very seriously. The worship style overall is going to be not all that different from the other Protestant worship styles with the exception of the Book of Mormon readings. Participation within the service will be encouraged with respect for the Scripture expressed within the sermon, songs, and prayers. Most importantly, this church is going to encourage missionary work. It will be rather normal to see these church members going door-to-door to offer people the gospel news about Jesus Christ. For some interested, this is a huge excitement because they have the chance to travel short and some far distances to bring the passionate gospel to other people, which is doing a huge service to humanity simply by being there for people who need it.[192]

Seventh-Day Adventists

The next church under this category is the Seventh-Day Adventists. This also originates back to the mid-1800s when William

---

[191] Milton V. Backman, *Christian Churches of America: Origins and Beliefs* (Provo: Brigham Young University Press, 1976), 149–159.
[192] Carmen Renee Berry, *The Unauthorized Guide to Choosing a Church* (Grand Rapids: Brazos Press, 2003), 245.

Miller began a quest to discover the chorological patterns within the Bible trying to examine why these important dates were not being recognized within the church. Miller analyzed the Bible with all its numbers trying to determine when the second coming of Jesus would be. Once Miller announced that he had discovered the date for the second coming of Christ (or so he thought), a massive amount of people left their respected churches and followed closely to what Miller began preaching most likely because of fear. October 22, 1844, was the date Miller had calculated to be the second coming. On this date, people hid in their homes waiting for Jesus to return; and since nothing did happen, the day became the "Great Disappointment." After this occurrence, many of the Miller followers returned to their churches, but a major number remained loyal to Miller who at that time in the Adventist churches became the Seventh-Day Adventist. This began the turning point of the church in which its formation took off.[193]

The Seventh-Day Adventists share some of the same beliefs as most Christian churches, but they are known more for their distinguished differences. The most well-known difference is that Seventh-Day Adventists firmly believe and recognize Saturday as the Sabbath day of the week. They will cease working from Friday night through Saturday night to recognize this importance. This day is a memorial to God's creative power and a sign of His authority over the world. In relation to God's authority, the Bible remains the reverent Scripture, but it is also accompanied by the writings of Ellen G. White who presented a lesser light that brings people closer to God's great light. The counseling and writings of White have long factored into maintaining doctrine unity for the church to follow. This includes believing that the Lord's Supper should only be available three or four years as needed to be the ultimate remembrance of Jesus's death for humanity. It is to be preceded by foot washing just as Jesus demonstrated within the New Testament.[194]

---

[193] Milton V. Backman, *Christian Churches of America: Origins and Beliefs* (Provo: Brigham Young University Press, 1976), 167–170.
[194] Ibid., 171.

In the older traditions of Seventh-Day Adventists, which some places still use today, they follow a very strict ruling to mimic the Old Testament. For example, many Seventh-Day Adventists are vegetarians because the Old Testament teaches not to eat meat. Many of them do not take or use tobacco, alcohol, tea, coffee, or any food substance that does physical harm to the body. The body is a temple made from God and should be treated as such. Related to this, in many cases playing cards, gambling, dancing, and being involved with modern technology can all take away from remembering the importance that God has in their lives. This is not to say that these actions are never done; they are simply frowned upon within the church community. More of the Seventh-Day Adventist churches now are more lenient about these areas, but they still hold their beliefs to be essential. In terms of those exploring this church, these areas of control can be a turnoff in terms of joining this church's membership. Yet on the flip side, if someone is seeking a rather stricter faith that holds closer to what they firmly believe, then the Seventh-Day Adventist would be a solid fit.[195]

Christian Science

Another church under this category is the Church of Christ: Christian Science. This Christian denomination was also founded in the late 1800s by a woman named Mary Baker Eddy. At the age of seventeen, she was diagnosed with a life-threatening fever by the family doctor. Instead of medication, Eddy prayed. Eddy claimed that immediately after her prayer ended, she felt "a soft glow of ineffable joy." Throughout her life, Eddy attended a formal education and was self-taught with a great many languages to further understand theology. After several failed marriages, and upon the death of her final husband, she sustained a painful leg injury after running out into the street overcome with emotion. A doctor had announced her injury to be fatal, but within three days after much Bible reading,

---

[195] Ibid., 172–173.

Eddy stood up on her feet alone freed from all pain. She had proven to herself and those around her the significance of prayer and trusting in God's miraculous healings. Now, she had officially begun the Christian Science movement. When she was asked to explain and theorize her beliefs, this became her famous answer:

> God I called immortal mind. That which sins, suffers, and dies, I named mortal mind. The physical senses, or sensuous nature, I called error and shadow. Soul I denominated substance, because soul alone is truly substantial. God I characterized as individual entity, but His corporeality I denied. The real I claimed as eternal; and its antipodes, or the temporal, I described as unreal. Spirit, I called the reality; and matter, the unreality.[196]

Throughout the century, Christian Science has fluctuated in following. Some people find it too irrational to believe, while others are willing to keep that strong faith in God that all pain and sickness can be healed through prayer. Christian Science teaches that "life, truth, and love" are the three components that make up who God is. God is the father-mother relationship, Jesus is the spiritual idea of the perfect child, and the Holy Spirit is known as the Holy Comforter. Christian Science believes that since the Bible explains that God is all and in all, there should be harmony within every living creature. The Bible is the significant guide to receiving eternal life! Likewise, salvation is the understanding of God and demonstrating one's own convictions by overcoming sin, sickness, and even death. There are no physical sacraments within this church. Baptism is considered a continuous act for cleanliness, and communion is shared twice a year when the church members silently commune with God.[197]

---

[196] Milton V. Backman, *Christian Churches of America: Origins and Beliefs* (Provo: Brigham Young University Press, 1976), 188.
[197] Ibid., 189–193.

What can be expected from the Christian Science church setting? Overall, there are not too many locations that have Christian Science as a huge religion, but it is practiced on various facilities in fairness to religious diversity. These churches place a great deal of emphasis on prayer. Being able to commune with God in silent prayer is essential. God's love for His people is a key factor into remembering that God's healing power comes directly to His people and the need for earthly medicines is not needed. The person will learn a huge respect for life both human and nonhuman. They will also learn that God's healing is the only true way for life to continue if God wills this to be so.[198]

Pentecostal

The final church under this Native American religions category is the Pentecostal faith. (Remember that Native American religions mean they have American origins.) Just as with the previous religions, the Pentecostal movement began post–Civil War focusing on the concerns of rebuilding the social, industrial, and intellectual revolutions that sought to preserve the central truths based on Christianity. The movement was based on protests concerning the evils of that generation. It was not until the early 1900s that this movement took off. The Pentecostal movement was now making it a requirement for a person to show evidence of being baptized within the Holy Spirit. If this had not happened, a second baptism was required with the expectation of an outward emotional reaction. The main goal was for people to begin speaking in tongues as it happened within the New Testament during the Pentecost event. Because of this huge emphasis on self-transformation, the Pentecost denomination has grown by incredible numbers. This was reasoned to be happening because the quest for truth is never going to be finished, and more people are

---

[198] Carmen Renee Berry, *The Unauthorized Guide to Choosing a Church* (Grand Rapids: Brazos Press, 2003), 245.

striving to know and understand how and where within Christianity they fit.[199]

What can be expected from a Pentecostal church community? A Pentecostal church is going to be very similar to some of the previous churches mentioned, yet different in other ways. This church will be very informal and rather spontaneous with people jumping into songs and laying hands on each other as encouragement within the Spirit. This spontaneous activity is also going to be accompanied by people sharing visions and words of knowledge that they have directly seen or heard from the Holy Spirit. Moving with and where the Spirit guides is a key part of this service. Visitors and newcomers seeking to be closer to God are always welcomed right in. If a student is a free-spirited type of person, then the Pentecostal faith will be a comfortable fit.[200]

United Church of Christ

Another denomination that is quite new overall, established within 1957, is the United Church of Christ (UCC). UCC founded many of its beliefs on the original early Puritan Church of England background. The evangelical side of this denomination along with the reformed background has made up the current UCC. One of the more available beliefs of this faith is that UCC is extremely liberal. They are an open community welcoming people of various backgrounds and lifestyles and with a desire to become more involved. UCC member and researcher Edward Queen describes the current UCC as follows:

> Next in size and historical importance is the United Church of Christ, which is the historic

---

[199] Milton V. Backman, *Christian Churches of America: Origins and Beliefs* (Provo: Brigham Young University Press, 1976), 197–199.

[200] Carmen Renee Berry, *The Unauthorized Guide to Choosing a Church* (Grand Rapids: Brazos Press, 2003), 315–317.

continuation of the Congregational churches founded under the influence of New England Puritanism. The United Church of Christ also subsumed the third major Reformed group, the German Reformed, which (then known as the Evangelical and Reformed Church) merged with the Congregationalists in 1957.[201]

One major key component that greatly makes the UCC different from nearly all other religions is it has no hierarchy. UCC does not delegate any one person to a specific leadership role in terms of making decisions for the whole. UCC believes that an individual community has to know what decisions, changes, and motives are important enough to adapt for their own needs. There is no so-called church doctrines or traditions that are imposed on people to follow. Because of this, the only main core belief for UCC is based on four principles: Christian, reformed, evangelical, and congregational.[202] The UCC motto is John 17:21: "That they may be all one."[203] UCC expresses freedom of the individual to decide what is right for that person. Judgment should not be made by any religious organization. If anyone wants to be educated about Christ, the UCC is welcome to all.

Amish

One smaller but greatly notable sect of Christianity is the Amish. The Amish community reaches back to early Puritan Swiss Anabaptist origins. The Amish are a people of simple dress and simple lifestyle, who engage in little technology or modern-day science. Today many of the Amish are found mainly in Indiana in secluded neighborhoods.

---

[201] Milton V. Backman, *Christian Churches of America: Origins and Beliefs* (Provo: Brigham Young University Press, 1976), 118–119.
[202] Ibid., 119.
[203] John 17:21.

Usually they continue to speak what is called Pennsylvania German or also known as Pennsylvania Dutch.[204] The simplicity of the Amish lifestyle can be rather difficult for most to understand considering our modern world is bursting with technology.

A person begins their Amish faith at baptism usually taking place during the teenage years or early twenties. Baptism is a requirement for faith participation. All Amish must be baptized prior to marriage and are only allowed to date and marry someone within the same faith community. A church is usually led by one bishop with selected pastors, and sometimes deacons are appointed in larger communities. The Amish rules are explained with the Ordnung, which is an extensive detailing of all Amish expectations. The Ordnung continues lifestyle clothing rules, technology limitations, prohibitions, automobiles, and nearly all areas of everyday life. The Amish do not have social security or insurance. These are not necessary for a religious community that maintains such simplicity. Related to this, the Amish practice resistance to society and will not ever be involved with military.[205] If or when actions are taken in violation of the Ordnung, the accused will be shunned by their own people and even ordered to be excommunicated by the bishop should the situation arise.

What can be expected while visiting an Amish community? The Amish are very separated from the modern English world. The Amish place a huge emphasis on education by having one-roomed classrooms for all ages to teach and learn. There is a constant desire for church involvement and much family dependency. The Amish are very community oriented. The Amish are usually welcoming to visitors and most often want to explain their lifestyle to others, but sometimes it does become easy to judge. Overall, the Amish can teach the Christian much about maintaining a structure that has worked extremely well for many years.

---

[204] Noah Zook and Samuel L. Yoder, *Berne, Indiana, Old Order Amish Settlement* (Berne: Amish Newsletter, 2009), 1.

[205] Ibid., 1–2.

Native American and Wicca

While Native American and Wicca sects may be different from Christianity, they are certainly not afraid to listen to, be educated by, and assist with Christian missionaries. In the Native American regions, theology can be vastly different. Some tribes are monotheistic while others are polytheistic. What makes the Native religions so unique is that many of their practices are not recorded. Native Americans have been telling stories, reenacting events, and celebrating traditions so many years but rarely have recorded their beliefs. There have been found cave drawings and abandoned tribes leaving behind markings and utensils used for worship practices, but nothing in print. It can be rather difficult to learn some Indian practices especially from tribes that are no longer in existence. What little information has been gathered does leave much to the imagination.[206]

Christian missionaries have been teaching certain interested Indian tribes about Christ and allowing the Natives to teach them as well. The most common practices within the Indian tribes are the elements of the earth and time. Native Americans place a huge importance and respect on the elements of earth, fire, air, water, and spirit. These five elements are also the five points of the Wiccan star called a pentagram. The Indians have learned that without the elements, the world would simply not exist. The soil of the earth makes the plants grown for food for people and the animals. In the same way water supplies the ground to grow, fire is the light, and the weather conditions are what control the growing harvest seasons. Related to this, the Natives are very thorough on evaluating time. The changes in seasons and the phases of the moon have helped them to create some of the earliest known calendars. Many farmers today base their growing seasons on these calendars, and our country time changes upon what the Indians had discovered and used for centuries.[207]

---

[206] John Rhodes, "An American Tradition: The Religious Persecution of Native Americans," *Montana Law Review* 52, 1991, 27.

[207] John Rhodes, "An American Tradition: The Religious Persecution of Native Americans," *Montana Law Review* 52, 1991, 29.

In terms of the uses of elements and time, the practice of Wicca can closely relate. Wicca is a pagan sect described by a term meaning "witch," specifically "witchcraft." Wicca is said to have begun during the early Salem witch trials, but in the same manner as the Native Americans, Wicca practices with the elements. Wiccans believe that since the earth supplies all that is needed for human survival, then the power of creation must be extremely real. Most often the concept of a deity is not that important. Wiccans believe in the triple deity of the sun, moon, and stars.[208] Along with the triple deity, Wiccans believe in the terms "mother earth" and "father time." Without these and the fruits of the earth to supply, the world could not go on. The importance of working toward a brighter future is based on the Wiccan belief of reincarnation. Reincarnation is believing that in the afterlife, a person of magic or witch will come again in another life possibly to redo unfinished business or begin an entirely new life. Not too many Christian religions are firm believers of reincarnation mainly because of God's promise of the heavenly kingdom mentioned in the Scripture, but other outside world religions do find a kinship to Wicca because of the reincarnation belief.

The worship of a Wiccan practice involves using the altar usually in a circular form with the elements, cardinal directions, and an athame. An athame is a dagger used for bloodshed for sacramental purposes and is considered to be a magical tool. In terms of documents or rituals to follow, Wicca has what is called *The Book of Shadows*.[209] This book contains various spells, instructions, chants, and the history behind how Wicca had begun and what is necessary to keep it going. Although Wicca has been looked down upon because of the witchcraft, it does not make it any less important as a religion. Even today, there are television shows and movies portraying witchcraft more as comedy, not as a religion. But it is not a laughing matter. As a show of respect toward this pagan sect, many Wiccan

---

[208] Joanne Pearson, Richard H. Roberts, and Geoffrey Samuel, *Nature Religion Today: Paganism in the Modern World* (Edinburgh: Edinburgh University Press, 1998), 6.

[209] Ibid., 7.

practices choose to remain quiet and private about their experiences, while others are welcoming for followers to have an open mind.

Nondenominational

Another branch within Christianity, which is probably fast growing, is simply Christian or nondenominational. The main difference here is that this group does not affiliate under a particular branch name. Nondenominational chose to follow the words of the Scripture as complete literal instructions laid out by Jesus. Just as those words were spoken two thousand years ago, they must mean the exact same today and then. Many nondenominational followers do not even allow translational differences or theories within the Scripture to be discussed. The Word of God is as is. For some, the literal instructions can be hard to follow. As compared to other more liberal branches such as the UCC and even the American Catholic, nondenominational can find it difficult to keep certain people for a longer amount of time, whereas in other cases, the long-lasting members find it easier to remain loyal and easier to reach out to others because relating back to the Word of God alone without any traditions, doctrines, and extreme hierarchies is appealing. More often too, these communities are greatly close knit and treat each other as family willing to assist whenever and however they possibly can. Since Jesus reached out to all people who asked Him for help, they do the same.

Atheists

A final not-so-religious group to mention is people who are called atheists. Atheists do not fall under any specific branch of Christianity or any other world religion for that matter, but what they do or do not believe in has intrigued many Christian followers for years. Atheists do not believe in any type of deity, creator, or savior. Some atheists might believe in Darwin's evolution or perhaps the big bang theory, or even still that the earth has always existed with no beginning and no end. Atheists believe that humanity has given life to which they choose and someday like all people will die into total darkness. Most atheists will likely explain their beliefs based on seeing all the tragedy in the world as an outward sign that there is no God. If God is supposed to be all good, then why are so many people and places in such peril? Why waste your time praying to an entity that does not exist and cannot hear you? These questions do make Christians wonder about their beliefs. Atheists' questions can cause doubts even within the strongest of believers. Also, those same questions can make their faith stronger knowing that Christ does exist and that humanity does have a purpose. In whatever reasoning an atheist may give, just as with all the current religions, treating them with respect while they share their beliefs has to be essential. A Christian is not a judge but is to be available when their beliefs are needed.

In conclusion, chapter 5 has scratched the surface giving an overview to almost all Christian denominations. The United States continues to harbor a vast amount of religious organizations, schools, and community efforts of several different backgrounds; yet all people are still searching for what makes their desires most at ease. Finding a purpose, achieving a goal, and especially carrying out Jesus's mission in everyday life certainly make the denominations here to stay.

CHAPTER 6

Christian Education in Culture

Definition of Culture

Christian missionaries do their best to travel as far as needed for the sole purpose of bringing Christian education where it may be needed the most. Psychology has certainly helped explain more and more regarding what makes a person want to learn and how they are able to maintain the knowledge gathered. Personal beliefs, which are usually based on a person's culture and surroundings, are apt to play a huge role in the education process for a person. The core here is that a person is basing the need for education on their senses. The senses create our understandings and perceptions of the outside world. When reaching out to a different culture, a person's senses can become confused. For Christian education, theologian David Tracey recalls that even science does not compute absolute truth and fact. Culturally, education has to be learned for adapting purposes to begin the teaching. Culture alone can be defined in a couple of different ways to include several other areas. One definition is that culture is "a set of important understandings (oftentimes unstated) that members of a community share in common."[210] For Christian edu-

---

[210] Barbara B. Gaddy, T. William Hall, and Robert J. Marzano, *School Wars: Resolving Our Conflicts over Religion and Values* (San Francisco: Jossey-Bass Publishers, 1996), 136–137.

cation, a culture can be defined as a community of educators, fundamentalists, mainline Christians, humanists, or secularists. These groups together are best described in culture through a paradigm. A paradigm is designed to explain how groups will intertwine, mix, and weave together by perception. This is also a way to see what does not work such as which areas may not be ready for some of the challenges included. Any paradigm is going to have strengths and weaknesses. The hope will be for the strengths to overcome the weaknesses especially for Christian education.

The paradigm to be discussed will include three focus groups: Christian fundamentalists, mainline Christians, and religious liberals. The paradigm in discussion of these three groups will be within the four realms of authority for knowledge and power, views of human nature and the self, values, and the nature of reality.[211]

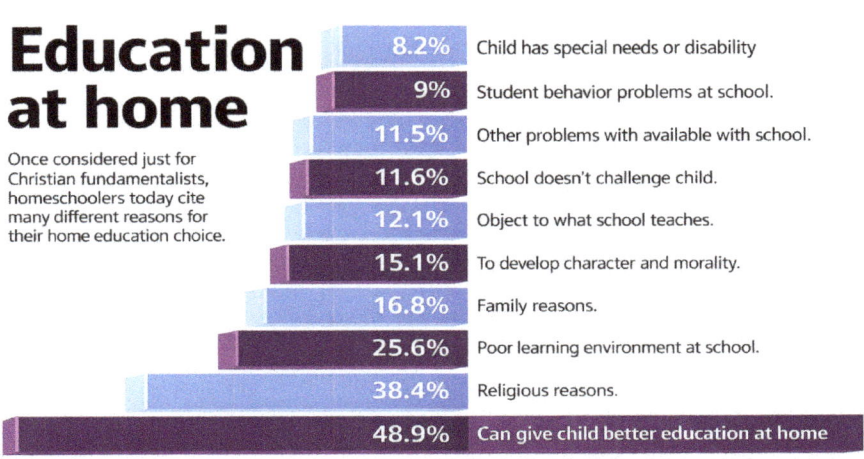

Education at home

Once considered just for Christian fundamentalists, homeschoolers today cite many different reasons for their home education choice.

8.2%	Child has special needs or disability
9%	Student behavior problems at school.
11.5%	Other problems with available with school.
11.6%	School doesn't challenge child.
12.1%	Object to what school teaches.
15.1%	To develop character and morality.
16.8%	Family reasons.
25.6%	Poor learning environment at school.
38.4%	Religious reasons.
48.9%	Can give child better education at home

Source: U.S. Department of Education   **ALLISON MARTINI**/Assistant Design Editor

The first circle within the paradigm is the authority of knowledge and truth. Overall, most people will share many of the same

---

211 Barbara B. Gaddy, T. William Hall, and Robert J. Marzano, *School Wars: Resolving Our Conflicts over Religion and Values* (San Francisco: Jossey-Bass Publishers, 1996), 139–149.

perceptions and understandings of several truths simply because they already believe in these truths based on their previous knowledge. Christian fundamentalists view the world as the Bible being the only single authority of religious knowledge and truth. From their perspective, the Bible provides the ultimate and unchangeable truth as God's message.[212] Ignoring the unquestionable message from God Himself can make individual salvation impossible and will further the work of Satan. This form of education can be a turnoff for the learners out of fear. There can be no question that science and history have created facts that have caused doubt and further exploration in certain passages for validity purposes.

Mainline Christians focus on the Hebrew Scriptures and the New Testament as making up the Bible together, but not to be taken literally. Mainline Christians focus and acknowledge the Bible as being divinely inspired and written by the spiritually filled humans. The Bible is a text showing the activity of God through the Jewish and Christian history. Outside of the literal aspect, the Scripture includes truths, insights, inspirational literature, ethical teachings, and moral examples. Along with all these other mentionable inclusions within the Bible, there is also a strong source of worship-style techniques and examples; however, alone it does not represent authority for knowledge and truth. The United Methodist Church is a prime example of mainline Christians considering they firmly believe the only four sources of religious knowledge are the Bible, experience, reason, and tradition. The main stress for mainliners is reasoning and experience. Mainline Christians already recognize that knowledge can come from other sources such as the society, history, and science; but these secular sources do not and will not conflict with the already placed sacred knowledge.

The religious liberals assume that all biblical knowledge is based on experience and reason. Liberals, either Jewish and/or Christian, view the Bible as a source of historical development for the faith and

---

[212] Barbara B. Gaddy, T. William Hall, and Robert J. Marzano, *School Wars: Resolving Our Conflicts over Religion and Values* (San Francisco: Jossey-Bass Publishers, 1996), 136.

personal spiritual growth. Likewise, liberals openly express that the Bible was not written by God, but rather by humans who cannot be considered infallible. Therefore, personal experience carries more weight. A person should feel dependent on God during such an experience while gaining the needed knowledge. It would be no surprise to learn that liberals are followers of science. The scientific methods of investigating, using hypotheses, and testing support human reason. Religious liberals are summed up as "an idea is only true when and if it is put into practice and works as predicted."[213]

The second paradigm is the views about human nature and the self. Many questions fall under this category such as are we all sinners from birth? Is this where original sin comes into our lives? Does the individual have limits? Are all people going to transform throughout life? How do people learn and grow? Is humanity formed by the nature of surroundings or the nurture of personal upbringing? What is the difference, if any? Human nature influences almost every aspect of a person's life whether the learning is conditioned by family upbringing, society, or education itself. The most common denominator for the human alone can usually be narrowed down to the attitude.

Christian fundamentalists who take the Bible literally as the key source of knowledge view the human being as an inheritor of Adam's original sin.[214] People have the nature as a creature fallen from God and to live in sin. Just as Adam and Eve were tempted by Satan, so will be every person born into the world. Further, Christian fundamentalists believe that a person cannot be saved by their efforts alone. Salvation is a gift given by God only to the people who truly repent of their sins and seek forgiveness. Salvation was made possible because Jesus suffered. By His crucifixion and death, Jesus paid God for all humanity's committed sins. For fundamentalists, the education of those seeking religious education should be in an attempt to be "born again" or start over but rather remember that salvation is a gift given to all. The true way to the fullness of self-worth is only to recognize God through Jesus Christ.

---

[213] Ibid., 141.
[214] Ibid., 142.

Mainline Christians also believe in original sin but not to the extreme method of the fundamentalists. Mainlines believe, as quoted by Reinhold Niebuhr, "to be self-conscious is to see the self as a finite object separated from essential reality."[215] Niebuhr, a mainline theologian himself, went on to explain that evil came into the world because of the irresponsibility of people. People are arrogant and self-centered and thus create evil intentions on their own. The only way for people to transform themselves is by correcting their actions and beliefs by the grace of God who already accepts humanity as they are. Most mainline Christians believe that it is not through salvation that we are cleansed of original sin but rather by the opportunity to learn and grow in self-understanding, self-knowledge, and self-discipline from past deeds. While holding on to personal dignity, Niebuhr once more points out that ignorance, lethargy, stereotypical thinking, cultural parochialism, and intense selfishness can and do overcome education as well as spiritual growth. For education alone, the purpose is to continuously guide children, youth, and all learners through the growth process to complete knowledge.

Religious liberals are much more open and optimistic regarding human nature so much that they do not give any credit to the idea of original sin. Liberals place a high human-centered belief and goal on the potential of human ability and wealth of goodness.[216] For this belief, liberals place an emphasis on the learning of children. Children and youth can be intellectually educated and morally nurtured to fully understand responsibility. Sharing a liberal view alone means an individual has the potential to reach total fulfillment. One of the fathers of Liberalism and well-known Unitarian, Ralph Waldo Emerson once stated his belief on the human soul,

> The human soul tends toward goodness and
> God-ness: Within man is the soul of the whole;

---

[215] Barbara B. Gaddy, T. William Hall, and Robert J. Marzano, *School Wars: Resolving Our Conflicts over Religion and Values* (San Francisco: Jossey-Bass Publishers, 1996), 143.

[216] Ibid., 143.

> the wise silence; the universal beauty to which
> every part and particle is equally related; the eter-
> nal One…There is no bar or wall in the soul,
> where man, the effect, ceases and God, the cause,
> begins.[217]

This single quote completely sums up the message of religious liberals by reaffirming that human ability has the potential to reach total fulfillment from within the inner soul.

The third paradigm is simply values. Most thoughtful religious people usually have many of these values including honesty, integrity, self-discipline, responsibility, generosity, human freedom, and courage.[218] Families and schools are openly trying to instill these values into students but may differ as the reasoning and sources behind each value. Society over the years has changed what exactly a value may be. Certain community traditions can become more prevalent than the actual importance value behind it. The danger here is that many people feel threatened when values of other countries and foreign places are taking a greater stand within America. Who decides what values are more important to keep or let go?

For the Christian fundamentalists, values are object as in being outside of human existence. Remembering that fundamentalists believe the Bible to be God's direct and infallible word, the values within the Bible are also absolute and objective truth. These words are written as the only natural law. Value is highly placed on the honor and worshipping of God, especially for children to learn this importance. Any religious tolerance and/or questioning of differing values and worldviews must not be considered.

Mainline Christians mostly agree with fundamentalists here only slightly disagreeing with the fact that human judgments and actions are influenced by religion and culture, which are essential for the well-being of all individuals and communities. There is not one single authority or absolute authority for the mainliners regarding

---

[217] Ibid., 144.
[218] Ibid., 144–145.

moral and ethics; instead, they tend to remember and acknowledge the civil government's laws, the Constitution, Bill of Rights, and other documents set forth by previous heroes of American history. The same is agreed with for morality issues. One theologian commented that "morality is a celebration of wholeness in which the integrity of the self and others is respected."[219] Some may not necessarily agree with this comment, but it does state how a mainline Christian would view morality. Likewise, mainliners will emphasize the values of understanding, accepting, and appreciating diversity originating from cultural populations, ethnicity, race, and religious beliefs unlike the rejecting from fundamentalists.

Religious liberals view values as ever changing and must take into account the situation from which the value is happening. Considering that the liberal stance is more relative, this may explain why liberals encourage humans to take a useful, beneficial, and right approach in discovering the best method for value use.[220] Again, morality plays a huge importance to the liberal viewpoint. Moral values are to include self-sacrifice, generosity, justice, responsibility, and freedom. Further, liberals pursue the commitment to human value by respecting freedom, dignity, and the opportunity for all to have happiness. Going one step further, liberals also want to ensure health and recreation to enhance pleasure and guarantee the ongoing values in place.

The final paradigm mentioned is the nature of reality. The other paradigms discussed beliefs and knowledge regarding authority, the self, and values. Now, the gears shift into reality. What is real? What is the deep understanding of a particular object, person, or belief being real? These questions are covered under metaphysics, ontology (study of being), and cosmology (study of time and how origins came to be). Christians, like many believers of religions, do believe that God is very real but may differ in their views regarding the nature

---

[219] Barbara B. Gaddy, T. William Hall, and Robert J. Marzano, *School Wars: Resolving Our Conflicts over Religion and Values* (San Francisco: Jossey-Bass Publishers, 1996), 145–146.

[220] Ibid., 146.

of God. Western cultures affirm reality in areas of materials, nature itself, social institutions, and human beings. Yet all reality does relate back and depend on the Creator. What does God do?

Christian fundamentalists believe wholeheartedly that the only ultimate reality is God. God is omniscient, omnipotent, and always alive within our world. God has always been and always will be. He is the sole creator of all the universe and is the only source for all that exists. Likewise, Jesus Christ coming to earth in human form was the perfect reality sent to humanity directly by God. Sadly, on the other hand, fundamentalists also have to acknowledge the reality of Satan and the presence of evil. Evil and sin are constantly seeking to destroy all values of goodness and love. Thus, this is why fundamentalists focus greatly on the need for repentance against sin and to live a holy and cleaned life.

Mainline Christians believe in the doctrine of the Trinity: God as the Father, the Son, and the Holy Spirit. Mainliners believe the same as the Christian fundamentalists do, only they challenge the idea of Satan's influence and sin being present in the world. Sin having the power to influence humanity seems to take away from the belief of God being the ultimate controller and cosmic power.[221] Mainliners still struggle with explaining how and why Satan would have as much power as he seems to when turning humanity toward sin. Ultimately, there should be nothing even close to ever taking away from God's goodness.

Religious liberals assume that ultimate reality, the core of all existence, is God. Liberals do not view God as a supernatural being but more as a person whose nature can never be fully known or understood. Liberals do not ignore sin and evil; rather, they believe that Satan is not literally the source of all evil. Human nature has a tendency to reject God in times of sorrow without the influence of Satan. These views add value to the liberal fact of God and science not being in conflict with each other. Here, some liberals would actu-

---

[221] Barbara B. Gaddy, T. William Hall, and Robert J. Marzano, *School Wars: Resolving Our Conflicts over Religion and Values* (San Francisco: Jossey-Bass Publishers, 1996), 148.

ally agree with mainliners by knowing that God is still present within the everyday world. Philosopher Alfred North Whitehead, who has inspired many theologians into liberal thinking, summarizes all religious liberal views of reality as this:

> God is in the world, or nowhere, creating continually in and around us. This creative principle is everywhere in animate and so-called inanimate matter, in the ether, water, earth, and human hearts. But this creation is a continuing process and the process is itself the actuality since no sooner do you arrive than you start on a fresh journey. In so far as man partakes of this creative process does he partake of the divine of God, and that participation is his immortality, reducing the question of whether his individuality survives death of the body to the estate of an irrelevancy. His true destiny as co-creator in the universe is his dignity and his grandeur.[222]

American and Midwest

Culture studies over time has been a comparative study influenced by art, history, and science. Especially with the rise of anthropology, the development of education compared with culture has become quite rapid. Even while education has continued to evolve, education still has the idea of culture along with the older Unitarian concept of what education should include. One such basis for early culture was civilization.[223] The colonial settlers of the 1770s in early America were on a journey for this specific purpose of escaping taxation and seeking religious freedom. This became a major influence

---

[222] Ibid., 149.
[223] Christopher Dawson, *The Historic Reality of Christian Culture: A Way to the Renewal of Human Life* (New York: Harper & Brothers Publishers, 1960), 60.

of culture in America. Civilization strives for all people to reach one specific goal or one ultimate way of life. "The democratic way of life," so to speak, might have had several different paths to reach that goal; but as long as the overall civilized people fell into the same universal understanding, an established civilization culture was developed.

If the civilization theory did not work as with some particular areas, cultures may have been introduced simply by the anthropologists' method of artificial creation. Ironically enough, the artificial creation is more open to the reality of what is actually happening with a particular group. These cultures take into consideration the vast differences of races, ages, languages, and even state-by-state divisions. By building a culture that is welcoming to people included, there has to be more adapting and outreaching to accommodate.[224] Some accommodations can be made from simply the land itself and geographic climate. For example, the Louisiana Purchase and the Western Gold Rush brought about many different people in search of one goal but were fully aware of not being alone. The different backgrounds and the variety of skills people brought together surfaced a difference of ideas and gifts for the culture to endure, as with all developments, changes, and challenges that will be faced; but some might argue that the artificial creation cultures strive stronger simply based on the openness of diversity.

Cultures can also be established based on locational achievements, mainly architecture. Before America, many other geographic locations have paved the way for cultures to develop by this method. For example, Egypt has the Great Pyramids while Rome has the Colosseum along with the Vatican treasures, to name a few. America has certainly made many of its own achievements over the past few centuries, but some of those achievements came with costly consequences that ultimately shaped cultural differences along the way. The most prominent example of this would the American Civil War. The Northern states valued human equality, business influence, and

---

[224] Christopher Dawson, *The Historic Reality of Christian Culture: A Way to the Renewal of Human Life* (New York: Harper & Brothers Publishers, 1960), 61–62.

government leadership while the Southern states valued the keeping and selling of slaves (as in those different from rich and powerful white men), remaining independent of Northern business deals, and simply preserving their own way of life that had been in place for over one hundred years.[225] Sadly, it took over four years of war, destruction, and major losses of life before this battle ended; however, the rebuilding took many more years. Even today some people still feel the effects and even resentment. Overall, massive changes came about that created huge cultural differences within America. Changes in religion, government, education, and everyday life took drastic turns to restore and rebegin American culture.

Cultural development begs a question: can culture be separate from religion including education? The answer would be no, claiming that religion cannot be separated just as human life cannot be separated from faith. Consider that religion and religious education greatly influence and transform the societal way of life that includes culture. So can culture be identified by religion? In America, terms such as the Bible Belt, Southern Baptists, and even Jesus freaks are used to describe certain areas. The Bible Belt refers to the Midwestern area based on the fullness of religious involvement through several Christian denominations. Southern Baptists use this term to distinguish themselves from other Baptist sects to maintain their own identity. The "Jesus freaks" term usually has a negative connotation relating to those who are fully and completely committed to teaching, preaching, and serving the Christian community by any means not always associated with a particular area.

Relating with religious culture, where does that leave education within culture? American Western civilization has an absolute standard of what the image of an idealized culture should consist of. Religious background originates greatly from history itself. First off, many of the religions within America were brought over from Europe as the new country began with many instituting their own educational systems.[226] Closely related to education, Judaism, Christianity,

---

[225] Ibid., 63.
[226] Ibid., 70.

and Islam share many similarities, creating a bond over the value of religious beliefs as opposed to government orders. Arguably, the culture of a particular religious community could often outweigh the other communities more based on family, state, and nation.

Second, education of American culture can be based on the traditions of sacred learning through the divine Scriptures, sacred laws, sacred history, and even sacred oral traditions. For some cultures, education done under these traditions is another absolute truth to represent a holistic learning pattern on the literary culture.[227] In most cases, the traditions including sacred learning would only apply to private schools. Considering that public schools teach little on religious texts, these traditions would be considered secondary or even supplementary.

Finally, culture can be based on social duty. Primary cultural activities can include education, government involvement by voting, and the importance of worship. Christian education relates with worship on a more public level. While education may be handled with a school, church, or community, worship is done within the community on an open level. Again, culture can greatly influence how, where, and why worship should be conducted.[228] Not only does worship reflect the importance of faith value, but the mere presence of people coming together creates a stronger community and outward language to other communities.

Yet there are times that communities can become further apart from these worship gatherings based on personal judgments. Perhaps in certain cases, some cultures need a boost to be more open, allowing further discussions and change to occur. Christian education has an added value in that not many cultures can illustrate a complete dualism within religion and culture by using conflict and spiritual tensions for a base.[229] Not all cultures of education can make this argument as strongly with much of their culture being based on

---

[227] Christopher Dawson, *The Historic Reality of Christian Culture: A Way to the Renewal of Human Life* (New York: Harper & Brothers Publishers, 1960), 72.

[228] Ibid., 72–73.

[229] Ibid., 77.

other attributes, usually politics. Whatever the culture may be based on, usually education whether religious or not does play into the shaping and continuing of the culture itself.

Culture of Gender

Culture certainly has shifted and changed throughout time due to various reasons. Culture has influenced religion, politics, and education perhaps more so than any other aspect. Taking culture down to another level can focus on other prominent areas where the cultural influence is recognized. One such area would the role of women. The roles, duties, and challenges of women have not always been as openly discussed compared to other moral or political issues in recent times; but that does not mean the cultural journey of women should not be addressed. Today many important roles within society are taken control of by women. The United States has more women in business, medical fields, military, and especially education than ever before.

History has shown that women have undergone some major changes of status over the centuries. Women of some cultures are basic property to be used and sold; some are servants or even slaves against their will, while others have more freedom, allowing for more opportunity. The battle of human rights explores two major components: cultural relativism and religious extremism/feminism.[230] Depending on what culture from around the world a woman may be will play a significant role in how she is viewed and treated. Some cultures continue to change their thinking while others may intensify theirs. During the European Age of Enlightenment, many documents were being produced for the first time expressing the importance of women in everyday society as needing to be recognized outside of women in royalty. Likewise, the United Nations produced a charter detailing the importance of human rights, especially in the

---

[230] Courtney W. Howland, *Religious Fundamentalisms and the Human Rights of Women* (New York: St. Martin's Press, 1990), 79.

treatment of women. Even in America, it was until many years after America had become its own individual country that women were given to right to vote, join the military, and become more available to other employment opportunities. One such opportunity that really became important for women was that of education. Education from those higher educated to be shared with children, other adults, and all those in need where education was not available. For those of Christian faith, this was a godsend waiting to burst.

Christian education alone has a huge growing number of women educators. Oftentimes, religious educators may sometimes overlook the fact that perhaps a woman's grasp of theology and religion may be different from men. Religious women and educators are usually fully aware of their own faith journeys and experiences that have assisted in getting these women into teaching.[231] Many obstacles and road-blocks continue to come up for some women seeking to further their education with other learners based simply on sexist viewpoints. For whatever reason, there are some people in the world who hold on to an earlier belief that women are only to be seen and not heard, or to clean, cook, bear and raise the children, and serve the men however men see fit. Women are still looked down as inferior to men. Mostly, in some traditions, especially within Catholicism, women are still considered less and/or different than men where liturgy is concerned. With a few smaller exceptions, nearly all of leadership clergy are still men and have been for previous centuries. Many other denominations are not as traditional and strict, although there are remaining exceptions and plenty of evolving still to come.

While learning their own faith through theological educa-tion, women of the Bible did not always have it so easy either. The Scripture expresses the lives of some women, but usually not too much may be known about them, or what facts are known may be more negative.[232] For example, in the creation story of Genesis, Eve was the one tempted by Satan to eat the forbidden fruit who then

---

[231] Jack L. Seymour, and Donald E. Miller, *Theological Approaches to Christian Education* (Nashville: Abingdon Press, 1990), 70.

[232] Ibid., 71.

gave it to her husband, Adam, thus causing both to be cast out of the garden of Eden. Later, Sarah, the wife of Abraham, laughed and doubted when visitors told her that within a year she would give birth to a son even in her old age. In the New Testament, Mary Magdalene is mentioned a few times in the gospels. History explains that Mary Magdalene may have been a follower of Jesus but was also a temptress and prostitute of her time. Likewise, the apostle Paul had close female disciples of his own whom he did not treat equally nor did the people of the villages in which Paul preached. One of the most famous gospel stories is Jesus stopping a crowd of people from stoning a woman caught in adultery. The powerful message in this story is Jesus making them realize that all people are sinners not any better or worse than the woman they are condemning, but the woman is never named or mentioned in the Scripture again. Did the gospel writers feel her name was not relevant enough to mention simply because she was a woman?

When asked about women in the Scripture, most people religious or not would quickly think of Mary, the mother of Jesus, although Mary would be thought of for different reasons. Mary was the young girl chosen by God to be the mother of Jesus. The Scripture explains that the angel Gabriel informed Mary that she would be overshadowed by the Holy Spirit to become pregnant with Jesus. She was to do this before her marriage to Joseph, which would have caused her public shame for that time. Regardless of the potential societal consequences, Mary did not hesitate to answer yes to God's plan, thus making her an incredible instrument of faith to many Christians.[233] For some Christian educators, Mary's story causes questioning that can cause doubt as to what the Scripture explains, such as how could Mary be pregnant without a man? Mary could not possibly be a virgin for her whole life. The Scripture explains that Jesus has siblings. What happened to Mary after Jesus's death? Why does the Scripture not explain how or when Mary died? Was Mary ascended into heaven as Jesus was? All of these and more are

---

[233] Jack L. Seymour and Donald E. Miller, *Theological Approaches to Christian Education* (Nashville: Abingdon Press, 1990), 71–72.

questions that the Scripture does not fill in all the blanks for. When the discussion of Mary comes up for many educators, a majority of her story has to be taken on faith. The point for women educators to learn from Mary is regardless of how her life really was, her answer of yes to God was the most powerful a woman can make. Each woman should strive for such courage.

Women in the modern age even in the United States may still deal with discrimination from time to time. As previously mentioned, the Catholic Church along with a few remaining Protestant denominations overall still do not allow women in clergy leadership roles as far as liturgy and worship are concerned. As a whole, the presence of women in religion raises some faith questions that would be slightly different from men. One main question that arises for women is sexuality. What is the relationship between sin and sexuality? How is sexuality different for men? These questions are usually placed more on women. In a Christian perspective, the purity and celibacy of a woman seems to be superior to the encouraged sexuality within marriage. Premarital sex can be rather frowned upon more for women. The Scripture even sometimes makes sexuality bleak for women. For example, Revelation 14:4 reads the praises of "male virgins who have not defiled themselves with women." Further, these men are seen as "the first fruits for God and the Lamb."[234] So how might women remember that their sexuality is a gift from God to be celebrated in love as opposed to a sin? Sin occurs when the gifts are rejected and personal gain, power, or desire becomes more important than using sexuality as a marriage gift.[235] For Christian educators, teachings about sin and sexuality can be tricky but should not be left out.

On the flip side of discussing sexuality and sin for women is salvation. When women are discriminated against, does this hinder the good works for salvation? Sometimes. Salvation for women under persecution can be rather difficult but never impossible with God's

---

[234] Revelation 14:4.

[235] Jack L. Seymour and Donald E. Miller, *Theological Approaches to Christian Education* (Nashville: Abingdon Press, 1990), 73.

help. Women will have their own education, experiences, and faith challenges along the way to overcome and grow spiritual from. The Scripture may have a few passages that are not so encouraging, but with the religious education from methodologies and scriptural context, women have passed personal judgments and strong traditions to keep moving forward.[236] Women can be and are usually more fully aware of God's gifts and mission for them so that seeking forgiveness, mercy, and salvation continues to allow the Holy Spirit's guidance.

By taking the Holy Spirit's guidance forward, women continue to seek the truth of Christ, the kingdom of God, and Christ's mission not only personally but professionally to educate those willing to learn the same. These courageous women grow to become powerful and influential church and missionary leaders. Can the mission of the Christian church be carried out by women? Do women educators have a strong-enough relationship with God, others, and their church to become leaders? Who decides what women are qualified? Tradition teaches that men are usually the more prominent leaders while women are the followers. Not as true. An active feminine theologist named Rosemary Ruether spoke of Christian ministry "as being centered within a community and that women also receive special callings to be witnesses against dehumanizing patterns of relationship in the church and society, and to raise up the Gospel vision of a new humanity in a new society."[237]

Women in ministry have taken on four strong challenges while continuing to educate. The first challenge is seeing that teaching ministry needs to be a partner with the church just as any other church activity would be. People should not ignore or isolate the importance of teaching. Instead, the entire church community should visualize itself as a whole teaching and learning community of believers. Closely related to this, the second challenge is seeking the participation in church leadership with values and encouragement that many

---

[236] Ibid., 78.
[237] Jack L. Seymour and Donald E. Miller, *Theological Approaches to Christian Education* (Nashville: Abingdon Press, 1990), 79.

women provide.[238] Participation needs to be open to all genders, ages, and abilities for the best leadership to be successful.

The third challenge is making space and allowing for leadership of different styles. These differences come welcomed especially when the mission involves people of different backgrounds. Understanding fully what participants bring in the mission helps with identifying personal and discerning of vocation.[239] When those three challenges are defeated, the fourth and most important challenge occurs: reflecting deeply on the true meaning of ministry. Many churches still question the ordination of women and the relationships of clergy with laity; but exploring these questions while remembering the importance, influence, and success of ministry with women in leadership roles sets an example for future generations to keep moving forward without sexist discrimination.

Culture of Ages

While the debate of women's roles within Christian education as well as in every day society may continuously be discussed, the role of age groups might also need to be considered. For most children and/or students, the classroom might possibly be their first interaction with cultural differences. Assessing the culture within a classroom has be determined by three key specific values. The first value is a genuine caring about individuals. Caring for other individuals includes the willingness to share and sacrifice time, money, energy, and other resources for the benefit of someone else. Many psychologists would agree that a genuine caring can only happen when all five relationship steps have been taken including attending, listening, responding, personalizing, and initiating.[240] People, especially younger learners, will often learn these steps without realizing it. It

---

[238] Ibid., 80.

[239] Ibid., 80–81.

[240] English W. Fenwick, Larry E. Frase, and Joanne M. Arhar, *Leading into the 21st Century* (Newbury Park: Corwin Press Inc., 1992), 102–103.

may take longer for some to become genuine in caring for others, but once caring becomes time investing as opposed to time consuming, strong and caring cultures can blossom.

The second value is obtaining a mutual trust and openness to different attitudes and feelings other than our own. Trust mainly derives from dependability and the openness to be dependable. The openness also assists with becoming more accepting of the difference in attitudes and feelings that others may express. The psychological breakdown within the Johari window best describes a positive correlation between a person's openness and their effectiveness. The Johari window consists of four individual "panes." Pane 1 is the public self, which is the knowledge that a person and the public already know about himself or herself mostly defined by personal behaviors. Pane 2 is the blind self, which describes information that other people already know about an individual whom they have yet to know. This information is collected from mannerisms and behaviors that are unknown to the self. Pane 3 is the private self, which contains information a person already knows about himself or herself personally that other people do not know about. Whether this information is kept from others intentionally or unintentionally, one has chosen not to share it. Pane 4 is the unknown self. The unknown self is as stated, unknown. This is information that is unknown to the individual as well as to the public including motivations, unconscious need, and possible potential. When all four panes come into realization, the mutual trust and openness will become stronger.[241]

The third value is the respect for authority, expertise, and competency of the principal. The principal within any school setting has the sole responsibility for the success or failure of the entire school. The principal is responsible for overlooking and monitoring all the teachers' actions, authorizing the school funds, assisting the school administrators, and maintaining a safe and educational school for all students. A principal's attributes are going to include all research on

---

[241] English W. Fenwick, Larry E. Frase, and Joanne M. Arhar, *Leading into the 21st Century* (Newbury Park: Corwin Press Inc., 1992), 104–105.

learning, teaching methods, and personal-professional leadership.[242] A solid school under the proper principal leadership, strong teachers, and welcoming students within any culture ensure positive feedback to others around.

For many religious faiths, the teaching and nurturing of children within a specific faith may be highly essential, while with other faiths children are more encouraged to make their own decisions at their own time. Some might argue that children within religious families do not even get to make their choices because the family of a specific religious culture would not allow them to. In the Catholic faith, the age of reason being age seven is when a child has enough knowledge and reason to make their own commitment to the faith. For others, the adolescent age around puberty is more appropriate. Still some others, especially within nondenominational Christian churches, a person can make their decision to become committed to the faith at any age they personally feel appropriate and called by God. Likewise, those of older ages also become the elders and decision-makers for the remainder of their church denomination. Advanced age usually is sanctioned with wisdom based on longer personal experiences. Some might argue that a specific age cannot also pinpoint when full wisdom, reason, and understanding are present. While this is a valid point considering children/adults are in a constant state of learning, perhaps it is better to allow the person to make their own decision. In any case, for many people, age may simply be a number; but for many cultures, age can determine a lot.

While the ages may vary for some and not mean as much to others, the Bible stories and lessons of Christian education are still presented. After speaking with a few Sunday school teachers, youth ministers, and homeschool educators, there seems to be a common flow containing the major areas in which younger-aged children are essentially taught. Many Christian educators began with the birth and life of Jesus including His travels and miracles leading through His crucifixion and resurrection, but the story and teaching do not end here. The discussion of Peter and Paul leading the Christian

---

[242] Ibid., 106.

people after Jesus's ascension beginning with Pentecost. Paul's many letters and journeys to those under persecution, and even some of the early Christians martyred because of their faith.[243] While also reflecting on some major events of the Old Testament, depending on the children's ages here, for most educators the teaching may stop until an older age of understanding. Again, for others, perhaps not.

The next area of Christian education usually addressed for younger learners outside of the Scripture lessons is early Christian history. Many of these lessons would include the persecution of early Christians, worshipping in secret beneath the ground in the Roman catacombs, the ongoing Holy Roman Empire with Constantine, early popes and bishops, along with various councils making decisions in church leadership and future directions. Further, the added split of churches between the Eastern and Western beliefs, differences of religious monasteries, and wars were impacts of the Crusades.[244] If the educator continues to be ambitious teaching the Christian history, they would explain the Protestant Reformation, the Catholic Counter-Reformation, the early American Puritans, Quakers, Baptists, Methodists, all leading into the modern world of the multidenominations of today.

For younger ages, the Bible lessons put simply would be sufficient while learning the history and ideologies over the past 2,015 years might be advanced for older-aged students even including adults. At an early age, children are taught to share and the importance of sharing with others who may be less fortunate. During the holiday season is when the outreach to support other people may be most obvious to children who may be learning this lesson for the first time, but what about sharing all year long? As Christian children get older, they begin to learn more about who are those people who take Christianity to people in remote places that most likely do not know anything regarding who Christ is. Sometimes children may learn that people within their own neighborhoods do not know about Christ or

---

[243] Jane Bingham, *Atlas of World Faiths: Christianity* (West Mankato: Smart Apple Media, 2008), 2–13.
[244] Ibid., 15–28.

may not wish to ever learn. These discoveries hopefully can begin to spark a real curiosity and desire to become more involved in assisting missionaries or perhaps later take on that very role.

When children begin asking, "How can I help reach those who are in need?" what answer does the educator give? In most cases, the answer will include more Christian missionary programs and world unity. In today's world, constant multicountry battles with one another make the mission of world unity rather difficult to accomplish, but not impossible. Christians remember that Jesus reached out to people of all different backgrounds and cultures outside of His own, as should we.

Cultural Missionary Outreach

One of the biggest areas within Christian education that continues to mesh cultural differences is through missionary work. What better way to learn about various cultures from all over the world than to learn from missionaries? Those who actively participate in missionary work dedicate much of their lives to ensuring that people from around the globe receive the same Christian educational opportunities that he or she may have already been blessed with. Today, when Christian educators teach about missionaries, one prime example that usually comes up is the work of Mother Teresa. Many people religious or not are well aware of who Mother Teresa was and how she completely dedicated her own life to the poor of Calcutta, India. Mother Teresa did not want recognition for doing what God commanded of all His people: being a servant to others. Mother Teresa once commented that

> I have the feeling that we are in such a hurry that
> we do not even have time to look one another

and smile. Do we share with the poor, just like
Jesus shared with us?[245]

For many educators, this quote can be rather difficult to digest,
but not impossible. Reaching out to other cultures outside of our
own is not only what Jesus expects of us but also a spiritual uplifting
experience that deserves proper recognition.

Just what exactly do people think about in terms of a religious
worldview? Does the Christian faith address worldviews and missionaries enough? Do people of other cultures within Christianity
share the same beliefs in heaven, hell, salvation, forgiveness, miracles, and the validity of the Bible? A Religious Worldview Scale was
created to stimulate interest in religious ideas while giving students
an understanding of their own worldviews. The scale was developed
by Malcolm McLean in 1952, revised by F. L Jennings in 1972, and
reviewed again by Michael J. Boivin in 1999.[246] The scale includes
twenty-five items presented in the Likert scale format ranging from
5 to 1 (strongly agree to strongly disagree). The items are thus scored
accordingly while assuming all religious backgrounds and knowledge. The results usually indicated that women were more religious
than men while older men used religious faith more often. For the
most part, the questions were to create personal thinking and feeling
for individuals to learn more about their own beliefs. The questions
include a wide variety of aspects such as God as Father and Creator,
Jesus as the Son of God and Messiah, the guidance of the Holy Spirit,
the validity of the Bible, miracles, free will, the existence of heaven
and hell, good and evil in the world, the fall of man, sin, forgiveness, grace, and human dignity.[247] After examining the full twen-
ty-five-question scale, many students' interest was piqued to learn
more not only about their own beliefs and those of fellow classmates,
but also those from other Christian cultures. Would they answer

---

[245] Jose Luiz Gonzalez-Balado, *Mother Teresa in My Own Words* (New York:
Gramercy Books, 1997), 23.

[246] Peter C. Hill and Ralph W. Hood, *Measures of Religiosity* (Birmingham:
Religious Education Press, 1999), 59–60.

[247] Ibid., 60–61.

believing the same? Do other cultures struggle with the same issues as our culture does? These and many other questions all arose that did stimulate more religious curiosity as the scale creators had hoped.

Outside of the classroom measuring scale, in the modern world, viewing places in other countries is relatively easy with the use of television, phones, and computers. We have the capability of communicating with people far away with the simple push of a few buttons, which, needless to say, is a huge step forward from days past. Television especially can bring to us vivid pictures of events happening worldwide. Sadly, more of the events shown are of violence and destruction as opposed to more pleasant occurrences.[248] Does the media aim to get under people's skin? Are their motives to show destruction in the hopes of positive responses? Maybe. Maybe not. In Christian education, it should not take seeing such destruction on television or news to create a reaction.

Jesus was never hindered or never stopped His mission because of unpleasant events, nor should Christians today; but as quoted by Mother Teresa earlier, people today are in so much of a hurry that many aspects of reaching out to others gets blinded from the busyness of personal life. Several Christian educators teach about missionary work and perhaps have information for their students to research on participating in such missions, but why are the missionary numbers not as high as they could be? Popular answers include there is not enough money to travel far away, people have too much to do at home, a fear of unknown people and places, and lack of interest. Of course, there can be other answers, but these in particular cover the personal important areas for most individuals.

Money can usually be the first and foremost answer to practically any cause in today's economy. People do not have as much money to donate and/or invest for other concerns outside of their own families. Churches quite often make a plea to their congregation members in hopes of receiving more funds for various church needs and for missionaries, but for people having the extra money

---

[248] Jack L. Seymour and Donald E. Miller, *Theological Approaches to Christian Education* (Nashville: Abingdon Press, 1990), 179.

to contribute can be challenging. Collecting resources and advancing technology can become rather expensive extremely quick too. Technology may be present for many educators to use in hopes of reaching out to missions without the expenses of travel, but in reality, the actual nonphysical presence can speak volumes to people who are desperately in need of education, companionship, and care.

People explaining that there is too much to do at home rather than be worried about what is happening around the world are not entirely wrong. The United States alone does have a growing need for assisting people who are unemployed, homeless, disabled, or simply forgotten. Many states contain major cities where the homeless and poverty rate is horribly higher than it should be. Perhaps missionary work does not have to include traveling so far from home to be helpful? Looking at the missionary concern in this manner is a positive approach. However, when people explain that there is too much to do at home, meaning working long business hours, driving the children around, planning events, attending sports, etc., perhaps a slowing-down breather focusing on someone else could be welcomed.

The idea of being in a new location with people different from me creates a major hesitation. This hesitation can be from previous experiences, media, or simple personal prejudice for whatever reason. The fear of the unknown has stopped people for centuries from exploring more opportunities, adventures, and cultures. Breaking down barriers of fear can only lead to the courage of truly making a difference. Holding on to prejudices of any kind will hinder the personal spiritual experience because the heart is not truly open to those in need. In extreme cases, there can be a complete lack of interest to even bother considering anyone else other than the individual himself or herself. It is not to say that these individuals cannot be useful or trusted, but rather, perhaps more education and/or personal experience can be mind-changing and hopefully life-altering for the better.

An extensive method of propping motivation for missions uses awareness. Simple awareness can change perspectives as to what people are in most need. The Christian experience should include practicing with the diversity of people while continuously reconnecting with ages, genders, and races of all kinds to keep a common focus.[249] People too often think of themselves as only living within a physical environment, not taking into consideration the importance of interrelationships and future generations, focusing on our examples. Cultural values play a huge role in teaching those future generations about faith and religious traditions while looking forward to evolving with a positive attitude.

In conclusion, when we remember what an incredible world of various cultures we are all already apart of, we can continue to connect and grow helping each other along the way. As Mother Teresa said,

> It is very possible that you will find human beings,
> surely very near you, needing affection and love.
> Do not deny them these. Show them, above all,
> that you sincerely recognize that they are human
> beings, that they are important to you. Who is
> that someone? That person is Jesus Himself: Jesus
> who is hidden under the guise of suffering![250]

For many, thinking of Jesus as being the one who is suffering can be rather hard to grasp. Christians are always encouraged to see Jesus within every person that they ever meet. What would the world be like if every person always saw Jesus in each other? There would be no more wars, conflicts, or disagreements. Peace would finally get to prevail in all situations. Maybe that ultimate peace could be a glimpse of what our heavenly home will be like when we finally get to see Jesus face-to-face and be united with all Christians from every physical world location and every moment in time. To repeat a statement made earlier within this chapter, when we are open to and aware of our world with all its various people and cultures, we become fully time-invested as opposed to time-consumed.

---

[249] Jack L. Seymour, and Donald E. Miller, *Theological Approaches to Christian Education* (Nashville: Abingdon Press, 1990), 180.

[250] Jose Luiz Gonzalez-Balado, *Mother Teresa in My Own Words* (New York: Gramercy Books, 1997), 84.

CHAPTER 7
Christian Education in the Home

Homelife can take on several different situations for many different people. The basic idea for home includes Mom, Dad, few children, pets, and a house with a big yard in a neighborhood full of people. Several homes are not so basic. Many people need to actually establish the difference between a house and a home. Perhaps the difference is not as simple to distinguish because the people within the house together do not make the place a home. Conflicts arise in every household over various different topics, but how are they often resolved? Are they resolved or just swept under the rug until later? Mother Teresa once commented that "there is someone who suffers in every family and in every human situation."[251] The problem with this comment is that many family members may not realize who that particular person in pain may be. In any case, breaking down a "home" as opposed to a "place where people live" will be this chapter's focus.

Family Structure

Christian education of the home begins back in the Scripture. Jesus and His apostles frequently visited the homes of many people.

---

[251] Ibid., 83.

Jesus was dining, preaching, and healing several people. He even often stayed in family homes for some time while traveling. The Acts of the Apostles explains Saint Paul visiting many homes, continuing the mission of Jesus. These early houses were often painted in the background of the setting of many biblical stories. Homes and businesses were used interchangeably in some cases where there was a head of household with many servants. Who was the rightful head? Those people, usually men, with greater fortune and property did create tension for others of the family/business wanting to follow the Christian mission. The argument was that the Christian mission could be carried out within their own home-community as opposed to traveling out. For many people wishing to truly become a follower of Paul and other disciples, this decision created conflicts, but also influence.

The influence of Christianity becoming a strong value within the home created an emphasis on moral authority known as the Christian paterfamilias. The Christian paterfamilias were the families who not only demonstrated Christian values in their own homes, but also were welcoming to others wishing to visit their homes for the purpose of learning more about Christianity and the Christian mission.[252] The real conflict here was the senior members of the household continuing to uphold generational long Jewish customs and beliefs while the young people were more open to the Christian values. Despite the conflicts occurring in the households of what religious beliefs were to be followed, Christianity was still spreading across the area. Much of the spread was attributed to those who did actively follow the disciples' leadership and by those who became more fluent in the translation of other languages. Paul had gained a great number of followers from various ethnic backgrounds that even he needed other Christians to assist him in translations.

These early demonstrations of Christianity continued to quickly take off and grow especially within the family. One could argue this is the earliest use of social networking for Christianity to evolve. During this social networking, people often became intermingled

---

[252] Beryl Rawson, *A Companion to Families in the Greek and Roman Worlds* (Chichester: Wiley-Blackwell Publication, 2011), 184.

with other families sharing the same beliefs, wanting to reach other newer audiences. In terms of "newer," this often meant people who were visiting the region to stay or simply pass through. History has confirmed that many new Christians were welcomed into the faith through the teaching, worship, and everyday lifestyles of the families who had fully converted to the Christian mission. Over the next several years, the Christian community grew from outside the family home and community into a dedicated church with its own leadership ultimately into the multidenominations there are today.

Considering a great conversion was beginning to deeply burst at this time, it is not uncommon for this time frame of early families to be carefully studied. A Christian author by the name of Arthur Darby Nock, in 1933, wrote a study titled *Conversion: The Old and the New in Religion from Alexander the Great to Augustin of Hippo*. The purpose of the study was to take a deeper look into how the Christian world of the early families evolved into an English-speaking conversion in America. Nock saw conversion as only a personal matter between the individual and his or her conscience. Further, Nock suggested,

> Conversion was the rein orientation of the soul of an individual, his deliberate turning from indifference or from an earlier form of piety to another, a turning which implies a conscience that a great change is involved, that the old was wrong and the new is right.[253]

Nock certainly did not hide his belief that the individual's encounter with Christianity was the primary reason for their own religious choices. Nock also claimed that Christianity had reached a "saturation point," which was when over 60 million people had acknowledged the Christian faith. Despite a great portion of the world accepting to follow the Christian religion, Nock continued to maintain that the following was a personal choice to be made

---

[253] Beryl Rawson, *A Companion to Families in the Greek and Roman Worlds* (Chichester: Wiley-Blackwell Publication, 2011), 191.

without the influence, motivation, or determination of the family to make the decision for the individual. Honestly, again history and likewise some more current statistics supported the truth behind "household churches." This indicated homes that the entire family would be committed to one religion. Often the chosen religion was also including the grandparents or older generations who had set their religious choices in motion to continue on.

Nock's argument was that regardless of the family religious model set in place, the individual still had the personal power to make their own decision often knowing of possible upcoming family repercussions. Would a child be allowed to choose their own religious path? At what age was this considered appropriate?[254] Does the choice have to be based solely on the family's wishes, or does their education have other influences? Earlier chapters have examined the breakdown of the school systems including differences between private and public in their teaching of religious education. A private institution may already be affiliated with a certain Christian denomination, but the teachers and students may not have much choice in what material is covered considering the curriculums are already in place. Suppose the students want to learn about another religious denomination but are too afraid to ask their own families for fear of rejection. How should this be handled? Careful planning is primarily a teacher's responsibility, but where does the student get to interject?

Teachers and parents are often afraid of children/students making bad choices and possibly being upset with choices going against their own background. Would some of these choices have such an effect as to ruin educational advances? Is straying away from the family religion going to damage their life choices? Selfishly, a family may be more concerned with their own reputation than anything else. In 1982, one teacher, Mortimer Alder, who refused to allow any students to make their own choices commented,

> To give the same equality of schooling to all
> requires a program of study that is both liberal

---

[254] Ibid., 192.

and general, and that is, in several, crucial, over-
arching respects, one and the same for every
child. All sidetracks, specialized courses, or elec-
tive choices must be eliminated. Allowing them
will always lead to certain number of students to
voluntarily downgrade their own education.[255]

Many people have argued against this, claiming it is not possible for a student to downgrade their education by asking or choosing
to pursue another form of education.

In America, homeschooling has become more prevalent today
than perhaps ever before. In the early 1800s, for the most part, only
the children of wealthy families were educated within their homes.
Children often learned more about what was expected of them as
young adults in the social world rather than as being academically
educated. For women, wives were to become mothers and were to
be solely responsible for child raising. After the War of 1812, families were not relying on European leadership and/or religious and
moral guidance anymore; so mothers began turning to early children's books, medical guides, journals, and magazines.[256] Some of
the most popular included *Advice to Mothers on the Management of
Infants and Young Children*, written by W. M. Ireland in 1820; *Hints
for Improvement of Early Education and Nursery Discipline*, written by
Louise Hoare in 1829; and the *Mother's Magazine*, which published
"To Mothers of Young Families," "Hints for Material Education"
in 1834, and "Domestic Education" in 1838. By 1840, the *Parents
Magazine* was published, becoming the number one source of parental advice for the entire decade. Child raising advice was written
strictly for the mothers. The literature rarely mentioned the fathers
because their role was not important for child upbringing.

[255] Nel Noddings, *Education and Democracy in the 21ˢᵗ Century* (New York: Teachers
College Press, 2013), 25.
[256] Eugenia Hepworth Berger, *Parents As Partners in Education: The School and
Home Working Together* (Columbus: Merrill Publishing Company, 1987), 43.

At this time, there was also great segregation in which black families were often torn apart being sold into slavery, usually never seeing their own families again. These mothers who could remain with their children had to raise them in slavery, basically just teaching them how to survive. It was extremely rare for many blacks to know how to read or white. Their slavery work was their entire life. During and after the Civil War when blacks were freed from slavery, some went on to find new lives for themselves and slowly evolved, bringing families together. By the early 1960s, segregation had reached an entirely different level. Blacks were finally allowed in schools to become more educated outside of basic survival. Sadly, even today there are still signs of segregation around.

Immediately following the devastation of the Civil War during 1870–1890 was called the Parent Education Movement. Since many mothers left at home while their husbands went off to war were home with the children, education became rather difficult due to basic survival taking over. By 1870 when this movement began, the extension of a kindergarten program began allowing children a place to go and allowing parents to use their techniques at home. For Christian households, a group known as the Woman's Christian Temperance Union strongly supported the continuance of the kindergarten programs, opening it further to poorer families and immigrants wishing to get their children educated.[257] From 1888 to 1920, women's groups continued to build up and expand the education system. Primarily children were taught to model their parents in religious beliefs, morals, and personal character development.

During the 1930–1940s, again, education began slipping as America was dealing with World Wars I and II along with the Great Depression. Mothers continued to keep their families together and going, but education was not as important. As America began piecing together again, education grew abundantly. Parents were hoping that their children being fully educated would contribute to the knowledge of making America a better place in the future. College and universities were showing a much bigger growth from the 1940s

---

[257] Ibid., 49.

on considering that older children were desiring to further their own education more. The ongoing need in America for military continues looking for many young men who were also interested in furthering their education, but the knowledge of the military was not lacking either. Education was blossoming inside the homes and slowly more outside.

The parents' education continued with a higher level of participation as well. Now that many fathers were taking a more active role in their children's lives, education within the home was no longer an occasional event, but an everyday part of life. The Pennsylvania Department of Public Instruction posted a bulletin called the "Parent Education Report," explaining that parents were learning from radio lectures, magazines, and millions of copies of *Infant Care*.[258] The bulletin remarked the importance of parent education by stating,

> More and more it is being recognized that educators have a responsibility for providing professional leadership and for furthering the coordination of parent education activities in their communities. The job of the school is only half done when it has educated the children of the nation. Since it has been demonstrated beyond doubt that the home environment and the role played by understanding parents are paramount in the determination of what the child is to become, it follows that helping the parent to feel more adequate for his task is fully as important from the point of view of public education and the welfare of society as is the education of the children themselves. Moreover, an educated parenthood facilitates the tasks of schools and insures the success of its educational program with the child.[259]

---

[258] Ibid., 59.
[259] Ibid., 59.

Clearly, the education in the home was being honored and greatly acknowledged. People agreed that children were learning just as much or more from their educated parents than some of the school systems were teaching. By the time the Pennsylvania Department of Public Instruction published their next bulletin, twenty-five states were offering parent education courses following six basic ideals.

1. Aiding parents to interpret their finding of specialists in regards to the various aspects of family life.
2. Giving parents the opportunity to allow change in children's attitudes and behaviors.
3. Serving as a device of personal adjustment.
4. Giving the opportunity to consider civic problems which are affecting family life in relation to the socio-economic life of the community.
5. Providing a place for parents to verbalize their concepts while attempting to adapt with personal conditions and trends.
6. Help to develop of strong understanding of the functions and purposes of education and the need for such services.[260]

Over time, these basic ideals continued to give a foundation to the importance of parental education. The idea of learning from and in the home had a strong backing, but as time progressed and both parents began entering the workforce, home education had shifted mostly into children attending public and private school. Homeschooling never completely died out, and today the decision for making homeschooling a priority is returning. Who are the decision-makers? Parents may be the ones choosing to homeschool their

---

[260] Eugenia Hepworth Berger, *Parents As Partners in Education: The School and Home Working Together* (Columbus: Merrill Publishing Company, 1987), 59–60.

children, but the role of the parents does not stop there. Most parents may believe that they are only spectators to observe what their children do in school and thus allow the school to be the authority figure in the educational process.[261]

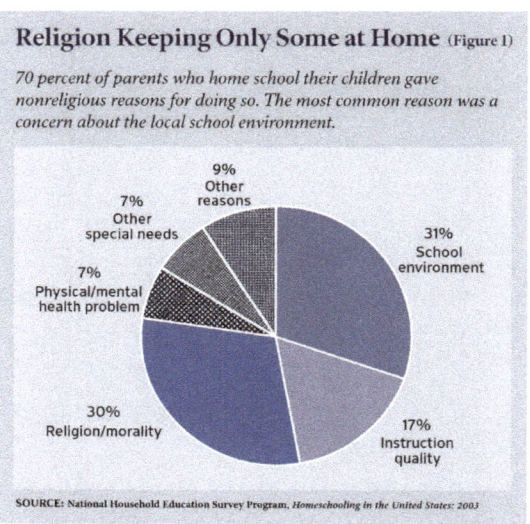

Religion Keeping Only Some at Home (Figure I)

70 percent of parents who home school their children gave nonreligious reasons for doing so. The most common reason was a concern about the local school environment.

SOURCE: National Household Education Survey Program, *Homeschooling in the United States: 2003*

The chart shows the six major areas covered under the roles of parents. As mentioned, some parents are seen as only (1) spectators allowing the school system and teachers to proceed with their child's education process as they see it. They are also seen as (2) accessory parents as those who volunteer to events unrelated to education, usually a community event offering time and tasks. Parents are often the number one (3) volunteers within the school offering to chaperone field trips and plan in school programs. While sometimes parents share prior/present experience from their own (4) employment, opportunities emerge for the students to learn more possible careers. Parents serve as community members and sometimes leaders within school meetings, making them the (5) policymakers. School administrators and board members may still have the final say, but active parental involvement shows strong support. Finally, some parents are

---

[261] Ibid., 103.

seen as (6) teachers themselves to their own children. Parental education can be along with the school system including extra home study or this can be complete homeschooling.[262] These parents are making a choice between a formal school system education and an informal education within their own home. Regardless of the choice, especially during the younger ages, the children are still under their decision-makers, the parents.

Homeschooling

Over the past twenty years or so, the concept of homeschooling has become a rather popular choice for the education of children. While there are some people who strictly believe that homeschooling is the only safe and practical way to educate children, there are many others who could not even fathom having the time, energy, or patience to teach their own children at home. Mostly people work daily, and the school system is designed for children to be in school while parents are out working. Parents have come up with many reasons as to why they will not allow their children to receive a formal education within a school building setting. Certain reasons may seem to be rather obvious while others may come as a surprise. Whatever the decided reason may be, the family has chosen to remain with it and continue their child or children's education in their own home.

Parent educational programs have grown and evolved a great deal over time. The Parent Effectiveness Training (PET) program enlists materials, techniques, outside communication, and technology into educational content that parents can use not only to teach their children, but also to maintain a school-like atmosphere. Several of the content materials include topics such as family relations, communication, interpersonal relationships, behaviors, and misbehaviors with more topics available upon request. One key factor learned

---

[262] Eugenia Hepworth Berger, *Parents As Partners in Education: The School and Home Working Together* (Columbus: Merrill Publishing Company, 1987), 103–105.

is how to not allow the child to own a specific learning problem by using active listening. Considering the situation, does the child own the problem? Is there a present problem in the educational relationship? Or does the parent own and control the problem? These three questions can be difficult to identify until the teaching process becomes more settled. It may take some time, but if the parent is truly dedicated, the child will learn.

Along with the parent learning from the PET programs, the parent within the teacher role will need to come up with goals to achieve in the educational process. Once the need or desire for homeschooling has been made, there are five usual goals that follow. Home-based school program goals might include the following:

1. Enabling parents to become more effective teachers of their own children.
2. Supporting the parents in the roles of caregivers and homemakers.
3. Strengthening the parents' sense of autonomy and self-esteem.
4. Reaching the child and family early in the formation years.
5. Respond to the family's needs and thus improve the home environment.[263]

Goals are going to differ depending on location and the specific needs within subject areas, language developments, health concerns, and everyday comprehension. Keeping the involvement and intensity strong will ensure the continued success for the homeschool to proceed.

By using the PET program and keeping personal/professional goals in mind, the education can usually begin. Obviously, the subject content will vary depending on student ages, and the Christian education would be no different. Those being educated in a Christian home are going to include religious teaching and Bible studies as part

---

[263] Ibid., 245.

of their daily routine. It should be no surprise that some families go as far as to make their homeschooling decision based on religious education options.

As opposed to the education of the Christian homes, others argue that religion is not nor has it been a real valid reason for parents choosing to educate their children in the home. Some suggest that children with disabilities and special needs have no reason to be in the school setting where extra care is limited. Other parents even suggest that school environments are not safe enough for children and/or their quality of teaching education is not sufficient enough. The following graph only displays 30 percent of the reason being religious/morality concerns. There were also a select few who chose to keep their reason private from public statistics.

Commitment and Reinforcement

The commitment and reinforcement of a person can be rather difficult to determine. Where does one draw the line of what are the qualities of someone being fully committed? What types of reinforcement are necessary, if any? Over the past fifty years, there have been some actual methods for getting a deeper understanding of what constitutes someone as being committed. Where is the motivation derived from? Just how much influence does a person's family or close friends play on religious decisions?

In 1957, researchers Ausubel and Schpoont developed a Religious Attitude Inventory. This particular inventory was designed to measure the intensity and/or extremeness toward four basic issues: God, immorality, religious doctrine, and the church.[264] The measurement was based on extremely orthodox beliefs from neutral all the way to extremely nonconformists. The questions of the inventory were based around ego involvement of the four topics along with a glimpse of self-image. Many personal characteristics of the individual

---

[264] Peter C. Hill and Ralph W. Hood Jr., *Measures of Religiosity* (Birmingham: Religious Education Press, 1999), 94.

questions would come to an open light hopefully further explaining the outcomes. For the outcomes, a person with a stronger orthodox view tended to be more positive in responses toward beliefs. On the flip side, a nonconformist's person tended to take a more negative approach to his or her beliefs. A neutral person might tend to show a medium balance of orthodox and nonconformists. The researchers pointed out that ideally a committed person would strive to fall into both categories.

The initial test run sampled ninety-five church members resulting in twenty-six falling into one extreme or the other, while the remaining forty-three were in the balanced neutral category. This inventory was further sampled with undergraduate students who were still considering their own religious paths at that time. Researchers Foy and Lenski in 1976 revisited this research by adding questions regarding religious background to visualize a correlation within the results.[265] Depending on the selections of sample groups such as ages, church affiliations, and personal bias, the correlations varied more than expected, thus continuing the inventory use.

Sample statements contained within the fifty-question Religious Attitude Inventory based on a five-point scale of strongly agree, agree, neutral, disagree, strongly disagree answers.

- God made everything.
- The church has acted as an obstruction to the development of social justice.
- God hears and answers one's prayers.
- God created man separate and distinguished from animals.
- The good done by the church is not worthy of the money invested.
- God is a figment of the imagination.
- The soul lives on after the body dies.
- Man cannot be honest in his thinking.

---

[265] Peter C. Hill and Ralph W. Hood Jr., *Measures of Religiosity* (Birmingham: Religious Education Press, 1999), 95–96.

- The church represents shallowness, hypocrisy, and prejudice.
- There is a far better way to explain the world than any God.[266]

Another development for measuring religious commitment came in 1963 by Poppleton and Pilkington called the Religious Attitude Scale. This scale was targeted primarily for Christian believers as opposed to the inventory that sampled all religions. Again, a positive or negative outcome was based on a person's attitude regarding God, social attitudes, religious beliefs, and the church. The scoring was weighted differently depending on the questions mixed up within the statements so as not to show any patterns. Based on the responses' weighted values, the researchers were able to correlate positive and/or negative attitudes regarding personal beliefs on Christian beliefs.

Sample statements contained within the twenty-one-question Religious Attitude Scale based on a five-point scale of strongly agree, agree, neutral, disagree, strongly disagree answers.

- To lead a good life, it is necessary to have religious beliefs.
- Jesus Christ was an important historical figure, but in no way divine.
- People without religious beliefs can lead just as moral lives.
- The miracles in the Bible actually happened.
- Christ atoned for our sins by His sacrifice on the cross.
- Without belief in God life is meaningless.
- The proof of Christ as the Son of God lies in the Gospels.
- International peace relies on worldwide adoption of religion.

---

[266] Ibid., 97–98.

- There is no survival of any kind of death.
- On a whole, religious beliefs make for a better and happier living.[267]

By 1988, the Religious Attitude Scales were visited again by Altemeyer and Hunsberger, only this time, the research was based on the religious doubts a person may or may not have. In several cases, some of the religious doubts were not even known consciously to the person until the statements were scored and revealed. The religious doubts covered more areas than perhaps realized at first, creating a breakdown of three subsections with the first being doubts of basic religious teaching. These ten statements were based on a six-point weighted scale including the following samples:

- Doubts that the Bible could really be the word of God.
- Feelings that religion does not make people better.
- Today's religion is only based on superstitions from the past.
- Overall religious teachings are contradictory.
- Religion makes people do stupid things; giving up a perfect life for no reason.[268]

The second subsection is the doubt vignettes. The vignettes are philosophical discussions and personal life experiences influencing religious doubts. Basically, this was measuring the difference in religion and science. Where does a person's belief lie? These ten statements placed an emphasis on a difference of a particular event in terms of religious belief or scientific fact. The doubt vignettes wanted to focus on one particular thought: was the participant brought up

---

[267] Ibid., 100–101.
[268] Peter C. Hill and Ralph W. Hood Jr., *Measures of Religiosity* (Birmingham: Religious Education Press, 1999), 102.

to have faith in religious belief or scientific fact? Sample statements include the following:

- Can both the Genesis creation story and Darwin's theory of evolution be correct?
- Do all the world religions believe in the same "truth?"
- As Jesus commanded, is loving your neighbor possible?
- How was the Bible divinely inspired?
- The science explains the universe, it seems God is not there.[269]

The third subsection is the secret doubts scale. This includes what psychologists refer to as the hidden observer. What about your own thoughts are being hidden? What thoughts must they hide? Is keeping a religious belief secret going to help or hurt personal spiritual growth? The secret doubts scale has only one question: "Do you have doubts that were created by Almighty God who will judge each person and take some into heaven for eternity while casting others into hell forever?"[270] Basically, how much doubt does a person carry toward belief in the afterlife? Should a person be doubtful of their everyday life because there is no good ending?

The researcher Altemeyer took the scale one small step further. He factored in a Religious Pressure Scale based on how much a person may feel pressured to remain committed to a particular religious sect. Altemeyer split his statements into two categories: a Religious Pressures Scale and a Religious Values Scale. Again using the six-point scale, the religious pressures statements included the following:

- Disappointment of parents.
- Tension in romantic relationships.
- Fear of punishment from God.

---

[269] Ibid., 104–105.
[270] Ibid., 106.

- Feel betrayed of ultimate purpose.
- Feel damned and condemned for eternity.[271]

The religious values category took into consideration the degrees to which a person could tolerate others' beliefs in comparison or contrast to their own. With the assistance of fellow researchers Morrow, Worthington, and McCullough, Altemeyer created the Religious Values Scales based on seven specific subscales: religious commitment, authority afforded sacred writings, authority afforded religious group identification, authority offended religious leaders, tolerance for others holding different views on the Scripture, tolerance for those with different group identification, and tolerance for those with different views regarding the authority of religious leaders. This scale contains sixty-two items that are resulted on a five-point scale describing the value of what statements express the truth of how a person feels regarding personal and religious values. Sample statements of the Religious Values Scale include the following:

- I am concerned that my behavior and speech reflect the teachings of my religion.
- I enjoy spending time with others of my religious affiliation.
- I feel there are many other important things in life than religion.
- I talk about my religion with family, friends, neighbors, and coworkers.
- I am willing to be persecuted for my religious beliefs.
- I understand my faith's scripture.
- I prefer to take advice from people who share my faith beliefs.
- I avoid doing things my church affiliation would disapprove of.

---

[271] Ibid., 108.

- I feel accepted by members of my local religious group.
- I share the goals of members of my local religious group.[272]

For some people who are active within a religious community today, taking the time to ask people to answer statements regarding their own feelings may seem a waste. Then again, for others, perhaps asking yourself these thoughts on a personal level can bring about some real understanding that might not have been present before. Regardless, simple thought statements are a useful way for someone to self-evaluate their own commitment to their religious beliefs. Maybe the results of these scales could trigger areas that the person may wish to focus on more and pursue other areas that are not so strong. Commitment after all does not always have to be in the public image. One person's faith commitment can move mountains.

Influence versus Choice

What exactly effectively describes the difference between influence and choice? Influence usually happens when someone else uses their own beliefs or techniques on someone else to try to get that person to follow their example or become like him or her. A choice is more of a personal decision made from one particular person based on how they see fit to proceed with a decision. Influence can certainly move a choice in favor of one side over the other. Perhaps some might even argue that choice can create influence in a bigger picture. Of course, not all choices are going to be on a life-changing scale, but that should not take away from the importance of weighing one's options.

For educational options, such as homeschooling, how does the student decide and/or express their feelings of what may be deemed

---

[272] Peter C. Hill and Ralph W. Hood Jr., *Measures of Religiosity* (Birmingham: Religious Education Press, 1999), 110–111.

the right option? Parents and maybe some close family friends will make the decision for a student to receive homeschooling, but what if being educated in the home is not what the student wants? Students especially at younger ages may often find it difficult to discuss personal feelings with parents. Education is such a huge part of a student's life considering it lays the foundation for what will become of the student in the future. Life goals and career ambitions are often based from education teaching the opportunities available later in life.

Communication between students and parents regarding education cannot be taken lightly. Parents may feel that they know what is right while making the student feel like they have no say in the matter. Period. The dangers of a student feeling trapped and controlled within their home without open communication can lead to some rather disturbing outcomes. For many students in today's world, social media is a huge way for expression.[273] Many of the parents' aged generation may not be as familiar with these outlets and therefore not fully know how to monitor or control what their student may be placing out for the social media world to read, but they as parents may know nothing about. So what can be done about this? Parents need to be informed and reach a common balance with their students regarding what is placed on social media. Perhaps using the social media as more of a learning tool rather than a place to vent could benefit both parties in opening up the family communication. Parents cannot be afraid of involving themselves with their student's desire for social media, popularity, and other internet uses. There is a difference between being involved and interfering. When this balance is approached respectfully and openly, the student usually can be more willing to comply when the parents are not waiting too long in which a real problem can occur.

The communication within families has been a popular topic for researchers over the past fifty years or so. Researchers including Stephen Chaffee, Jack McLeod, and Dennis Wackmanm in 1973

[273] Lynn Clark, *The Parent App: Understanding Families in the Digital Age* (New York: Oxford University Press, 2013), 126.

detailed two major differences in family communication. On one side, a family is concept-oriented, meaning that the parents do encourage their children/students to express ideas.[274] These families have a much easier time with homeschooling considering the education has more of a give-and-take method between student and teacher as opposed to parent and child. The concept-oriented families usually have a healthier family home while the respect of listening to each other continues to speak volumes. The openness hopefully offers a beneficial balance in which the student can more freely express what he or she would desire to learn more about.

The other side of family communication is to be socio-oriented, meaning that the parents strictly enforce the importance of getting along with others. More often these types of families are not going to be welcoming to the idea of homeschooling considering that they value the importance of social interaction. Those socio-oriented families who do choose to homeschool might often be in favor of allowing other students into the home so as to make more of a classroom setting.[275] Parents feel that their students can learn more from other students their own age than by simply reading a textbook in their home. Socialness leads to stronger conversation skills inside and outside the home. Students can also feel that they have the openness and confidence to speak freely with their parents while engaging others outside the home. Still, communication within a family whether by choice or influence will shape a student's present and future success.

Homeschooling and Technology

When looking at the world around us in this modern age, it is nearly impossible not to mention all the advances of technology there are. People were slightly reluctant when the internet first became part of society, and now many people cannot seem to go one day without using the internet somehow. The uses of electronic email, bill

---

[274] Ibid., 128.
[275] Ibid., 128.

pay, personal notifications, calendar reminders, and even ordering a pizza or two can be done with a simple computer, iPad, cell phone, and customized watches. For education purposes, many schools have adopted recent technological advances that have created the need for homes to have them as well. For those students who may be enrolled in a school setting, it is common for them now to watch and listen to their school classes while at home. In fact, more and more education systems encourage students to be Skyped in if they for some reason cannot physically be in the classroom. The mere uses of chalkboards and paper/pencils are now replaced by web boards and typing. Some educators think that this technology is a godsend making teaching so much easier while others seem to think that this makes learning too easy without enough thought, especially when a computer's spelling/grammar check corrects mistakes before a teacher will.

What does this have to do with homeschool? There are a few homeschooled classes that are linked to an educational system using the same type of technology mentioned here. Parents can encourage students to further research by using computers, accessing library catalogues, group discussions, and even grading systems. For those homeschooled who wish to be around other children, discussion boards and Skyping can make a world of difference for learning social skills. Parents as the teachers can often be using the same web boards, computer programs, and web designs that classrooms may be using. Again, there are some parents who would rather keep their students more focused within the home while not being totality connected to other students through technology does not seem a priority. Technology does allow more communication not only through emails, but also with social media including Facebook, Twitter, and Instagram pages. When these programs are carefully used and monitored, students can have learning opportunities from others usually their own age to socialize with. Students can create and allow their own identities and personalities to show through on social media.[276] While this may be a tremendous privilege to have, parents/teachers

---

[276] Lynn Clark, *The Parent App: Understanding Families in the Digital Age* (New York: Oxford University Press, 2013), 212.

do need to be sure and monitor social uses to ensure they are being used for educational purposes socially and not divulging too much personal information.

Does technology really assist learning, or can it be hurting it as well? There are arguments leading to both sides explaining that technology makes learning so much better and efficient, while some may say technology can be too complicated and be getting in the way. What about the families who cannot afford to keep up with the most modern technology available? Or what about the families who may have too much technology in their homes? Is it even possible to have too much technology? Consider this: has technology changed the numbers on teen suicides, teen pregnancies, drug and alcohol uses, or juvenile crimes? Maybe. Maybe not. Those student dangers are still here today as they have all along. In fact, media research has suggested that the use of internet connections has caused students to open up more than they would in their own homes. Communication through the internet especially with social media may be booming, but it can also be hurting the family communication. How many times do you see people out to dinner, in the grocery store, or sitting at home with their eyes glued to their phone as opposed to speaking with the person they are with? Maybe too often.

There can be a danger with a student's involvement with technology that can be easily overlooked not only for the student but for the parents too. A digital trail. When students remain attached to social media too much, they leave a trail of the websites visited, people communicated with, and emails received and sent. Today it is not difficult for computer hackers to easily view someone more closely simply based on their internet usage. Lynn Clark, in her book *The Parent App: Understanding Families in the Digital Age*, explains that the digital media is composed of four specific characteristics that pose a risk to social media uses and trail. The four characteristics are persistence, constant mutability, scalability, and search ability.[277] The awareness of these characteristics and the dangers they cause may not

---

[277] Lynn Clark, *The Parent App: Understanding Families in the Digital Age* (New York: Oxford University Press, 2013), 213.

seem important at the time when a student may be simply checking their email, but are they considering what trails are being left behind? What might their parents discover? What would a future employer determine should they do an internet search on a job candidate? More seriously, is the student being set up for cyberbullying? Are the risks of technology use worth the dangers of losing control? The Cyberbullying Research Center offers a simple slogan: "Pause before you post."[278] Although this may sound simple enough, it does require the full careful attention of parents and students to ensure safety and secure the learning environment.

What constitutes as full careful attention? Are parents supposed to physically see any and all emails, chats, and postings that their students make online? Are parents supposed to be sitting right next to the student at any time technology is being used? This may perhaps be a slight overkill, but there are boundaries that can be set in place. For example, some parents keep the family computer in the living area so students cannot be behind closed doors and the parents can see what their students may be working on. Nearly all computers, as with televisions, come with parental controls that can be preset to stop access into websites that may not be suitable for the student. In the same manner, parents can decide when and if their student receives a cell phone. They can also determine what capabilities the phone will be allowed to have. Features such as texting and internet usage can be turned off in a phone so the student would not have the option of using social media this way. While many students, especially those who may be older, would certainly not like this option for whatever reason, it could just the safety net needed.

Have the technological advances of today become too saturated of an environment? For some families, putting these precautions in place may not be so easy. Students can quickly begin to feel like they are being left out of conversations and activities their friends may be having without them. When this is the case, students can often turn their anger or frustration out on the parents, claiming there is no trust in their family, causing difficulties. A student might

---

[278] Ibid., 213.

immediately go into a retreat mode and isolate themselves from their parents. Parents usually expect their students to earn their trust and prove they can be trusted with less or no parental monitoring, but when is that to be determined? Is there a magic age for this to occur? Sometimes students often do not realize that the parents may selfishly be looking out for their own family reputation that can quickly be damaged through social media. Regardless of the reason, parents being aware of what their students are doing is essential.

Education within the home may have a more difficult time with technology than perhaps realized. All hope is not lost. There are some effective ways in which parents can change or rethink their parenting decisions that will create a healthier form of communication between parent and student. Researchers have identified several methods for being more respectful in maintaining a connected relationship with their students, especially when education is given in the home as well. One basic method is to make monitoring less work intensive and more rule specific.[279] Putting a student's electronic usage off for a long period than keeping close parental controls will enable the parents to be assured of safety. Do not forget that using a well-educated conversation regarding media can and should be done with and away from the media itself.

Another helpful method for furthering healthy family communication and keeping the respect of the parent to the student could be for the parent to model what they want from their students. If a mother will be playing solitaire on her computer as opposed to helping the student with homework, then how can the mother expect the student to study when he or she would rather be chatting on social media? Parents should be expected to follow the same rules they place for the students. Making a distinction between what should be family time and work time needs to be respected by both parties. The differences between using the internet for education purposes and using the internet for social purposes need to be addressed in a manner that

---

[279] Lynn Clark, *The Parent App: Understanding Families in the Digital Age* (New York: Oxford University Press, 2013), 219.

will be beneficial to both.[280] Also, remember to make time together without electronics or technology. Scheduling a time when the entire family can be together whether for dinner, game night, or a sporting event should not be a challenge. Families need to have time together to relax and focus on strictly being a family. Should family time turn into a use of the internet, then make it an event that touches everyone and does not single out one person to become distracted.

On the flip side, there are a couple of methods in favor of using social media in the family. First, let the students take the lead in teaching parents.[281] Sometimes the student can be more technologically advanced that he or she can teach the parent some techniques and uses that can further their teaching. Parents can even challenge their students to use technology more by suggesting to complete an art project only using the computer or create a family video email card that can be sent to distant family members. Families who have members in the military especially benefit from the technology of Skyping because they can see and hear their families who may be across the globe from them. These technology challenges can close a generational gap between children, parents, and even grandparents by simply learning and exploring the available educational and communicational opportunities that they may not be aware of.

Technology has certainly changed our world in many different ways, and it seems there are more technological advances in the making every day to be introduced. Education may be benefiting from the technological advances in some ways and yet still suffering in others. For those who receive their education in their home, technology can be just as effective or defective depending on the rules set in place by the parents. Although technology has created great changes in almost every aspect of life including education, culture, society, economics, and everyday life, the importance of keeping up with what is best for a student's progress should always still be at the core.

To wrap up, the educating of students within their own homes has taken many twists, turns, and challenges along the way in some

---

[280] Ibid., 220.
[281] Ibid., 221.

of the same ways that school systems have. Parents of homeschooled students have taken on a huge responsibility that goes above and beyond the simple raising of children by making it their personal mission to educate their own students whether Christian or not. When Jesus walked the earth, He was in a constant state of being in the teacher role and was always direct with the truth of the disciples' benefit as well as Christians today. What greater compliment can a parent get than being compared to Christ as the educator? Jesus said, "Let the little children come to me."[282] Parents are taking Jesus's words to heart every time they make a decision for what is best for their own children's welfare and growth in education.

---

[282] Matthew 19:14.

CHAPTER 8

Education in Schools

Chapter 8 will be taking a look into the various types of Christian education within the school system. Schools have certainly changed and evolved over the centuries. Some of the earliest schools were more word of mouth, later, the use of writing and artwork, followed by printing and typing, and now even Skyping. Technology has most likely been one of the causes for many of these changes, but technology cannot cover all education alone. Various factors of environment, ages, genders, and the educational economic status can all play roles into the school system. By remembering the incredible importance and value of a solid education, some learning obstacles can be overcome. Christian education is the same way.

History

When America settled into a new nation until around 1787, the same year as the Constitutional Convention, everyday life and education were primarily Christian based. Basic knowledge included recognizing God as the Creator, humanity being made in His like-ness, the capability of knowing God and entering a fellowship with

Him, and the destiny of living an eternal life.[283] Related to this, the Bible was fully recognized as the Word of God; and it was the supreme answer of authority in all faith, morals, obligations, and relationships. In the early New England area, the typical elementary and secondary schools were controlled by the political state, but the church had such a huge influence on the schools that the educational goals were more religious than civic. Further west, the middle colonies chose to have their schools as religious and general combined into one. The Southern states chose private schools only by strict parental control, which was often church influenced too. Most colleges founded prior to 1787 were a basic training for ministers. The Scripture, theology, and church history were the core curriculums for colleges. This religious curriculum was also used as the model for the younger generation schools keeping God as the first and primary understanding.

From 1787 to 1850, there was a shift in the educational system that had turned to God being left out. The development of human intelligence and the great divisions occurring with Christianity were making it rather difficult for families and states to select a specific religion to follow. The impact of these divisions created a stress on the community to allow more public schools to be opened that were only permitted to teach general education with full exclusion of religious teachings. Following the American Revolution and the Civil War, religious education had greatly taken a back seat. The government control and constant loss of life and property made it extremely difficult for religion to be expressed. Where was God during all these horrible times?

Finding an answer to the previous question was not an easy task. From 1850 through 1900, the churches found a way to further keep religious instruction going outside of the public schools. The churches developed Sunday school as a chance for those wishing to further their religious education to do so. One prominent way this Sunday school concept was going to bloom was by training lay

---

[283] Charles B. Eavey, *History of Christian Education* (Chicago: Moody Press, 1964), 305.

teachers to teach these classes. The shortage of ministers and finding ministers to teach after a Sunday service was not always an option. Training lay teachers and using the religious curriculum while guiding the students back to a religious foundation over time proved to be a great success.[284] Or so it seemed.

Related to this, by 1900, the upcoming Sunday school curriculum was the beginning of vacation Bible school. By the turn of the twentieth century, religious education had spread into even further different directions. The Sunday school concept was beginning to lose credibility after so many years of practice. Many of the teachers did not know much about basic educational teaching, which caused frustration among students and parents. Likewise, some teachers chose to teach what they personally believed to be accurate as opposed to what the religious curriculum had in place. The branching of religious education into vacation Bible school or other simple Bible studies was now forming based on denominational differences. Such programs even seen today developed including youth fellowship, summer conferences, camps, various denominational publications, evangelism, more colleges, seminaries, and Bible institutes.[285] These programs laid the groundwork for private educational schools to be led by education boards and church leaders. However, the vast denominational divisions still caused a hindrance that the term "Christian education" was not to be used. At this time, these programs were to be referred to as "religious education."[286] As the various denominations broke off with their own religious education, it became a church choice as to what they wanted their own education to be labeled.

Just as previous history had shown, differences usually lead to challenges or conflicts. The proper instruction of the educational system was not any different. While over time the dissatisfaction with state schools using or not using religious education continued to

---

[284] Charles B. Eavey, *History of Christian Education* (Chicago: Moody Press, 1964), 306–310.
[285] Ibid., 311.
[286] Ibid., 312.

grow, a member of the Philadelphia Presbyterian Board of Education, named Dr. A. A. Hodge, of Princeton Theological Seminary, spoke out just as the movement of state education was being introduced:

> A comprehensive and centralized system of national education, separated from religion, as is now commonly proposed, will prove the most appalling enginery for the propagation of anti-Christian and atheistic unbelief, and of anti-social nihilistic ethics, individual, social, and political, which this sin-rent world has ever seen. It is capable of exact demonstration that if every party in the state has the right of excluding from the public schools whatever he does believe to be true, then he that believes most must give way to him that believes least, and then he that believes least, must give way to him that believes absolutely nothing, no matter in how small a minority the atheists or he agnostics may be. It is self-evident that on this scheme, if it is consistently and persistently carried out in all parts of the country, the United States system of national popular education will be the most efficient and wide instrument for the propagation of atheism which the world has even seen.[287]

Needless to say, Hodge was not afraid to openly express his belief in the upcoming danger that could potentially stem from the separation of education and religion. He would be followed by several others especially within the religious community wanting religious instruction to remain the first importance of education. Over the years and even now, the separation of education and religious

---

[287] A. A. Hodge, *Popular Lectures on Theological Themes* (Philadelphia: Presbyterian Board of Education, 1887), 283. Quoted in: Charles B. Eavey, *History of Christian Education* (Chicago: Moody Press, 1964), 315.

instruction is ongoing. Families continue to follow their own beliefs regarding education whether the choice be based on religious beliefs, cost of education, proximity, or basic necessity. Each of these reasons will be examined a bit closer throughout this chapter based on history, current statistics, and personal experiences.

Factors of Education

Education can be found, given, expressed, and even chosen by a variety of factors. Despite the fact that the various school systems have changed and continue to evolve over time, many parents and older students have kept their idea of what the ideal education should include. Whether students and/or parents decide on a private education, a public system, or homeschooling, certain educational requirements must be available. Throughout the year 2000, the Department of Education conducted a survey within the United States asking parents what information they would like to see available regarding their school of choice's success. This survey was done already assuming the differences between student demographics, geographical locations, and school populations. The survey ended up including seventeen factors that parents expressed interest in the most by percentages of the total surveyed.[288]

Item	Percent
Qualifications of teachers/administrators	85%
How is money budgeted and spent?	78%
Results of financial audits	78%
Graduation rate	75%
Scores of standardized tests	75%
Student attendance rate	73%

---

[288] Henry M. Levin, *Privatizing Education: Can the Marketplace Deliver Choice, Efficiency, Equity, and Social Cohesion* (Cambridge: Westview Press, 2001), 91.

Curriculum	73%
Governing structure	70%
Methods of teaching	66%
Mission/Philosophy of school	65%
# of students suspended and/or expelled	61%
Teacher turnover	55%
Class size	55%
Requirements of parental involvement	49%
Race/Ethnicity of student body	33%
Economics of student body	29%
Graduate placement	27%

Needless to say, these seventeen factors opened the doors to several questions for many school systems. Are these factors as important to the school as they are to parents? What are schools doing in response to these factors? Where is the area for changes and/or improvements? How often should these questions be revisited? Who should be required to gather and record this information? Should it be available only to the school board and administrators? Or should it be allowed to all the school families? Is this the proper information needed to make the necessary adjustments? If so, how and will the adjustments be monitored, budgeted, and performed?[289] A continuous effort by the school, students, families, teachers, administrators, and benefactors all working together will create the necessary information to ensure educational success.

Public Education

Public education to most people may be simply "the education system controlled by government and taxes," but there is much more to public education. The everyday community has much more say

---

[289] Ibid., 92–94.

in how the public school systems operate than perhaps most tend to realize. Citizens have the responsibility of electing the public officials who ultimately make the education decisions. For many parents with students in the public school system, choosing a candidate with educational background and focus might be a key importance for their vote, while other families may value other political situations more than education.[290] On a local community level, a typical school board is made up of five, seven, or even nine members who have voting rights. The next level up would include the state officials including the governor, the state superintendent of public instruction, the state senator, and the state representative. For many community voters, it may seem incredibly difficult to access these officials at a state level, but people need to remember that they are decision-makers for public education as well. Ultimately, there are the federal officials including the president, vice president, two assigned state senators, and a representative from Congress. When voters remember that these chosen-elected people are in their offices for a reason, many families hope that the public education system will continue to progress successfully and wisely depending on their decisions.

Throughout history, public education has certainly taken many turns, changes, and criticisms especially when being compared to private institutions. Many politicians within the past twenty-five years or so have been pushing more money into what is called excellence in execution. Public schools are continuously challenging to education more so students will come out with higher ACT and SAT test scores to be placed in the best universities.[291] The stronger the academic background that can be taught to these students, the better their future as these select students grow up to engage in more influential professions.

A report made in the early 1980s challenged public education, arguing that its goal of having better education decreased. The

---

[290] Myron Lieberman, *Public Education: An Autopsy* (Cambridge: Harvard University Press, 1993), 67.

[291] Barbara B. Gaddy, T. William Hall, and Robert J. Marzano, *School Wars: Resolving Our Conflicts over Religion and Values* (San Francisco: Jossey-Bass Publishers, 1996), 67.

American Educational Research Association (AERA) stressed three major reasons to explain the decline in public school education. First, the AERA suggested that the children today are not as intelligent as the children of previous years.[292] Many psychologists jumped on this claim, stating that intelligence was certainly higher than previous years because of evolution and technological advances. Many newer IQ tests were greatly administered into schools trying to determine where the average student was intellectually. Was there a difference in gender? Was there a difference in economic backgrounds? Or was there a difference in ethnicity? The AERA desperately tried to find an answer to change the minds of those questioning intelligence as a reason in public school decline.

The second reason the AERA reported was that despite the decline in basic test scores, the overall Scholastic Aptitude Test (SAT) had shown a significant decrease resulting from American education. Considering that the SAT was the key exam for students entering college, these low scores greatly troubled the public school parents and prompted the media to ask for more information. In certain cases, the media used these lower scores as a way to publicly insult or criticize the value of the public school system. Many public schools greatly changed their educational systems to correlate with the test questions of the SAT. Over the next fifteen years, there was an average of 41 percent increase in SAT scores, and those students were accepted into major universities.[293]

The third reason the AERA gave for the decline in public education was that American students simply do not know as much past generations did. This reason forced a stronger focus on improving certain subjects such as history and literature. Perhaps the emphasis on rediscovering subjects based on long ago would develop the intelligence of students. The strong belief in history repeating itself did not seem to faze many. Overall, the push on history and literature

---

[292] Ibid., 69.

[293] Barbara B. Gaddy, T. William Hall, and Robert J. Marzano, *School Wars: Resolving Our Conflicts over Religion and Values* (San Francisco: Jossey-Bass Publishers, 1996), 73.

provided a nearly 60 percent increase of students recalling the lessons of past generations. So the changes were reacted to rather quickly, giving the public school system a much-needed boost, but was it going to be enough?

From 1988 to 1990, the Aurora Public School System in Aurora, Colorado, began an approach that would improve the outcome-based education system or OBE, as it is known. The learning areas primarily included the subjects math, science, and history. The outcomes were based on previous education backgrounds and especially the current classroom subject direction. The sample of the life-long learning outcomes is as follows:

Outcome 1: A self-directed learner:

- Sets priorities and achievable goals.
- Monitors and evaluates his or her progress.
- Creates options for himself or herself.
- Assumes responsibilities for actions.
- Creates a positive vision for himself or herself.

Outcome 2: A collaborative worker:

- Monitors own behavior as a group member.
- Assesses and manages group functioning.
- Demonstrates interactive communication.
- Demonstrates consideration for individual difference.

Outcome 3: A complex thinker:

- Uses a wide variety of strategies from managing complex issues.
- Selects strategies appropriate to the resolution of complex issues and applies the strategies with accuracy and thoroughness.

- Assesses and uses topic-relevant knowledge.

Outcome 4: A quality producer:

- Creates products that achieve their purpose.
- Creates products appropriate to their intended audience.
- Creates products that reflect craftsmanship.
- Uses appropriate resources and technology.

Outcome 5: A community contributor:

- Demonstrates knowledge about his or her diverse community.
- Take action.
- Reflects on role as a community contributor.[294]

This lifelong learning outcome sample did change the subjects being taught and for some schools seemed to improve, although the greatest criticism was that there was no research evidence to support its effectiveness. However, other states such as Kansas that used the same approach reported that a 94 percent increase of positive outcomes were attributed to using this sample. Primarily in the Midwestern region, this system was being used more and more, and nearly all reported a successful outcome.

Public Education Cost and Higher Education

Public education being funded and regulated through the government could arguably have more cost restrictions than private schools. Public schools, both grammar and high schools, are located

---

[294] Barbara B. Gaddy, T. William Hall, and Robert J. Marzano, *School Wars: Resolving Our Conflicts over Religion and Values* (San Francisco: Jossey-Bass Publishers, 1996), 95.

within different areas throughout a city not only to accommodate the location of education, but also to be available for those students of families that are in need of education without the added expenses. Related to this, often students of various demographic backgrounds are more likely to seek out public education simply for the diversity. City census counts, voters' registrations, and hospital birth records all indicate the number of possible students current and in the future. These numbers are observed each year in comparison with the totals of enrollment with the public schools. City, state, and federal taxes are calculated along with the numbers as taxes are also used to finance the public school system. Each year a set budget is laid out to include as many areas of finance as possible; however, as with many costs, some items in need are placed on a waiting list, which can create difficulties such as faulty materials and outdated resources. Whereas the public school may be more convenient and cost efficient for education, the necessary needs may not as be as convenient to find.

The public school is often viewed as the main preparer of students to enter into higher education. The students in public high school who chose to excel with honor courses and several extracurricular activities are already preparing to make their college application more appealing. There is a rather large dynamic correlation between public high schools and college entry.[295] Considering that the government has already made the credentials for the public school system to follow, a set number of credits including the proper number of core courses is required for all to graduate. Many of the courses that are requirements are for college admittance purposes.

Along with the course credits, the public school system has a few other options for students to easily continue through higher education that many private school do not offer. One major option is that public school students have the choice of early enrollment into certain college credit courses while still finishing high school. This option is called the Advanced Placement Program.[296] Some

---

[295] Myron Lieberman, *Public Education: An Autopsy* (Cambridge: Harvard University Press, 1993), 233.
[296] Ibid., 235.

high school teachers are qualified to teach such courses within the high school itself to those students who are eligible, while others may be allowed to attend the local community college for courses with a morning or afternoon session. If a student participates in the Advanced Placement Program, he or she will be allowed to waive certain general requirement courses at the college level. Each school year, more colleges have been allowing these courses more and more to increase the overall enrollment, thus creating academic growth.

Another reason public schools have a higher option for college entry is the inflated grading system. Some high schools will begin grading on a college-level grade point average for students to learn the importance of maintaining better grades. A typical undergraduate college application now will ask for a student's high school GPA and sometimes a class rank number. Considering that nearly all college courses are graded on a 4.0 grading scale, this GPA number in high school will not be quite a surprise in college. In the same manner, select college courses can also be determined by a simple pass or fail credit. These courses may be necessary as preliminaries to other courses or simply an extra task for one course, but these are not graded within the GPA calculations yet are still required.

One other reason students may find continuing through higher education not as intimidating could simply be based on athletics and extracurricular activities.[297] While grades are always important to maintain, colleges will personally offer students scholarships and grants to attend certain schools based on athletics, music ability, and countless other activities depending on the students' earlier performances. Sometimes these chosen students may be publicly viewed as only going to college for their activity and not the education, but every college and university is under strict ruling that all students must maintain a set GPA or the extracurricular activities are automatically not allowed. Regardless of the activity, a student's choice should include considering the academic program before committing.

---

[297] Myron Lieberman, *Public Education: An Autopsy* (Cambridge: Harvard University Press, 1993), 235–236.

Public Education Proximity and Necessity

As previously mentioned, with public educational costs, the proximity or location of educational facilities does make a difference. These selected locations are also chosen to help grow the community around so the educated students will hopefully carry on their education efficiency.[298] Each school will have goals to achieve already set in place by the government, but the school itself wishes to continue on by showing their students' accomplishments and growing graduation numbers. The students' efficiency is based on their learning scores showing from standardized testing usually involving math, science, and social studies. Again, the government may have a set score in place, but the teachers may make it a personal challenge to educate a little extra to push the test scores higher. High schools in particular are going to try to push students' learning for their testing outcomes to impress various colleges as these students may wish to pursue higher education options. Most high schools and especially colleges will be closely looking not only at the scores and grades in math, science, and social studies but also at literacy, writing styles, history, and literature. The college tests ACT and SAT are inclusive of these subject areas and score them individually by subject and as a personal total.

Many cities have had ongoing debates of public schools producing better-educated students than private schools, which in many cases is true; but as with all educational measurements, there are four main complicated issues.

1. For all subject instruction, there are disagreements as to what the learning objectives should be and how specifically to be taught.
2. A student absence has agreed-upon standards already in place, but measuring the

---

progress of outside classroom make up work can be difficult.

3. The achievement of learned objectives include certain unknown factors that can cause various ranges of education obtained knowledge.

4. At some point, all learning objectives will include inconstancies and contradictions. Who handles these? And how?[299]

Public education did not totally disregard the necessity of teaching certain religious factors within public schools. Considering that some more rural schools did not have access to private religion-based schools, the public was allowed to teach some religious areas. The National Council of Social Studies specified fourteen defined guidelines that could be used with the public system. Here is a brief description to each of the fourteen guidelines:

- Study of religion should strive for awareness and understanding of diversity, experiences, and expressions.

- Study of religion should stress the influence of religion on history, culture, arts, and contemporary issues.

- Study of religion should promote and encourage a balanced examination of ideas and attitudes.

- Study of religion should investigate a broad range of geographical and chronological beliefs, values, and practices.

- Study of religion should examine religious dimensions with human existence in terms of political, social, and economic relation.

---

[299] Myron Lieberman, *Public Education: An Autopsy* (Cambridge: Harvard University Press, 1993), 144.

- Study of religion should deal with world religions' perspectives.
- Study of religion should be objective.
- Study of religion should be academic in nature in awareness and understanding.
- Study of religion should express the necessity and important of tolerance, respect, and mutual understanding as a nation.
- Study of religion should be descriptive, no confessional, and conducted free from advocacy.
- Study of religion should strive to develop skills, attitudes, and abilities that are essential to history and social sciences.
- Study of religion should be academically responsible and sound, using the methods and materials of social sciences, history, and literature.
- Study of religion should use a range of materials that provide balance in the treatment of the subject.
- Study of religion should be conducted by certified and qualified teachers selected by their own academic knowledge.[300]

These fourteen guidelines should be revisited each new school year by reevaluating what is working and what challenges are possibly being faced. The effort to maintain a solid understanding of what should or should not be included with these guidelines is constant. Certain schools especially in more populated areas may find it more difficult to maintain while the rural areas may be more accepting, but nonetheless, the need for teaching religion in some manner has been adopted by the public school system for some time now.

---

[300] Barbara B. Gaddy, T. William Hall, and Robert J. Marzano, *School Wars: Resolving Our Conflicts over Religion and Values* (San Francisco: Jossey-Bass Publishers, 1996), 200–201.

Private Education

Private education is primarily based on a religious affiliation. More often, children who attend private schools are following the example of their parents as most likely the parents did before them. Various students and their parents have been asked for years several different questions regarding what they would like to receive in their education and why such education is so important. Similarities in answers showed that children are greatly influenced by what their parents' desires are; however, as the age of the student increased, there was more of a tendency for students to be questioning education in terms of what appealed to them possibly against what the parents wanted.[301] Especially where religious education instruction is present, children may or may not as always be consistent.

When the statistics were taken, certain unexpected surprise findings surfaced. For example, there was a difference between males and females based on religious-based education. During the late 1960s, when these early statistics were taken, 83 percent of girls were fairly confident that God exists while 61 percent of boys shared the same feeling. Here, for the current religious families, the percentages of children believing was actually lower than expected. Such lower numbers could be attributed to personal experiences, parental doubts, or the urgency of independence to think for himself or herself. Overall, there were very few instances where the children within religious households came up as complete nonbelief.

While asking the same questions to families of nonbelieving parents, the daughters showed a small belief in God's existence or at least the existence of a particular deity, while the boys showed nearly a complete nonbelief at all almost similar to the parents. On the other hand, these percentage numbers could be based on the children having a desire to believe in a deity that the parents may not for simple rebellion, peer pressure, or again personal experiences. As with both the religious and nonreligious background families, the difference in

---

[301] Edwin Cox, *Sixth Form Religion: A Report Sponsored by the Christian Education Movement* (London: Billing and Sons Limited, 1967), 49.

believing in God as opposed to believing in Christ surfaced. Some believed in both completely while some saw these as two separate entities, then a few saw God and/or Christ as nothing.[302] Again, the background of the families' beliefs certainly influenced the outcome of the students questioned.

Private Education Cost

The continuous inflation of the economy hinders many choices that people need to make on a daily basis. Sadly, one such choice is concerning education. Private institutions can range exceedingly higher than public institutions. In certain states, there are currently private high schools that are costing more than a college year of tuition. From a consumer perspective, cost is certainly a major roadblock but possibly for the wrong reason. A case study in defense of the cost argument suggested that there are two major objectives obstructing the private education growth. One objection is that the consumers suffer from lack of information that allows devious businesspeople to take advantage of their ignorance.[303] This objective was based on the professions and household of registered students from various higher end private schools. On the other hand, the claim regarding the "taking advantage" is not quite as easy to be proved outside of personal prejudice. Those families who already have higher incomes argue this to be a solid method for ensuring the future of the school and keeping a promise to their children by providing the best education opportunities possible.

The other objection claims that private institutions could not gather the proper research, development, and quality control to raise the necessary school standards. Related to this, since the government has a role within the educational system anyway, the resources will

---

[302] Ibid., 50.

[303] James Tooley, *The Global Education Industry: Lessons from Private Education in Developing Countries* (London: Institute of Economic Affairs, 1999), 21.

ultimately be limited.[304] Again, the higher-income families do not see this as a threat. For these people, the education system can be more viewed as a business venture with the opportunity for expansion of students, resources, educators, and profitability for the future. Perhaps evaluating the education system in this way could allow one to profit in more ways than one or perhaps not. Regardless, the growth and expansion of wealthier private education institutions within the United States is not easily overlooked.

One area of education that correlates with cost is the relationship between a parent's occupation and the student's interest or goals. Studies recorded that parents who were brought up in single-sex schools were more apt to be employed in a management or professional occupation. Parents who were brought up in coeducational schools came out relating more into agriculture and the industrial occupations.[305] Granted that regardless of the profession in which the parent was currently working, there was little association to what the students believed. On a few occasions that have increased more recently, students are more aware of the families' occupation income sources against the cost of education. For some students, the lower income and struggle of the economy has motivated them to pursue higher education for stronger-paying professions to avoid the struggle that the parents experienced.

Private Education and Higher Education

Just as with public education, cost is an ongoing struggle for private education, perhaps even more so. The costs are affecting not only the students' families, but also the administrators, teachers, and faculty. Remembering that private education is not under government control and finances whereas the public educational system is, financing certain costs and budgeting has to be obtained from

---

[304] Ibid., 22.
[305] Edwin Cox, *Sixth Form Religion: A Report Sponsored by the Christian Education Movement* (London: Billing and Sons Limited, 1967), 50.

other sources. In private education, the term "privatization" is used to simply define as not being under the government control or educational independence.[306] Privatization relates specifically to teachers, administrators, and all those responsible for education to occur. Considering that private education more or less has to overcome financial situations on its own, who are the benefactors to keep this system functional?

Benefactors and/or stakeholders that maintain the financial success or failure of private institutions surprisingly include a large number of people. First, the teachers and teachers' unions alone are benefactors by the way they agree to teaching conditions and salaries and reach educational goals for their students' levels. Likewise, the teacher unions include membership and sometimes contract agreements to maintain a fair and supportive system. Second, by direction of the educational administrators including the school board decision-makers, the students become benefactors. The direction given by the administrators is based on the curriculums of student interests, successes, values, and various social attributes.[307] Just as with the teachers' roles, the students' progress benefits the school's growth potential. A solid teacher-student relationship is the most important internal benefit any school can hope for.

The third and perhaps largest group of benefactors for private education includes those outside the school itself, those who previously attended the school and are now active and supportive alumni who wish to further sponsor current students. Related to alumni possibly is their places of employment. Oftentimes, when several alumni work under the same employer, it can become an office support. In some cities, the popularity of a particular school can be an entire community effort including everyday businesses, politicians, and even outside investors. Community involvement can include educational support, religious involvement, sports fundraising, club

---

[306] Henry M. Levin, *Privatizing Education: Can the Marketplace Deliver Choice, Efficiency, Equity, and Social Cohesion* (Cambridge: Westview Press, 2001), 279.

[307] Henry M. Levin, *Privatizing Education: Can the Marketplace Deliver Choice, Efficiency, Equity, and Social Cohesion* (Cambridge: Westview Press, 2001), 280.

organizations, along with countless others.[308] Granted that not all schools are fortunate enough to have a strong backing as others, but each year brings about new challenges, new people, and new goals to continue.

Along with these educational goals previously mentioned with cost comes the concept of higher educational learning. Higher education includes the education levels of college and beyond. More students are going on in school to receive a master's degree while some others continue on to a doctorate degree. More often than not, the higher education degrees are for the purposes of career advancement and possibly exchanging roles from student to teacher.

For the past thirty years as higher education has continued to become more prevalent, the Board of Education has pinpointed six specific overlapping reasons as to why more students wish to continue on with higher education specifically within a private institution. The first reason is the rise of our information within the economy.[309] Today gathering information is easier than it ever has been thanks to numerous methods of technology, resources, and quicker communication. Using this technology available, reaching out to educators from anywhere in the world can be as simple as one click away. Related to the rise of attainable information is reason 2: changing students. The student population in higher education is in constant change of ages and demographics.[310] These students are outside the realm of grammar and high school ages; instead, these students are more adult aged and further. Many of the student changes can be linked to adults being more comfortable learning education at their own pace.

The third reason is cost. Education within a private institution can usually be quite expensive, but those who continue on with higher education are more able to keep the costs lower. Many colleges will offer financial aid to those who are in need of course, but many

---

[308] Ibid., 282.

[309] Myron Lieberman, *Public Education: An Autopsy* (Cambridge: Harvard University Press, 1993), 144.

[310] Henry M. Levin, *Privatizing Education: Can the Marketplace Deliver Choice, Efficiency, Equity, and Social Cohesion* (Cambridge: Westview Press, 2001), 135.

students seeking higher education who are attending for the purpose of career advancement might usually be sponsored by their place of employment. Likewise, many students seeking higher education in a religious field will find individual parishes willing to cover educational costs.

In addition, reason 4, much like reason 1, is use of newer technology. Considering much education can be conducted electronically now, this saves costs of using paper, printing, some textbooks, and mailing. Again, those receiving financial sponsoring from various outside locations oftentimes will be allowed to use the sponsor's technology resources as well.[311]

The fifth reason for the rise in higher education is the change of the public societal attitude. People who have attained higher education degrees generally do move on to higher positions with their specific career choices and in some cases receive more respect for their accomplishments.[312] In some industries, such as medical, a doctor is going to usually be quite busy with many patients, often telling nurses and other medical personnel what to do. The doctor has already put in years of education and training to put himself in that particular position. Most often the public does recognize those with higher education, sometimes using their educational knowledge for help and personal direction.

The sixth reason may tie all previous five reasons together: higher education has a demand for more patrons. In other words, the educational system itself wants to see more people with higher degrees inside using their education to further others.[313] The productivity of those with higher educations can often be easily seen in workforce and many educational institutions. Keeping these six reasons for the increase of higher education in mind, the potential is present in hope for other students to continue on realizing just how many possibilities are really out there.

---

[311] Henry M. Levin, *Privatizing Education: Can the Marketplace Deliver Choice, Efficiency, Equity, and Social Cohesion* (Cambridge: Westview Press, 2001), 136.
[312] Ibid., 139.
[313] Ibid., 139–140.

To summarize these six points, remember that teachers and their unions are benefactors to the educational success. Likewise, the decisions made by the administrators caused the students themselves to be benefactors in their own educational system. Closely related to this, the everyday educational costs and need to keep up with the advancements of technology continue to be ever changing and usually growing. Finally, higher education has a huge impact to societal attitudes usually for the better while continuing to allow various companies in the workforce to expand. While higher education may seem like a huge turnoff to many people, the factors involved and future benefits are well worth the effort.

Private Education Proximity and Necessity

From an early time, schools were geographically divided by three separate regions. The first region is the early colonial areas or eastern coast. The second region is the northern area into the Midwest. The third region includes the western and southern portions of the country.[314] Over time these divisions have continued in some educational areas such as comparing colleges and universities but may not be as different today. Mostly the school divisions were based on the population of major cities. The population usually determined the number of schools that would be available to students. The larger populated cities would most likely have public and private choices as well as single-sex and coeducational schools. The lesser populated areas would be more rural where the schools would be less available in that all children could be placed again.

For private education, there are various internal and external factors that illustrate the successes of these institutions. One factor was the awareness for efficiency.[315] The private school that maintained this awareness kept their spending at a lower cost, relying on

---

[314] James Tooley, *The Global Education Industry: Lessons from Private Education in Developing Countries* (London: Institute of Economic Affairs, 1999), 50–51.
[315] Ibid., 44.

other resources such as asking the business owner families within the school community to assist. Also, a select few of these families had a parent or two come in discussing their line of work for business and/ or economy classes. To further the resources, the need for technology was closely monitored to only advance the school's technology on an as-needed basis as opposed to as-wanted basis. By keeping the awareness for efficiency in mind, the success rate increased.

Another internal factor examined was innovation. Innovation had to be distinguished between being a "process" and being a "product."[316] Since the education system was and still is viewed as a financial business to maintain operation, innovation was defined as having a level of curriculum development, availability to technology, well-recognized brand-name backers, and guaranteed certification. The certification was necessary to provide proper teachers within specific fields and to provide student goals. Once a student would graduate from a private high school wishing to further his or her education in a college or university, he or she needs to choose which certification and/or course of study to pursue. By having been educated earlier by certified teachers, the students are already familiar with the openness of course choices to complete for beginning in the professional world.

By monitoring the progress of these internal factors, the external factors become clearer and easier to prove. The financial growth from capital, population expansion, and overall outward reputation are all going to be present within the community speaking volumes to future students desiring the same qualities.[317] Again, the factors have built the success of the private school system. There will always be a challenge of year-to-year changes and overcoming those interested families who may be intimidated by the school's finances and success, but the promise of providing the best-quality education possible will ensure continued success.

---

[316] Ibid., 45.
[317] Ibid., 55–57.

Educational Goals

Education in general, whether public or private, has certain goals that all educators would like to achieve in their education of all students. These goals are not based on age group, educational level, and even academic choice of study. Christian education most often shares these same goals in hopes that all those seeking to learn more about Christ will achieve this educational success too. Certain goals are targeted toward costs, others toward the teaching system, and others toward decision-making, while others toward the students in general. The educational agenda goals are a list of twenty-six key points in which twelve are included here:

1. Students should be allowed to choose their school of public or private without worry of denominational or profitable consequences.
2. Education restrictions should not apply to schools only for profits.
3. Financial aid should be an option for all families with financial hardship wishing to send a student to a more expensive school.
4. Schools should not be required to accept all students who apply; restrictions should be enforced.
5. At the high school level, families should be required to pay some out of pocket costs.
6. By age 16, students should have option to seek employment in addition to school.
7. Students should have options to complete education is shorter amounts of time.
8. Ethnic and racial issues should not be a concern for educational success.
9. Educational institutions need to use proper caution when labelling a students as "learning disabled." Certain professional guidelines should in place for these students.

10. Teachers should have to take and pass all examinations within the fields they will be teaching on a regular basis.
11. Federal reports on the education system should include a total breakdown of all school system academics, costs, challenges, and successes.
12. Primary focus should always be on what the students want to learn, are willing to learn, and can be taught.[318]

The list of educational goals is certainly inclusive of rather specific educational areas, but the results of each school year are going to cause these goals to shift and possibly evolve with time. Needless to say, each school year, causes for change are not always going to be easy to make happen. Transitioning into different methods of obtaining these goals can cause more problems than it will solve, which too many educators can be let down. Sometimes the need to reassess goals, finances, and leadership is an area of education that many administrators would rather not deal with. Considering the old phrase "If it's not broke, don't fix it" sadly can become the attitude of some teachers who are rather set in their ways, refusing to change their teaching styles or even entertain the idea of new technology.

Whether these school systems and/or teachers refuse to evolve because of their own teaching methods or simply because of budgeting issues, the fact remains that education has to evolve along with the students. Christian education can have the same problem. Granted that the Christian faith has been taught for over two thousand years now, but educators are discovering different ways of teaching and providing resources to students that were not available earlier on. Christian education is primarily about learning about what Christ has put in place for His followers and how Christians are to take those lessons out into the world by their own lives. Christian education

---

[318] Myron Lieberman, *Public Education: An Autopsy* (Cambridge: Harvard University Press, 1993), 273–277.

may not be more test and essay learning based, but more a personal experience and discovery based. Sometimes experiencing Christ on a personal level can be more influential than their twenty years of book reading education. As previous chapters have mentioned, people do learn at various levels, speeds, and methods; however, Christian education does distinguish itself from basic general learning by the great amounts of religious influence surrounding many younger generations, especially those who grow up in an already religious home. Even in places throughout the world where religion may not be as present, Christian missionaries are doing everything possible to reach them as well. This once again proves a distinguishing trait that Christian education can and does have a unique value that cannot be taken away.

Most education does not have an age limit on it; however, Christian education is a lifelong lesson that many people will continue to explore and learn until death. Christ will never stop amazing us with His promises, words, and miracles. Christians already have the mission in place of taking Christ's Word out into the world as He commanded. In some cases, a person filled with this mission could be further educated in their own actions rather than others' words. People all working together and helping each other as Jesus did can be the best educational experience possible.

Chapter 8 has explained the separating differences of public versus private education on a general level and a closer exploration of Christian education from both sides if present. From my own experience, growing up in a split religious denominational home and attending private grade school and high school education, I was not entirely familiar with public education until I attended a public undergraduate college. While attending classes with people of various ages, backgrounds, and faith beliefs, I was amazed at how many options there were for me to study and practice my own beliefs. I ended up being an inspiration to other students later on taking on a teaching role myself. My intention was always to be as inclusive as possible of everyone. Answering questions about faith, life, and personal belief was empowering for me to share with people I barely knew. I am most proud to admit that some of those students are now colleagues and still close friends. My personal prayer will always be for everyone to continuously practice, question, and explore their faith in constant wonder of where their education road may take them next.

CHAPTER 9

Christian Education as a Community Effort

Family, School, or Church Based?

The community of a particular school plays a more vital role than probably most people ever realize. A school is made up not only of the students, but also of the parents, teachers, administrators, perhaps the government, alumni, and financial supporters. When there is a successful relationship within the community network, a school has an easier time thriving with community involvement. Hopefully, if the relationship is strong enough when controversies arise, the network will already have a plan in place to reach the best outcome.

Creating the community needed for each school is never an easy process. In fact, it is continuous and constant, ongoing, evolving, and changing as necessary. For the educators, this requires being aware of questions and concerns that arise, keeping parents informed, and maintaining the school's goals by their philosophy and mission. For the parents and community, this requires involvement, volunteering to help out, gathering committees for decision-making, and interacting with those in the educational roles.

For a successful school community, the development of policies is needed for the educational materials used and the development of challenges. These policies are going to lay the philosophies and goals for each classroom in a step-by-step detail explaining the criteria and selections used. These selections are going to ensure the best resources available to students while keeping parents and the community involved to understand the educational objectives. The policies should clearly express the following:

- A statement of philosophy that guides the school district to recognize academic freedom and responsibility which also included the importance of a shared school community.

- A statement that the educational materials selected include more than simple textbooks such as library resources and supplemental in newspapers, charts, films, and current computer programs along with advanced technology.

- The overall goals and objectives of the school district must include the need to teach specific facts and the knowledge to develop analytic thinking skills.

- A clear description of each step in the selection process beginning from consideration to final approval and the identification of all those involved with the process.

- The specifics of the regular review process for revising and updating all materials used in this process.

- The criteria used by qualified professional to select the specific age-appropriate educational materials.[319]

---

[319] Barbara B. Gaddy, T. William Hall, and Robert J. Marzano, *School Wars: Resolving Our Conflicts over Religion and Values* (San Francisco: Jossey-Bass Publishers, 1996), 214–215.

On the flip side, developing a written reconstruction policy is another open step for community involvement should the need for changes occurs. Reconstruction policies need to be well organized and written out in preparation for the educational challenges that will arise. These challenges can come from anyone involved with the school community to question the validity of nearly every possible subject area. So the reconstruction policies should always include the following:

- A statement encouraging complainants to read the entire work, rather than select excerpts, to consider work in light of the program's overall goal.
- A clear and detailed description of the steps in the review process which includes steps to follow complainant's wishes to appeal a review committee's decision.
- Clear guidelines on filling out written detailed complaints that cite specific examples.
- A requirement that the review committee be a broad-based committee with teachers, parents, administrators, and librarians, as well as students when appropriate.
- A statement that encourages ongoing communication between parents and teachers that recommends every effort be made to resolve the concerns, questions, and complaints, at classroom level on individual basis.[320]

Every opportunity for these regulations and reconstructions to be made public should be taken. The community can only assist in the reconciling process should they know what is included. The pur-

---

[320] Ibid., 215.

pose of parent-teacher associations within many schools is simply to keep everyone informed of progress reports, challenges, and future goals. Other schools may use mailing, special meetings, and possible local media to simply "get the word out" to the entire school community. The importance of keeping the community fully informed cannot be stressed enough for all people to follow. Once again considering the community to be a foundation for educational success only pushes all community members to be well educated.[321]

Experience has shown that the best way to work out problems whether large or small is simply by sitting down and having a one-on-one discussion. For the educational process, a one-on-one with parents to the classroom level can be just as effective. Teachers often wonder, "What do I do when a parent approaches me with a question that I cannot answer? Am I using the correct materials? Am I educating incorrectly?" A publication written by the People for the American Way, among others, strongly suggests these five points:

1. Talk with the parents and listen. Find out all possible in regards to his or her concerns about the material. Review your reasons for choosing the material and explain the needs for it within the educational plan.

2. Find out if the parent has read the book or material in question before answering. If not, encourage the parent to do so. Sometimes reading smaller portions is not enough to be completely informed. A whole perspective is always better than a partial.

3. If after reading the material in entirety, the parent still objects to his or her child reading it, offer an alternative assignment.

4. If the challenger wishes to have the context removed completely, refer him or her

---

[321] Ibid., 218.

to the written reconstructive policies which should already be in effect.

5. Remember that challengers are individuals. The media may report on extremists on any issue, however many challengers are rational people who care just as much as about the students' education to become thinkers as the educators do.[322]

There are many people who will object to methods and policies within the school system whether based on personal agenda, religion, or moral grounds. Perhaps they worry about their student's outcome or the future of the school community together. Regardless of the reason behind community challengers, remembering that all people have their own view of the world, society, and the future sometimes overshadows what really matters today. Respect the differences of all people and let their voices be heard too.

Leadership

A community strong with a commitment to Christian education as well as the strength of community has to realize one major detail as most communities will. A community involvement opens the doors to many opportunities for those within the community itself to further explore, but as with all groups of people, the differences of the individuals can complicate the group's influence or outcome. So what can be done to help organize, facilitate, and inspire people to assist in community development? Maybe not so much what as who? A leader. Leadership is not always the easiest word or quality to understand. A leader has to maintain stability, adapt to

---

[322] Barbara B. Gaddy, T. William Hall, and Robert J. Marzano, *School Wars: Resolving Our Conflicts over Religion and Values* (San Francisco: Jossey-Bass Publishers, 1996), 218–219.

changes, and evolve with the times, along with several other aspects and challenges that will come about.

A rather helpful model to demonstrate the importance of a leader is by describing a one-practice, two-commitment method. This model contains five practices with two commitments each for a total of ten. The first practice is to model the way. Modeling the way will gather the rights and respect of one in leadership through directing the community. People must first follow a person than a plan. Commitment 1 with modeling the way is finding a voice through expressing personal values. Commitment 2 is setting an example through actions with the shared visions of the community in question.[323] A leader may ask himself or herself, *In what ways do I implement this first practice? How can I improve?*

The second practice within the leadership model is to inspire a vision. A vision is the desire a leader has to make something happen hopefully to create a new idea specifically to change a present weakness. The leader must be sure that followers are on board by speaking the instruction to them in a proper language. Commitment 3 is to envision the future by expressing new and exciting possibilities to pique and maintain interest. Commitment 4 involves enlisting others who may share the common vision by appealing to their beliefs as well. The warning here is not to exclude anyone from this vision simply because they may not agree or may want to see something completely different take place. A vision will lead to a strong idea to be put into plan form, preferably without exclusion.[324]

Practice 3 may be the most difficult: challenging the process. The leader will strive to recognize ideas, support, strengths, and weaknesses by having a willingness to challenge the process in the hopes of growing into a stronger process, system, and service. Commitment 5 explains searching for opportunities by seeking different ways to grow, change, evolve, and improve. Commitment 6 is experimenting and taking the risks while challenging the process. Perhaps taking

---

[323] James Kouzes and Barry Posner, *The Leadership Challenge* (San Francisco: Jossey-Bass, 2002), 5, 6.
[324] Ibid., 5, 7.

smaller wins for starters and learning from mistakes may be a wise place to record the progress of challenging.

Practice 4 is ever important: enabling others to act. Leaders have the sole responsibility to engage and encourage people to make any project work. Not only wanting the project to work may be enough. For some communities, especially within Christianity, people need to also live the results for people to feel capable and committed to success. Commitment 7 teaches that fostering collaboration is best accomplished by promoting cooperative goals and establishing a positive trust. Commitment 8 values the importance of strengthening each other by sharing the power, decisions, and discretion. Some leaders struggle with this practice by wondering, *How can I engage people without trying them away? What actions can I designate people to take over?* Leaders need to exhibit courage and faith within their own ability to answer these questions best.[325]

To finish the one-practice, two-commitment model is practice 5: encouraging the heart. Strong leaders should know that encouragement, praise, and celebrations build a stronger identity and can greatly raise the community's spirit. The high spirit is most effective during difficult times by simply remembering that a celebration will be pending once the challenges are met. Commitment 9 involves recognizing the contributions of individuals by showing appreciation and boost for excellence. Commitment 10 also finishes with celebrating the values and victories achieved and reminding everyone involved that the collective spirit is what community is all about.[326]

When in doubt, a leader can refer back to these five practices as often as he or she may see fit. Not every leader will ever be perfect at all five areas, but by reaching out to others involved and gaining support from a trusted advisor, perhaps the leader can find other qualities present. This model can also be referred to as MICEE: Model the way. Inspire a shared vision. Challenge the process. Enable others to act. Encourage the heart. Mice may be difficult to organize, but as long as the leader does become a cat, the cheese can be obtained.

---

[325] Ibid., 5, 9.
[326] Ibid., 5, 10.

Motivation

A leader will have many difficult tasks to face once he or she has been placed within the leadership role. One rather tricky aspect that creeps up on nearly everyone is motivation. A leader might often ask, "Do I have enough motivation to make this work?" Or "Why am I not motivated?" Considering the leader will be gathering volunteers, creating plans, and focusing on the community goal, motivation of all the community members especially the leader is ever so important.

From a psychological standpoint, motivation has been best broken down by researchers David C. McClelland and John W. Atkinson. These researchers emphasized that all people are motivated by three distinct minimotives relating to work behaviors.

1. Need for Achievement.
2. Need for Power.
3. Need for Affiliation.[327]

McClelland and Atkinson visualized a bowl of energy. The entire bowl is the motivation. The bowl has three values or openings allowing the energy to flow. The values are power, achievement, and affiliation. Each motive (or valve) leads to a different behavioral type, but the amounts and sizes are all going to vary per person. One could say that a strong motive is an opening that opens easier so more energy can enter to keep the person more fully motivated. Likewise, a more closed opening or a tighter fit might not allow as much energy into the motive, thus creating a weaker influence or commitment. McClelland and Atkinson actually developed a test called the Thematic Apperception Test, which involves showing a person various pictures of work-related situations and then asking the person to tell a story about the picture. When people begin to express thoughts, feelings, and actions regarding the picture, the researchers

---

[327] Marlene Wilson, *How to Mobilize Church Volunteers* (Minneapolis: Augsburg Publishing House, 1983), 29.

gather accurate information based on which motive behavior the person has described. To visualize this method, look at this diagram.[328]

9.1

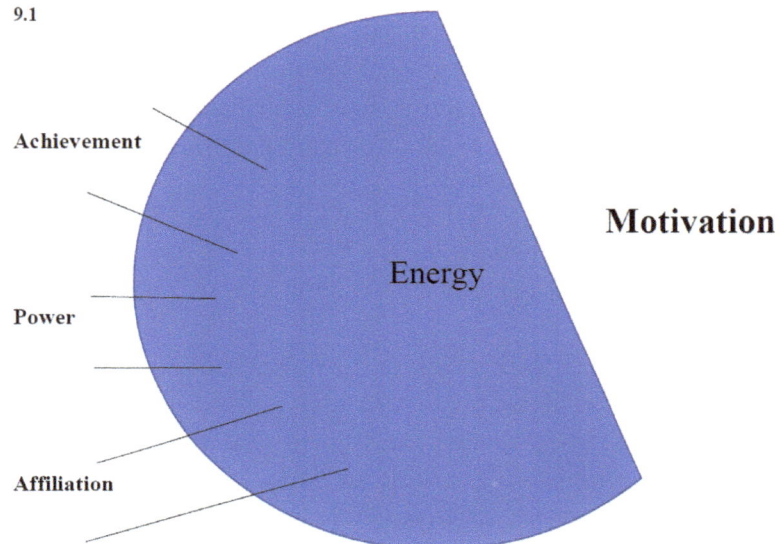

Each of the three motives individually creates their own goal based on their own particular characteristics along with what they may usually be thinking about.

Achievement-Motivated

Goal: Achieve success in situations that require excellent performance.

Characteristics: Concerned with excellence and doing a personal best while setting moderate goals and taking risks. They like to take personal responsibility for solutions, have a desire to accomplish unique tasks, and are usually restless and innovative. Achievement motivators also take pleasure in striving, need feedback, and are usually much better organizers than maintainers. Sometimes interest is lost when all project bugs are not worked out but are ready to

---

[328] Ibid., 29.

move on to a new challenge. Achievers are usually very goal oriented, remembering that they never like to fail.

Spend time thinking about: How do I handle my jobs better? How do I accomplish something usual? What goals can I accomplish? How will I overcome the obstacles? How can I make this meeting quick and to the point? An example here is Sir Isaac Newton. When Newton was asked about how he discovered gravity, he replied, "By thinking about it all the time!"[329]

Affiliation-Motivated

Goal: Want to be with others and enjoy friends.

Characteristics: Concerned with being liked by others and accepted for who they are. They need warm relationships and inter-actions. Affiliation-motivated people are concerned about being separated from other people. They are rarely loners. Affiliates are nur-turers and caregivers while enjoying the company of others. These people are more likely to be ready to receive a call to welcome people, host an event, or greet at church.

Spend time thinking about: I want to be liked, but how can I? How do I be there and console others? Where can I find warm and friendly relationships? I need to recognize my feelings and be open to the feelings of others. I want my meetings to be full of discussion, socializing, and building each other up as much as possible.[330]

Power-Motivated

Goal: Seek to have impact or influence on others.

Characteristics: Concerned about personal reputation and what other people other think of the power already in place. They always

---

[329] Marlene Wilson, *How to Mobilize Church Volunteers* (Minneapolis: Augsburg Publishing House, 1983), 30–31.
[330] Ibid., 31.

want to give advice. Power-motivated people have strong feelings about their status with a strong need to change other people's behavior to how they see fit. Many times the power motivation can be verbally fluent to somewhat argumentative while seen by others as forceful, outspoken, and maybe hardheaded. They are the movers and shakers by raising funds, negotiating, and often holding people accountable for actions.

Spend time thinking about: How do I gain influence and impact others? How will I use my influence to win, change people, gain status, and grow in my authority?

While the power-motived people may seem to be more negative, it is not always so. People need to remember that there is positive and negative within all the motivation valves. Perhaps it does become more clear when the motivations are not merely discussed as positives and negatives but rather as personalized and socialized.[331] A person's personal beliefs and characteristics may be useful to them on a personal level but lack in social openness or vice versa. When using as much of both areas, personalized and socialized, motivation can be at its strongest to further success of the community and also the leader.

Community Negotiation

Once a prominent leader has been chosen with a community/group to lead and be a decision-maker, the next most important element to present is negotiating. For some people, the idea of trying to negotiate can be really difficult especially within a community where a large number of people are involved. Ideally, a community gathering would want as many people to become involved as possible, but it does raise some challenges along the way. There is a common human interaction that occurs with larger groups called the win-win. The win-win is not a technique but rather an interaction containing the values of the heart and mind that desire mutual benefits. Win-

---

[331] Ibid., 32.

win strives to be mutually beneficial and satisfying and wants a solid decision so all parties involved will feel positive and committed to an action plan with more cooperation as opposed to competition.[332]

Ultimately, there are seven ways for the entire win-win system, but for community assessment, we are going to look specifically at three ways. The first dimension of the win-win is recognizing what a person will be looking for or secretly desiring to make most human interactions positive. He or she will be seeking personal character, relationships of trust, shared agreements, a supportive environment, and a process for the negotiating to happen. Of course, each person will have their own ideas of what should be included with these listed qualities, and it is quite that other qualities that are not on this list can come up too depending on the desire of an individual.[333]

Second, the win-win negotiating has six possible outcomes of interacting, and ideally a leader should be aware of all six to further the process along or stop it completely depending on necessity. The six possible solutions are win-win, win-lose, lose-win, lose-lose, win, or no deal. The last two mentioned being win and no deal are possible outcomes that are considered with little explanation. A win is simply a win. Take the win and be gracious. No deal means that perhaps the circumstances were not ideal for the time or not fitting into the plan correctly. Therefore, the idea was a no go or no deal.

The third dimension of the win-win negotiation process includes four smaller steps of its own. The third dimension is stated as the guidelines. Step 1 under the guideline is to see a problem from another's point of view. The best way to seek and fully understand the needs and concerns of others is by using perception: putting yourself in someone else's shoes, emotion: understanding your emotions before others, communication: listening actively and acknowledging

---

[332] Sean Covey, *The 7 Habits of Highly Effective Teens* (New York: Fire Side Books, 1998), 145.
[333] Ibid., 147–148.

what you have heard, and prevention: build a working relationship by facing the problem and not the people.[334]

Step 2 under the third dimension is identifying the key issues involved. Identifying issues is best done by being hard on the problem and not the people. For a wiser solution, remember to reconcile the interests as not the positions. Recognize the shared and compatible interests present as well as the conflicting ones for a whole picture. Ask yourself, "Why these interests?" Or perhaps "Why not these?" Consider all the choices, remembering that they come from various points of view within the group. Also, be sure to really talk and discuss the interests so they come alive by being acknowledged for a certain answer. Look forward for answers, not backward, and remember to be concrete but flexible too.

Step 3 under the third dimension is to determine what results would constitute a fully acceptable solution. What would the win-win solution look like? How to get there? What method will best include and cover everyone's concerns and needs? There may never be a complete right or perfect answer to this question, but solid boundaries can be agreed upon for success. Again, while considering both sides, one might deeply consider how to complete this personal statement: I can be happy with any solution as long as it includes…?

Step 4 and closing out the third dimension is to identify possible new options to achieve results. This can be done by a simple brainstorming meeting with all people involved. Remember that identifying new options will also include obstacles of premature judgments, searching for a single answer as opposed to an open solution, assuming the "fixed pie" effect, or thinking that fixing their problem only applies to them.[335] Each leader will have their own method including these guidelines along with others along the way, but each leader should be clearly striving for as much success with their plans to further the community in a direction that expresses the most open awareness to those looking on.

---

[334] Ibid., 150.
[335] Ibid., 151–152.

Involvement and Frequency

The involvement of a community while encouraging the direction of students' education plays a much larger role than many people often realize. The entire community atmosphere or what is usually better known as society teaches students certain behaviors, certain skills, and certain beliefs. For many student-aged children into young adulthood, the major external area that greatly influences their life is through socialization. Socialization is a process of learning "the way we do things around here." While schools may have the task of preparing students for joining society someday, it should also be noted which domain of socialization a student may be heading. The first domain of socialization is the primary. Primary socialization happens within families during the early years directed toward emotional stability, cooperation, and respect for authority. Also, the primary includes learning how to form affective relationships.

The next domain is secondary socialization. Secondary happens with formal education, everyday activity, and various experiences. The result is competence, preparation for specialized learning, and the real socialization into both the political world and everyday work.[336] Secondary differs from primary in that more primary is usually family based within the home while secondary will occur more within a school setting with early exposure into what the outside community has to offer.

Finally, socialization's last domain is the tertiary. Tertiary happens within the legal, religious, social, and/or voluntary organizations. More often these occur through media, contracts, political rallies, and the everyday economic system. The purpose here is to gather the individual into a specific social order while recognizing the individual's uniqueness in the system. Ultimately society would expect this person to develop vocational competence along with independent responsibility.[337]

---

[336] Ibid., 59–60.

[337] Fenwick W. English, Larry E. Frase, and Joanne M. Arhar, *Leading into the 21ˢᵗ Century* (Newbury Park: Corwin Press Inc., 1992), 59–60.

Socialization within all three of these domains increases the awareness of diversity within communities through differences of values and beliefs. Learning to understand these differences with the help of school systems is best examined through the lens of cultural, economic, and social context to further the operation of socialization. For many rural-agricultural families, socialization is handed down from their parents. Children even at young ages learn their families' values, habits, and vocations. Parents often teach their children these lessons in the same manner as their parents perhaps taught them. Mostly, the similarities of the home, school, workplace, activities, and everyday values will be shared within the same community again as the parents previously did. At one point within this generational learning, there had to be a distinguishing between "schooling" and "education." Are these terms the same? How would they be defined any differently? In earlier society, the school was only seen as one of many educating facilities while later in the nineteenth century, the school was identified as the primary place of learning. School at this time had also overtaken many of the functions previously performed by other educating locations. Schools derived from a greater community purpose now shared the vision expressed by John Dewey in 1916:

> The school has the function...of coordinating within the deposition of each individual the diverse influences of the various social environments into which he enters. One code prevails in the family; another on the streets; a third, in the workshop or store; a fourth, in the religious association. As a person passes from one of the environments to another, he is subjected to antagonistic pulls, and is in danger of being split into a being having different standards of judgment and emotion for differing occasions. This danger imposes upon the school a steadying and integrating office.[338]

---

[338] Ibid., 61.

The split of different standards that John Dewey mentions has been related to how diversity within a community is present. Most communities may often be rather similar just as mentioned earlier by the values and beliefs being handed down from previous generations. It may be some time before children will really get to experience the vast differences that diversity can bring. Mass media can shed some light onto diversity that may often hinder or scare some children away from not wanting to learn more. Some environmental issues within their own community can contain growing poverty, less family care, language difficulties, health risks, and an increase of industrial living, which are outside of a community's comfort zone.[339] For many students who are already involved with these situations whether by choice or by chance, the outcomes can be rather difficult to overcome. Such incidents that arise include substance abuse, early pregnancies, and possible suicides. These can all stem from lack of involvement within the community or a feeling of alienation of participation from those who can help.

Based on these demographics, has a reform from the community made an effort for positive changes? Depending on the location of this particular community, many would argue no given the following reasons:

1. Dropout rates have continued to increase.
2. Youth poverty has changed little.
3. Students' test scores show little to no improvement.
4. Funding for better school resources is lacking.

Other communities perhaps within bigger cities with more school resources could easily counterargue those reasons.

1. Dropout rates are lower than before.
2. Youth poverty has lowered due to more community involvement.

---

[339] Ibid., 67.

3. Student test scores have increased despite ethnic/diversity backgrounds.
4. School funding is quite strong in providing adequate learning resources.

The socialization from both examples can teach the community a valuable lesson in maintaining where the importance for involvement should be placed. Examining the various areas within the family life, school systems, and everyday community involvement could very well change the entire perception and direction for a community striving to maintain proper education, especially Christian education.

Commitment

Considering that leadership, a community's involvement, and frequency of involvement all play roles in the success or failure of community goals, there also has to be a question of commitment. Sometimes simply asking a person or family to describe their commitment level cannot be enough. In 1995, a pair of religious researchers, Pfeifer and Waelty, developed a five-point religious commitment scale ranging from a three-item answer to a seventeen-item answer. Two of the scales deeply focused primarily on Christian commitment and involvement with religious emphasis. During their initial testing, to their surprise, the researchers were confronted as to whether their questions could be used to evaluate other religions outside of Christianity. After some careful modifications, the test was approved for other uses. Because the research was being considered by other religious groups, several Christian churches took to trying the religious commitment scale to help evaluate their own commitment levels.[340]

---

[340] Peter C. Hill and Ralph W. Hood Jr., *Measures of Religiosity* (Birmingham: Religious Education Press, 1999), 205.

The other remaining scales focused more on behavioral practices as opposed to simple questionnaires that people were asked. These behaviors were measured by religious beliefs, religious practices, and the influence of those beliefs on personal behaviors. The religious emphasis scale focuses primarily on religious practices of the home and church community. These questions measure deeper based on childhood backgrounds and where they have led the religious commitment to be today. What were the factors? And why did he or she remain loyal to a specific religion?

The questionnaire regarding religious orientation and daily life is a fifty-one-item evaluation with each response being weighed differently so as not to show a regular to maintain testing validity. All of these questions are a basic yes or no response with various point values known only to the person administering the test. The questions include topics such as personal religious beliefs, prayer, Christian celebrations, parents' faith, children's faith, God's true existence, discrimination, morality, the Scripture, sin, life's difficulties, and the true meaning of Christian life.[341] Many people did not think that answering yes or no to such loaded questions would be able to create valid results, but it turns out that many of those doubters were fascinated with their own outcomes.

The second half of the questionnaire is the questions regarding religious emphasis. The religious emphasis is not a yes-or-no-based system, but rather a 0 to 5 scale on how much or how little a person may agree or disagree with certain statements. These items were based on a person's upbringing to consider the nurturing factor to what makes that person motivated to commitment with a religious community today. These statements included attending Sunday services, attending Sunday school or other religious classes, praying in the home, reading the Scripture together or personally, morality choices, youth groups, and personal aspirations from a young age to where they would like to see the future ahead.[342] These results have various correlations between some people remaining loyal and some-

---

[341] Ibid., 207–208.
[342] Ibid., 210.

what strict in the ways of their childhood, while others showed more of a disgruntled manner in being unhappy with their community and religious choices.

Commitment on any level for most people is not a quality that can be measured, although these psychological tests and church information cards seek to gather as much information about a person and their families as necessary. Many people believe that when the time is right and/or when they are specifically being called to service, their commitment will speak volumes for itself. Arguably, trying to determine the amount of commitment one has can quickly make some rather uncomfortable and hesitant. Regardless, if the leader keeps their guard down and has a little trust and faith in their followers, the dedication within will certainly show through the commitment on the outside.

Obstacles

Leadership, community involvement, and commitment can all support the outcome for a stronger community. Yet not every aspect of community will always be smooth sailing; in fact, it can be downright difficult and sometimes not successful. Gathering a community usually requires reaching out for volunteers. Volunteers are people who are not getting paid for their services but rather offering their time and talents for the community goal. Within a Christian community, there are a handful of common obstacles that can greatly hinder the community's success if not addressed properly. One more obvious obstacle is that volunteers especially within ministry may not fully know or understand what is to be expected of them. The position description is usually not written down or clearly defined, causing confusion upon working details. Many times a leader may verbally state, "It will not take you long to do" or "There is really not much to do the task." Only after these words are spoken that the volunteer may come to find out that the exact opposite may be true.[343]

Another common obstacle, some might argue happens only in the Catholic communities, is that tradition often overtakes new and creative ideas. First, the Catholic Church is not the only community that values tradition. Consequently, valuing tradition does not have to overtake any approach to use newer ideas. Several Christian denominations are led by the elders of the church or people advanced in age chosen by the church community to be leaders. It is not uncommon for many people in these positions to comment, "We never do that here. It has always been done this way." Those words can quickly become a turnoff to people wishing to make a difference already thinking outside the box. Sadly, there are many leaders who do feel this way, relying on the old phrase "Not broke, don't fix it." This can show closed-mindedness to some and will cause a variety of service opportunities to become lost.[344]

The use of time and talent sheets or a collection of volunteer names can cover up a person's gifts. For the people on a list who are never called or asked to assist with certain projects, a feeling a worthlessness or lack of trust can become present. Some volunteers simply choose not to return because they feel left out and not wanted. Ironically, Christian fellowship is about reaching out and accepting the stewardships given in time and talents, so when a person feels that his or her gifts are not needed, the Christian mission suffers, as does the community.

Slightly referring back to the tradition obstacle, when the clergy or lay ministers are automatically in a position of leadership, they can be poor delegators. Some have not had the proper education themselves to be in the leadership position let alone know how to further a community. To avoid this, some clergy would rather do the work and projects alone so as not to bother giving the task to someone else. Perhaps they feel no one else can handle it or there is no trust.

---

[343] Marlene Wilson, *How to Mobilize Church Volunteers* (Minneapolis: Augsburg Publishing House, 1983), 22.

[344] Ibid., 22–23.

The major negative here is that how can a leader grow in leadership skill without learning to delegate? Where will the advancement of the community head?

The most controversial obstacle of all is allowing the volunteer's job to become more important than the person performing the job itself. Most communities will have a list of job slots to fill or taking turns with the same people as opposed to who has the right gift for the job. Sadly, this occurrence happens way too often considering it can be most difficult for volunteers to describe: what they are good at, what they are tired of, what they do not like, what they want or need to learn, where they are being led, or when they simply need time away.[345] Each of these questions can and should be answered on a regular basis. These problematic questions can be avoided once people begin to care more about the gifts of the individuals rather than the job tasks. The gifts of each person are truly a blessing that need to shared and grown within a community for all to express. In her book *Eighth Day of Creation*, Elizabeth O'Connor states,

> We ask to know the will of God without guessing that His will is written into our very being. We perceive that will when we discern our gifts. Our obedience and surrender to God are a large part our out into the world and make us participants in life, the uncovering of them is one of the most important tasks confronting any one of us.[346]

Once our gifts are fully recognized, a person's volunteering desire can be unstoppable. And for those who have not yet discovered their fullest potential, be prepared for a couple of surprises.

---

[345] Marlene Wilson, *How to Mobilize Church Volunteers* (Minneapolis: Augsburg Publishing House, 1983), 23.

[346] Elizabeth O'Connor, *Eighth Day of Creation*, 117.

Church and State

A community of most types within the United States is almost certain to have a moment when the division of church and state can be confrontational. People have their religious views and their political views. The two of these views may or may not always match up with each other or with what others in their community may believe. For a community to maintain the importance of its education, some confrontations need to be addressed. For many, discussing church and state is viewed more as a private personal matter; but when a community is coming together for a common belief and purpose, those who may be harboring other ideas can really create tension. That same tension has happened numerous times in American history and still does today, especially when subjects that fall into both categories cross over.

Previous chapters have mentioned the differences in private education against public education, but one particular dilemma makes public education even more or a challenge. Public education is controlled and financed by the government. Since the government has a great deal of heresy on the educational process, the question of boundaries on the government and religious relationship consistently unravels. For several years, defenders of both sides argue the rights listed within the First Amendment of the US Constitution. However, the rights and applications for this amendment greatly differ based on their uses. Where exactly does government control end and religious liberty begin?

Even from the earlier colonial times, Thomas Jefferson cited both sides of public school debate by calling religious liberty "the most inalienable and sacred of all human rights."[347] The First Amendment, and perhaps the most important one, embodies two clauses that are known as the religious liberty clauses. One is the establishment clause: "Congress shall make no law respecting the establishment of

---

[347] Barbara B. Gaddy, T. William Hall, and Robert J. Marzano, *School Wars: Resolving Our Conflicts over Religion and Values* (San Francisco: Jossey-Bass Publishers, 1996), 181.

religion." Two is the free exercise clause: "Or prohibiting the free exercise thereof." Remembering that these clauses were written at the time when the New American colonies were separating from English religious rule, it almost seemed that these were to protect the state from the church, when actually the church was to be protected from the state.

"The wall of separation" was a phrase coined by Thomas Jefferson while explaining the importance of keeping church and state separate, but as time went on and the United States continued to evolve and create its own identity, the First Amendment received some rather challenging moments. In 1879, the *Reynolds v. United States* decision was the first case before the Supreme Court dealing with the context within the First Amendment that also relied on Jefferson's "wall of separation" metaphor. Chief Justice Morrison Waite argued Jefferson's metaphor to be an "authoritative declaration of the scope and effect of the First Amendment." Sixty-eight years later, in 1947, in the *Everson v. Board of Education* case, Everson affirmed the reasoning from the Reynolds case. Court Justice Hugo Black famously said after this case took place,

> The First Amendment has erected a wall between church and state. That wall must be kept high and impregnable.[348]

For nearly twenty-five years after the *Everson* decision, the Supreme Court continued following the "wall of separation" doctrine in several cases involving public education. In 1948, the Court outlawed sectarian religious teaching in public schools in *McCollum v. Board of Education*. Further in 1962, in *Engel v. Vitale*, the Court banned state-sponsored prayer in public schools. And once more in 1963, in *Abington School District v. Schempp*, the Court outlawed required Bible readings in public schools, also declaring that government could neither advance nor inhibit religion.[349] The bigger

---

[348] Ibid., 183.
[349] Ibid., 183–184.

court decision was made in 1968, when the Court struck down an antievolution teaching in the *Epperson v. Arkansas* case, which was a total reversal of the *Scopes* decision forty years prior.

The free exercise clause sometimes works together with religious freedom, but there is often an inherent tension between the two. This tension is often visited by the courts as previously mentioned and also by legal scholars. The government's accommodation of an individual's right to religious freedom could also be viewed as an establishment of that religion.[350] Remember that when the First Amendment was written, Christianity was the predominant religion of the time. A question of motivation has been asked over the years regarding this time frame. Were the writers trying to keep one religious sect from overpowering another by only supporting Christianity? Was Christianity supposed to be the only religion for the country? Even if these questions may have been thought of at the time, the United States certainly went on to break down into several different religions along with numerous branches within Christianity.

Since the writing of the free exercise clause, several other court cases have challenged this clause just as with public religion. In 1963, a decision in the *Sherbert v. Verner* case introduced a three-pronged test involving a strict security standard. The test consisted of the following: (1) the state's action is not to impose burden on the free exercise of religion unless (2) there is a compelling state interest for the action and (3) the state interest is accomplished through the means least restrictive to the religious practice.[351] Considering that the free exercise clause protects an individual's right to religious belief, applying the three-pronged test requires the courts to determine whether the state has enough of an objecting party to take actions that will conflict with religious beliefs. Most importantly, simple exposure to an offense does not and will not be enough evidence to violate the free exercise clause involving school controversies.

Another important court case to mention is the highly controversial and perhaps most misunderstood case in the 1950s, *Engel v.*

---

[350] Ibid., 185.
[351] Ibid., 187.

Vitale. Ten sets of parents brought about the lawsuit against the New Hyde Park, New York, public school district, challenging the daily reciting of school prayer. In particular, the daily school prayer that was being challenged read as follows:

> Almighty God, we acknowledge our dependence upon Thee, as we beg Thy blessings upon us, our parents, our teachers and our country.[352]

The case eventually reached the Supreme Court, and by 1962, a decision to remove the school prayer was made based on the "wall of separation" given by the Constitution. Even through today, prayers within public schools read by school officials, parents, or teachers are still considered to be unconstitutional. The one common misinterpretation that still arises from this case is that all religion was to be taken from the public schools, not just the daily prayers. The Supreme Court had to further explain this decision by referencing that the court did not use hostility against religion, but in turn, the government was protecting religion from government interference since "a union of government and religion tends to destroy government and degrade religion."

Moral Education Influence

So does religious right have too much political influence? Within the past ten years, it can be an overstatement to suggest that some politicians have either won or lost elections simply based on their own "moral values." Most politicians do not fully understand the depth and severity of discussing moral issues, especially where these issues have the strongest religious backing. Jim Wallis states that "the Religious Right is comfortable with the language of religion, values,

---

[352] Barbara B. Gaddy, T. William Hall, and Robert J. Marzano, *School Wars: Resolving Our Conflicts over Religion and Values* (San Francisco: Jossey-Bass Publishers, 1996), 187–188.

and God talk, so much that they sometimes claim to own the territory or even own God."[353] Many people are not so comfortable speaking out about moral issues, and even fewer are comfortable teaching these. Arguably for the sake of education, the moral issue of poverty needs to be addressed especially since younger students will eventually have the power to change the world and further control poverty issues of the future, but that goal starts now. Poverty can be attributed to several different areas including decline in the economy, overseas wars, and a weak employment status. The wars and conflicts with other countries create questions of ethics and not so much looking into the severity of consequences it's leaving within America. Are poverty and war social, moral, or religious issues? All three.

What can be done regarding these moral issues as well as others? One solution is the moral-value strategy. Moral-value is simply what it states: basing a moral issue on the value it has within a particular environment. In some cases, this strategy may win over debates on a short-term basis, but ultimately have a low outcome rate in the long term simply because it can be rather difficult narrowing down the moral issues on one particular group.[354] Politicians who ultimately make these strategic decisions may be open to discussing the issue head-on while hoping that the short-term clarifications will be enough, but most decision-makers will completely ignore most moral issues because of the amount of questions and conflicts that arise with it. The truth here is that regardless of religious, political, or personal views, the separation between church and state does not mean that religious views should be excluded from politics.

In 2005, Edward Harrington, a United States senior district judge for the district of Massachusetts, wrote in his book *The Metaphorical Wall,*

> The idea that political figures should not be influenced by their religious beliefs, or that religious

---

[353] James D. Torr, *How Does Religion Influence Politics?* (Farmington Hills: Greenhaven Press, 2006), 24–25.
[354] Ibid., 25.

views should not inform public policy debates, is misguided. People who hold this view often invoke the metaphor of a wall between church and state. However, that metaphor was originally coined to convey the idea that religion should be protected from government control-not that government should be protected from citizens with religious beliefs. Rather than calling for the regulation or curtailment of religious speech, the First Amendment encourage religious expression and protects it from government control.[355]

The separation argument has long been used to distinguish the teachings of religion, especially religion with morality involvement from the participation of political debates toward the public. Sadly, many of the people who fight such moral teachings in an attempt to shape the public agenda are quickly cut down, ridiculed, and often judged rather harshly. The battle of church and state, religion and politics, society and culture might never come to an end; but the beliefs of standing up for what the community feels to be right can never be wrong.

Community Wrap-Up

Communities of all sizes, ethnicities, and backgrounds continue to be a huge support to the Christian faith often more so than people may realize. The church leaders of a community are always pleased to see people coming together in a group especially when it benefits others. Outwardly, the community is making a statement to those around whose interest may be piqued to want to know just a little bit more. Individually, a person may have all the strength and

---

[355] Edward F. Harrington's *The Metaphorical Wall*. Quoted in: James D. Torr, *How Does Religion Influence Politics?* (Farmington Hills: Greenhaven Press, 2006), 43.

confidence possible, but even the most proud people every once in a while have to take a step back and ask for help. Perhaps only thinking of community as a give-and-take may not be the correct approach; doing one act of kindness to someone spreads like wildfire. When someone takes even a little time to do something nice for you, do you not just feel like doing something nice back? Even if it is not for the same person, spreading the feeling of community and reaching out to those who may benefit from community can grow into proportions that can move mountains. Christ has given us the power and mission to spread the welcoming love that He showed to all people while on earth. We are to see Christ in one another, and what better way to see Christ all around us than by being a part of a strong Christian community?

CHAPTER 10

The Future of Christian Education

Christian education has come a rather long way over the course of two thousand plus years, but there is still a long journey ahead too. Over time, we have seen many changes in teaching styles, technologies, methodologies, and people of influence on the realm of Christian education. Mother Teresa openly expressed her delight in a conversation with a Hindu man. Mother Teresa asked a Hindu man, "What is a Christian?" He responded, "The Christian is someone who gives."[356] That giving has to continue into the future for Christian education to remain strong while getting stronger for future generations to carry on Christ's mission.

What does the future have in store for Christian education? Are we carrying out the Christian to the best humanly possible? Have we lost too many people along the way? Are we not as motivated as people from earlier times were? Perhaps many of these questions are not asked near enough for those who are dedicating their lives to service. Have Christians allowed the times and technological advances of our world hinder what really matters? Many would not entirely know how to ask these questions fully. Each individual Christian needs to remember that carrying out the Christian journey always begins with one step.

---

[356] Jose Luiz Gonzalez-Balado, *Mother Teresa in My Own Words* (New York: Gramercy Books, 1997), 17.

Christ Himself gave us four incredible teaching ministries that we are to use as windows for looking into the future of Christian education. The first window is Jesus's resurrection from the dead. This divine happening restores the body and souls in a full relationship with God. The resurrection completes the salvation offered by Christ to all His people. Therefore, Christian education needs to be focusing not only on the mind learning, but also on the body's ability to serve. We are to apply all the God has created into our mission. Saint Paul reminds Christians that to really know Christ and make Him known is the essential element of who we are. Jesus's resurrection makes possible the transformation within our own lives when faced with death. Jesus's resurrection is also the promise of our own resurrection into a new life.[357] John 6:35–40 reads,

> Jesus said to them, "I am the bread of life. Whoever comes tome will never be hungry, and whoever believes in will never be thirsty. But I say to you that you have seen me and yet do not believe. Everything that the Father gives me will come to me, and anyone who comes to me I will never drive away; for I have come down from heaven, not to do my own will, but the will of Him who sent me. And this is the will of Him who sent me that I should lose nothing of all that He has given me, but raise it up on the last day. This is indeed the will of my Father that all who see the Son and believe in Him may have eternal life; and I will them up on the last day."[358]

Christian education should always be uplifted in remembering this great promise for our own lives now and in the future.

---

[357] Robert W. Pazmino, *God Our Teacher: Theological Basics in Christian Education* (Grand Rapids: Baker Academics, 2001), 135–136.
[358] John 6:35–40.

The second window for the future of Christian education is the return of Christ. The second coming of Christ is the true hope for all people that we will be with Christ someday. Christ's second coming completes that first coming with the promised teaching of a new humanity and a new creation all with God that He will bring to full fruition. This too is explicitly detailed in 1 John 2:28–3:3:

> And now, little children, abide in Him, so that when He is revealed we may have confidence and not be put to shame before Him at His coming. If you know that He is righteous, you may be sure that everyone who does right has been born of Him. See what love the Father has given us, that we should be called children of God; and that it is what we are. The reason the world does not us is that it did not know Him. Beloved, we are God's children now; what we will be has not yet been revealed. What we do know is this: when He is revealed we will be like Him, for we will see Him as He is. And all who have this hope in Him purify themselves, just as He is pure.[359]

The hope of Christ's second coming is the Christian motivation to live a life full of service, continuing the mission forward. As 1 John pointed out, Christians are called to be righteous because we are the recipients of God's grace, forgiveness, salvation, and adoption. Only by living in and with this complete confidence can Christians come to a life abiding in Christ. Christians will continue to reach their most possible fulfillment of the mission to complete the earthly mission with the ongoing hope and promise that Christ will return.[360]

The third window into the future of Christian education is the last judgment. The last judgment provides Christians with the ulti-

---

[359] 1 John 2:28–3:3.
[360] Robert W. Pazmino, *God Our Teacher: Theological Basics in Christian Education* (Grand Rapids: Baker Academics, 2001), 136–137.

mate basis for accountability and responsibility in all human affairs. Sin and salvation continue play against each other in our continued struggles, but the Holy Spirit still leads us into God's light and His path. Matthew's gospel reminds us to see the face of Jesus in the hungry, the thirsty, the naked, the sick, and the imprisoned. In doing so, we are accountable for our own eternal life or enteral punishment based on what the last judgment determines. Those chosen for judgment are gathered because they have followed the Great Commission of baptizing, preaching, and completing the task of teaching all the nations. The Scripture has certainly given Christianity a clear picture as to what we should be constantly doing—His mission.[361] God's love never fails even when humanity often fails. Despite all that has happened, is happening, or will someday happen, all Christians can be assured that "Jesus always be with us until the end of the age"[362] (Matthew 28:20).

The fourth window of the Christian education future is our everlasting life. Everlasting fulfills God's original plan for humanity after the fall of all creation. Christ's life, death, and resurrection make eternal life possible for all of the fallen humanity. There is no greater love than what Jesus did for all His people. The promise of eternal life brings all Christians together along their earthly journey ultimately knowing where they will finish. The book of Revelation describes images of heaven and what eternal life will be like for us to one day share in. We see the worshipping of God and the Lamb who are worthy of glory, honor, power, blessing, wisdom, and might. All our adoration of Christ should be the central focus of our education and efforts to celebrate and worship the Triune God.[363] The complete reconciliation of nature will occur as Revelation 21:1 and 22:1–2:

> Then I saw a new heaven and a new earth; for
> the first heaven and the first earth had passed

---

[361] Ibid., 138.
[362] Matthew 28:20.
[363] Robert W. Pazmino, *God Our Teacher: Theological Basics in Christian Education* (Grand Rapids: Baker Academics, 2001), 138–139.

away, and the sea was no more…Then the angel showed me the river of the water of life, bright as crystal, flowing from the throne of God and of the Lamb through the middle of the street of the city. On either side of the river is the tree of life with its twelve kinds of fruit, producing its fruit each month; or the leaves of the tree are for the healing of the nations.[364]

While examining the four windows of the theological future for Christian education, one has to be wondering how I could possibly live up to these expectations. What can a person do within their own life to ensure the future of Christian education? A person can consciously remember the five-task model: community formation, service, worship, proclamation, and advocacy. By using each of these five tasks, a Christian will certainly ensure a successful and promising future of Christian education for many years to come. By using all five of these areas, any and all Christians can certainly rest assured that they are fulfilling all that Jesus commanded of His people. Our faith community formation is always present for our assistance, our service to others should always be an ongoing process, our worship to God should never be taken lightly or ignored, our proclamation of God's Word is ever essential to reach our global destination, and our advocacy to show our beliefs through our way of life could never be exhausted. Christ is always with us.

Dedication, Participation, Service

Dedication to continuing the Christian mission on through the years to come may seem rather intimidating to some people but a real joy to others. For those who may feel like shying away from teaching others about Christ, it could be a reflection of their own inner struggles. This very thought was the key to developing a Purpose in Life

---

[364] Revelation 21:1; 22:1–2.

Test created by researchers Crumbaugh and Maholick in 1964.[365] The test was developed for people to assess their own meaning to the fulfillment of life or the lack of fulfillment. The test would focus on personal motivation, interests, personal developments, and normal daily functioning. The scoring is based on a three-part breakdown. Part A responses are objective on a four-point scale usually beginning with an "I am usually…" phrase. Part B consists of incomplete sentences that the test taker responses as sees fit. Part C has the individual write about his or her life goals, ambitions, hopes, plans, past meanings, and motivation for the future.

The Purpose in Life Test is a compilation of twenty items to be answered with a single response as best fitting the test taker. The responses are given on a seven-point scale ranging from worst to best. The following are examples of certain testing items:

- Life to me seems…
- Every day I…
- If I could chose, I would…
- If I were to die today, I would feel that my life has been…
- My life is…
- Facing my daily tasks is…
- I have discovered…[366]

Many psychologists over the years have continued to evaluate the core of a person's inner thoughts, feelings, and personal bias toward various topics; but not too many are eager to ask about faith. Perhaps the old cliché of never talking to people about religion and politics holds more truth than realized. Regardless of what the reason may be, a deeper researcher to what drives a person's commitment and/or dedication to religious beliefs only strengthens the faith basis of the whole church mission. Also, remembering that there are

---

[365] Peter C. Hill and Ralph W. Hood Jr., *Measures of Religiosity* (Birmingham: Religious Education Press, 1999), 503.
[366] Ibid., 508.

plenty of others who may share the same thoughts, struggles, and even doubts is an encouragement for stepping out of the shadows and into the light by mere participation.

Participation within a mission will always be a prime directive to success in achieving a mission while guaranteeing its continuance. Yet there are some select people who take this a step deeper by answering a call to make the mission their entire life's work through vocation. James W. Fowler wrote a detailed book regarding vocation called *Weaving the New Creation: Stages of Faith and the Public Church*. In this book, Fowler commented that

> vocation is the response one makes with one's total life to the call of God to partnership... Vocation...involves a process of commitment, an ongoing discerning of one's gifts and giftedness in community, and of finding the means and settings in which those gifts—in all the dimensions of our living—can be placed at the disposal of the One who calls us into being and partnership.[367]

Thinking of a vocation as a partnership with God and His community is not an easy concept to handle, but what a truly remarkable compliment for those who have said yes to the vocational call.

While dedication and participation are truly important aspects on their own, service is the key that makes all mission work come together. Service has been described in so many different ways. Service can be doing the good for one's self, community, family, strangers, and the church. Service has been stated as not being a code of ethics, but as a way of living. True Christians believe that service is a three-fold word. First, service is a teacher proclaiming the here and now. Teachers make this personal and urgent as opposed to theoretical and historical. Second, service is a leader calling the people to follow. A leader calls out to those followers to become helpers along the way.

---

[367] Certificate of Youth Ministries Program, *Foundations for Ministry Leadership*, July 2006, 4.2.

Third, service is a healer to release people from human suffering in any way possible.[368]

How does service get accomplished? Is service measured or recorded as a reference? In Richard Foster's book *Celebration of Discipline*, there are several options of service that are presented. In terms of ministry, considering these options of ministry could be quite beneficial while discerning the direction of each church community's mission. Here are nine of the options of service that could and possibly should be applied with the Christian mission.

1. Service of hiddenness. This contains all of the gifts, charities, donations, and other services that are done anonymously simply because a person receives great joy in giving. Nearly all the time, these people do not wish to be recognized or acknowledged. It is a truly personal enrichment.

2. Service of small things. The small things are described as the insignificant day-to-day possibilities that surround all of us in our homelife, school, work, and communities. The terms "pitching in" and "lending a hand" best describe this option. Sometimes the smallest things can make a person's day, with maybe a simple gesture of small, holding the door for someone, or offering to assist someone in need of help. For the mission, these small things are acts of love to see what needs to be done.

3. Service of guarding the reputation of others. This service makes us accountable to stay away from anything negative that can harm another person. Many times, the leader of a group may be the first and only person to receive harsh words when a plan does not go well. The old saying "Sticks and stones will break my bones, but words will never hurt me" is simply not true. Words can be incredibly damaging. The best way to handle this is speaking *to* the person directly, not speaking *about* them.

---

[368] Marlene Wilson, *How to Mobilize Church Volunteers* (Minneapolis: Augsburg Publishing House, 1983), 105–106.

4. Service of being served. Many are full believers in that it is better to give than to receive, but sometimes it can be wonderful to be the receiver too. Sometimes being the person always wanting to give can become an act of pride and even resentment. Human nature prefers a give-and-take ability while not simply give, give, and give more. Remember to use service as a balance.

5. Service of common courtesy. People today are so busy with their lives that simple acts of courtesy can speak volumes. The gifts of service here are best described by the most polite and wonderful words—"please," "thank you," and "excuse me." These are words acknowledging a person's worth and courtesy.

6. Service of hospitality. First Peter 4:9 urges us to "practice hospitality ungrudgingly to one another." This means opening up our homes, lives, and actions to other people. Perhaps a simple coffee or meal can be an invitation to make some feel welcomed rather than like an inconvenience. Sharing one's own resources and valuables with others while feeling a personal reward from their hospitality service.

7. Service of listening. The only true way to learn about other people is by listening. We cannot assume that we always know everything there is to know about a person, place, or event. People do not always have all the information beforehand without really listening. The danger of not listening can at times have some very horrible consequences. Active listening is strongly recommended over basic listening. All Christians involved need to constantly be in a state of listening.

8. Service of sharing the word of life with one another. Sometimes we feel afraid to share what we have learned due to guilt or rejection. In reality, we are the witnesses who need to share all of what we have learned about God through the Scripture, our experiences, and what God has done within our own lives. Example shown here:

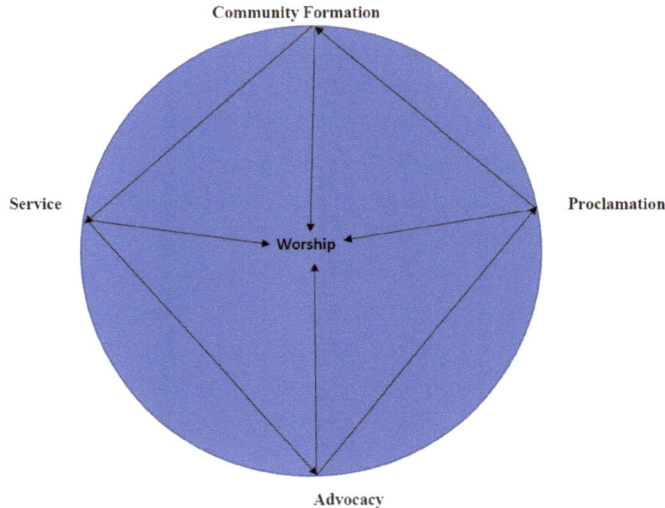

- Service of bearing the burdens of each other. Having compassion for others has to originate by discovering the feeling of our own existence. We need to feel the burdens of other people along with our own to help each other carry on. Jesus tells us to come to Him when we are burdened and He will give us rest. We can do the same for others. A word of caution should be to remember that showing pity and sometimes even too much sympathy can turn people away. Compassion and empathy when appropriate can keep people closer and trusting.[369]

Global Reach

Education has never been classified to one particular culture, country, or race of people; rather, people all over the world have learned and evolved. People have an internal inkling to learn regardless of who they are, where they are, or by what materials may be

---

[369] Marlene Wilson, *How to Mobilize Church Volunteers* (Minneapolis: Augsburg Publishing House, 1983), 107–110.

available to them. The truth is that people using their desire to learn creates more alternatives for other people to be inspired and learn from them. As previous chapters have discussed, education does take on many different forms, technologies, teaching strategies, and patience. Expanding education on a global level may take the most intense work of all.

For the mission to expand globally, one should consider what the mission includes in addition to the educational aspect. Does simply educating a person give them all the knowledge needed to keep Christianity going, or is there more to be considered? A rather deep understanding of these exact questions come from *What Color Is Your Parachute*, which is a research documentary by Richard Nelson Bolles. Bolles explains that there are three separate stages of a mission in addition to the educational part. First, the mission is to always stand in the conscious presence of God, since God is the One to whom the mission is derived. Bolles says, "The Missioner before the Mission should be the ultimate rule." In other words, Christians are to know God, enjoy Him forever, and see His hand in all His works. What a powerful thought to bear in mind while encountering all of God's people.

Second, the mission must be done by what a person can do each second, moment, day, and every step taken. All are called to make the world a better place than could be imagined, and the only true way to accomplish this is by following the guidance of the Holy Spirit. By overcoming fear, challenges, and disbeliefs, the Holy Spirit will never leave the mission's aid nor anyone who is a part of keeping the mission going. Using His leadership into God's mission can create such a strong assurance of success that many people would be truly inspired to follow that same example.

Third, Bolles describes that mission is to fully exercise the talent that all of us are given. Each has a talent or talents that are particular to him or her alone. No one else can duplicate the talent that one particular person has been blessed with. Talent is a gift from God that He wants Christians to delight in using as often and fully as possible. This talent should be used in the place or setting to which you are in whether by choice or not. If a person feels driven to use their talents in another location, then go for it. Remember that the talent we each possess is given for the purposes of God's people for whom He sees are in need most.[370] These three steps certainly require a more in-depth personal thought within ourselves as to what, where, when, why, and how God wants His mission to be done. We can only pray daily while still placing one foot in front of the other moving forward to the best of our own abilities.

Mission Leadership

While reaching out through the globe spreading Christianity's mission whether by participation, motivation, dedication, vocation, any or all of the above, the mission has to begin with a leader. Leadership has been mentioned in other chapters describing what makes a strong leader, what leaders should be aware of, and the challenges they may face; but this time we are going to consider leadership in the Christian mission. The Foundation for Ministry Leadership explains four major areas of focus for providing the best leadership possible along with a couple of thought-provoking questions to consider.

1.   The church is the body of Christ, and through our baptism, we are members of the body of Christ.[371]

Saint Paul reminds all of us that each person within a faith community is called to ministry and is already blessed with gifts for that ministry. By baptism, we are called to our own ministry with our church community; our baptism is our empowerment. All Christians share in the mission of Christ through the Spirit to continue serv-

---

[370] Certificate of Youth Ministries Program, *Skills for Christian Leadership*, July 2005, 4.1–4.2.

[371] Certificate of Youth Ministries Program, *Skills for Christian Leadership*, July 2005, 4.2.

ing the mission. All who share in the ministry also share in Christ's priestly, prophetic, and royal office.

Questions: Do you believe that every person is called to ministry? Blessed with gifts? How do we practice this belief? Do you view ministry as a service? Do you limit or encourage others' gifts?

2.   Individuals and the community are blessed with gifts for ministry.

The Christian ministry is completely gift based. Through the Holy Spirit, the sacraments and the special task involved within the church community keep the mission going. Many are called by the Holy Spirit to serve. Some will answer the call, others will struggle, but there are always ones who will continue on no matter what. In a perfect world, all people would realize that they are called to serve in the mission and to use their gifts for the greater good. People also need to remember that their gifts are accompanied by interests, motivations, styles, values, passions, hopes, dreams, and their own life journey. The gifts are not always recognized until the person focuses enough on their entire life considering all the factors around and how they relate.

Questions: Do you consider every gift a person has? How do you practice gift discernment?

3.   There is an abundance of gifts for ministry.

Finding and discovering the gifts within our own church community can be viewed as more of a mental challenge as opposed to physical. Sometimes the person may not see their own gift, but others will catch on to that gift sooner. Sadly, leaders can be more limited by simply choosing the people that they may think to be in the proper role without recognizing what everyone involved is bringing to the group. Missing gifts or not applying them properly can become a drastic mistake to the leadership position. To fully avoid this mistake and perhaps several others, consider again as number one suggests: we are all the body of Christ; therefore, no one person should be left out. Do not worry if their own gifts have not been recognized; it will happen.

Questions: Do you believe in the abundance of gifts in your church community? Do you only rely on filling positions rather than discerning? William Easum summarizes the abundance gifts by saying, "Ministry is to be delivered any time, any place, by anyone, no matter what."[372] How do you empower people for this type of ministry?

4. Ministry leaders are called to empower and equip individuals, teams, and in the end, the entire community to utilize their gifts for the mission of the Church.

All Christians need to view themselves as servants to church and stewards to their resources. We all can play a huge role in the church's mission by discovering, developing, and utilizing all the gifts our communities bring forth. Christians are always to strive in securing the ministry for now and always. By doing this, Christians continue to pass on the mission to the following generations, allowing the times to evolve but the mission to remain.

Questions: Is equipping your ministry a strong priority? Why or why not? How much time do you spend considering this? How do you empower your teams in ministry? How do you practice empowering and equipping? Most importantly, have you learned to "let go" so the other group members can shine along with the leader?

Perhaps some leaders have considered these four, perhaps not. Although they may seem to be a great deal of questions to bear in mind while leading any type of mission, they certainly cannot be overlooked in importance. A leader for any mission will have more than enough work cut out for them to make completion a possibility. The Christian mission would be no different. Each and every

---

[372] Ibid., 4.4–4.5.

Christian needs to remember that with or without a leader, the mission must still continue on. Christ gave us the perfect model to follow, words to heed, and instructions to be carried out. What more could a person working toward the mission need?

Another Millennium Moving Forward

As of 2000, we have been in another millennium that has already brought about many changes with many more years of change to come. There have already been thousands of traditions, beliefs, histories, and instructions brought over from the last millennium into this one. Stop and consider for a moment just how many incredible events, disasters, and other world-changing events happened in the past one thousand years. Where will the world be in another thousand years? More importantly, where will the world of Christian education be?[373] Will Christians still be needing to teach others about Christ? Will the Bible finally be available everywhere possible? Will there finally be an end to all religious persecution, Christian or not? These are rather loaded questions that could and should prompt action to ensure that the answers will all turn out to be for the greater good and a much brighter future.

For Christian education, does the future require a change in the Christian vision? Is the mission of Jesus still going to be as relevant, or will we move forward in time, making us realize that we are also moving further away from the time that Christ was on earth? Perhaps what He taught then does not apply to now. Or should Christians be more focused on moving closer to the second rather than further from the first? In order for the mission to drive forward in the twenty-first century, we should maintain Christ's truth, which has been

---

[373] James Riley Estep Jr., Jonathan Hyungsoo Kim, Alvin Wallace Kuest, Mark Amos Maddix, and Michael Douglas Barton, *C.E.: The Heritage of Christian Education* (Joplin: College Press Publishing Company, 2003), 16.2.

the foundation of Christian faith for over two thousand years.[374] Jesus was and always will be the teacher of perfection. His truth is above all history, changes, and outcomes that will one day come. The Christian educational mission will continue to be challenged through society, culture, technology, and new methodologies that will likely arise; but remembering the foundational truth keeps the Christian education, message, and mission forever moving on.

What about the Christian education processes already in place? In terms of educational context, the new millennium brings about several more opportunities for improvement and change for the direction ministry. The present time has brought about two possible issues that are near certain to create more change in the mission where the educational context is becoming blurred. The first area that will need growing Christian attention is multiculturalism. Consider in today's American land how many people are presently living there who are from other countries. Immigration has grown so much that the American culture may not be as truly American as it was in the past.[375] For Christianity, there has become such a blending of other cultures, ethnicities, and religions that teaching Christianity might be challenged in certain places. In schools, children from various backgrounds might struggle to learn about another faith to which could very well be alien to. This places more effort on the part of the teacher to make sure that there is little to no confusion making the Christian education effective.

On the flip side, Christianity should be ready and welcoming should the people not of American descent wish to learn more about the Christian faith, seeking a fuller understanding of what exactly makes up Christianity. Christianity has not had to deal with as much cultural change occurring at one time as it may be in present-day America. Certain reevaluations and redirections may need to be visited more often. Although this task may seem like a large one, it will not be impossible. Keeping the faith, the focus, and the future open for whoever may walk in the door will guarantee the continuance

---

[374] Ibid., 16.2.
[375] Ibid., 16.4.

of Christian education. The ultimate goal is coming together for all God's people to experience His love as a whole.

The second issue facing Christian education, which has also been the ongoing point of this chapter is globalism. The first issue was taking on multiculturalism by relearning how to keep Christian education strong in teaching those from different backgrounds. In globalism, Christianity has the opportunity to learn from the other cultures too. Many places in the world besides America are blending in various cultures, but there are still places that do not allow other people inside who do not share their same beliefs. If Christianity relies heavily on reaching out into the world, then the learning cannot be limited or restricted.[376] Going into places where the Christian faith may not be welcomed could potentially be dangerous, but not impossible. Educational learning is branching out now more than it ever has in the past. Whether the reason is technology, more resources, or personal motivation, Christian education reaching a global scale is truly commendable. Within Christianity, the Catholic Church is the universal church considering the Catholic Mass is celebrated in the manner all over the world; this is a remarkable example to the Christian faith that global reach is not only possible but achievable in even the most remote places. With this being pointed out, the necessity of Christian collaboration will also be a factor in encouraging the mission to continue on strong. There is always strength in numbers, and Jesus did explain that when two or more are gathered in His name, He is always there.

While the millennium moves on each day, the voices of Christian people will continue to carry on also. People from various backgrounds may wish to offer suggestions and ideas using their own cultural origins to assist in the education process. Likewise, the ones who are already taking on the role of Christian educators need to be aware that they are not alone. Regardless of who may be present within a particular church community, the voices of those wishing to

---

[376] James Riley Estep Jr., Jonathan Hyungsoo Kim, Alvin Wallace Kuest, Mark Amos Maddix, and Michael Douglas Barton, *C.E.: The Heritage of Christian Education* (Joplin: College Press Publishing Company, 2003), 16.6–7.

move forward have to be recognized.[377] Local church communities, clergy, and geographical locations will become hazy as the lines separating them might gradually be more open to those wanting the education of Christianity. These voices are a chance at progress looking forward into where the church's direction could and should be heading. Being a voice for the voiceless is never wrong. Opportunities can pop up from anywhere or anyone. Christian education must always stand steadfast in the challenges that this new millennium may bring while keeping the promise of leading God in the direction He has chosen for us.

Conclusion

For over ten chapters, the world of Christian education has been explored on several different levels over a wide range of time, technology, opinions, and worldviews. Now, a brief recap and revisit to each chapter will properly conclude our exploration into Christian education. Chapter 1 explained the very basic statements with a few details on what Christian education is on a surface level while giving an introduction of what all the chapters would cover by a brief description. It also provided a glimpse of the purpose of realizing and understanding the impact Christian education has in our world as a whole.

Chapter 2 covered an in-depth look at the history of Christian education. The history broke apart "Christian" and "education" dating back to various known origins or where and how each began. For example, what is the difference between education and Christian education? One might easily argue that education by itself would date back way before Christian education even became known. People have had to learn basic survival, family life, and working skills simply to get by; but people also knew of the Christian promise even centuries before Christ was on earth. Taking up when Christ was on earth, noted as AD 0, AD 0–1600 will be the first half or era dis-

---

[377] Ibid., 16.10.

cussed in terms of education and Christian education. Naturally, the remainder of the chapter looked into AD 1600 through our present day. The past two thousand plus years certainly will cover many historical events, and it would be nearly impossible to list all of them, but pinpointing what specifically led to the greatest educational and Christian educational occurrences is the goal.

Chapter 3 explored Christian education as philosophy. The history lesson from chapter 2 opened up more questions to be asked regarding how Christian education continues to be as prevalent as it is. Many times philosophical questions are more answered by personal belief as opposed to cold hard facts, but does that make it any less logical? Throughout history, there have been several various philosophers who openly asked the deeper questions, which many people were not and may still not be eager to address. Such is true with Christian education.

The goal of chapter 3 was not to ask the challenging and somewhat annoying questions such as "Could God make a rock so big that He could not move it?" No, the purpose was seeing what various tests, measurements, factors, and results have come up. What have we learned from these results? How have tests and measurements been used or perhaps not used? What factors have been included with the development or cessation of Christian education? The most significant factor of this chapter is discovering the use of technology. Today our world is every day changing with technological advances that it is oftentimes rather difficult to keep up with. However, technology was not always an influence on the education system as it is now. Long before computers, phones, and iPads, most of education was simply done by word of mouth. Listening. Sometimes, especially here in America, we easily forget that other places within our world still learn best by word of mouth. Technology is not available for educational purposes in third-world countries and sometimes at our own back door. Different circumstances, either with or without technology, does not necessarily hinder the learning process. Despite worldwide-reaching technology, Christian education may not even be known in all parts of the world yet. What can and should be done about this? Who is responsible for making sure that Christian education is where it needs to be?

Chapter 4 was probably the most intense chapter yet. Christ as the educator. Christianity, defined as "followers of Christ," is referred back to Jesus Christ of the New Testament in the Bible. The Bible is also known as the Sacred Scriptures. Christianity believes the Scriptures to be divinely inspired by God as the absolute truth. Since Christians are the followers of Christ, Jesus would be the absolute educator. Christian education strives to model Jesus and follow His example to the best of our abilities. Needless to say, no one living today was present two thousand years ago while Jesus walked the earth, so Christians rely and believe firmly in the words of the Scripture as resource, guide, and reassurance for the human mission.

The first four books of the New Testament—Matthew, Mark, Luke, and John—are called the gospels. The gospels contain the stories and truth of Jesus's life while He was on earth. During this time, His ministry and the Christian mission began. Jesus is the educator! Jesus gave His life to the people, His followers. Therefore, Christians always view Jesus as the model of leadership. Clergy today strive to follow Jesus's example of leading people to and through their faith. Being a leader requires having followers who are open and willing to follow. Giving a follower's life to the leader is being a disciple just as Jesus's followers were in His time. Discipleship takes on an earthly job in itself by making Jesus's mission, the Christian mission goal known as Scripture instructs.

Chapter 4 finished with another aspect of Jesus as the perfect model in terms of human morality. The education of morality inside and outside of the Christian umbrella is not always an easy topic to cover. The morality of heavier topics including abortion, capital punishment, euthanasia, and homosexuality is vastly viewed in complete opposites by people, especially today. Yet the Scripture and Jesus do address these topics. Granted these topics were not as prevalent as they are today, which easily allows the context to be construed. Regardless, the truth of what is right and what is wrong has been and will always be an ongoing debate.

Chapter 5 looked over the various denominational faiths included within the Christianity realm and their educational emphasis. The biggest and most recognized Christian faith is Catholicism. Catholicism is known as the universal church because in every Catholic church across the world, the exact same service or Mass will be celebrated. Catholicism does have its own separations too, such as traditional, Greek Orthodox, and the New American, just to name a few. Although the Mass liturgy maybe the same, the faith practices could differ greatly.

The next major Christian faith realm is Protestantism. The Protestant Christians include many different faiths, again all the same core beliefs but very different worship styles. Some of these include Baptist, Methodist, Lutheran, Episcopal, and Presbyterian. These branches of Christianity are known as transplanted Protestant faiths or more Native American based. As opposed to the transplanted Protestant faiths are the American faiths or American based. Native American includes Latter-Day Saints, Seventh-Day Adventists, Pentecostal, and the newer faith of Scientology.

Chapter 5's exploration of the Christian denominations' emphasis on education concluded by a brief look at the remaining faiths within Christianity that are nondenominational or not under a specific title heading. Nondenominational Christians take the gospel scriptures extremely literal, desperately trying to live their lives to the near perfection as Jesus did.

Chapter 6 visited Christian education in culture. Culture is another vast spectrum that extends all over the globe. For starters, this chapter began locally looking into the American culture and even closer in the Midwest. It is rather surprising how different culture can be simply going into the next city without leaving the same state. Culturally differences within education are going to differ as well. Just as in the previous while discussing the denominational differences, culture can and does impact worship values too.

Extending Christian education globally is a really difficult task; however, a strong understanding of cultural differences can make the global outreach achievable. Global outreach should be a job for all Christians, but more often Christian missionaries make taking Christian education their sole purpose. It is not difficult to find places in our world that have never even seen or heard anything related to Christianity! In various third-world countries, people are struggling for basic survival by lacking food and clean water. When missionaries visit these locations, their mission has an even greater purpose—bringing hope.

Also within chapter 6, in culture, it is important to remember that educational roles can be vastly different but equally significant. For example, Catholicism especially places a huge emphasis on men being in clergy with the leadership role, while some Protestant churches welcome women clergy. Likewise, many school systems are dominated by women teachers rather than men. In the same manner, the age of educators can make a difference. Again for certain Protestant faiths, the older members of the church are the leaders and decision-makers. Other faiths encourage youth ministries for the goal of youth taking on leadership roles within the church. Is education influenced by men, women, young, or older teachers?

Chapter 7 explored education within the home. Homelife plays a huge role in the education of individuals especially for children. The homelife discussion revisited these questions. What kind of family background does this learner come from? Is there a religious base in the household? How important is a Christian education to all the members within the house? Do they know? Who decides? In some cases, a family may be very structured into attending church and school within a specific denomination that can date back for generations. Other families may be newer to Christian education perhaps learning through a new family member in marriage or a better school choice.

When a decision is made regarding what is best for the family, the most important element will be making a commitment. The commitment must be solid through both parents as well as for the child or children. Families of split religious choices can usually place a huge strain on what will happen with the children. Regardless of the circumstances, religious education must be reinforced. Positive reinforcement results in a happier and healthier relationship for the family's homelife. Children asking questions about wanting to learn more about their faith and other faiths should be addressed and welcomed. Perhaps this can become a learning experience for the entire family to evolve.

Homelife education may not always be the easiest choice to make. It is quite common for parents to defer their child's education not only within school but also within the religious community. Most often a family's religious choice is greatly influenced by the parents' upbringing or perhaps a new choice made by the marriage. It is rather common for a spouse to change denominations or faith practices to become the same as the new spouse, but again it can also be a joint decision for beginning their lives together. What happens when a child reaches an age to make their own decisions? The adult age is eighteen; but many times children, especially teenagers, find church to be boring or not "cool." When is he or she allowed to make another choice? Why is it so difficult for some families to comprehend?

Homelife plays a huge role where education is concerned. How does this fit in with school education? Homeschooling. Many parents have decided and are deciding to homeschool their children. Education in the home is more private and personal to the child's learning ability. Along with regular education, parents will also be teaching religious education especially if the family is already committed to a religious affiliation. Does learning about Christian education in the home change the mission? Or does Christian education in the home enhance the mission more so than school learning?

Discussing education in schools by whether public, private, or homeschooling still required one more component: exploring the various age levels. In America, children are usually in school from age five to eighteen. Many psychologists have theorized and explained that a child's mind contains and grows with years of education. Each student is going to learn and mature at their own pace. For example, it does not make sense for a sixteen-year-old to be learning the alphabet, a system they have known for many years. Christian education is no different. Many simple Bible stories are told to children at young ages; but as they grow and mature within their faith, more questions will arise, causing curiosity and possibly some doubts. How much of a factor does age play?

Chapter 8 discovered educational differences and similarities within schools. The main question is the difference between public and private schools. Religious education is certainly much more emphasized with private schools considering many of them are already affiliated with a religious denomination. Public schools are on restriction as to how much or little teachers are allowed to educate religiously, but this does not stop curious minds from wanting to know. In this case, several churches have available classes to accommodate students who want to learn more that are not taught in public school.

Chapter 9 analyzed Christian education as a community effort. Recapping from chapters 7 and 8, Christian education can be very strong within the home, church, and school life; but what about the everyday community? Consider asking another person, "Are your religious practices influenced by church, school, family, or community?" A person might look puzzled. Many communities are so vastly different in ages, races, and cultures that perhaps it is not as simple to identify. On the other hand, one may be shocked to know there is more in common within the community than there is awareness.

Some communities regularly make an open effort to host gatherings, game nights, or dinners to welcome people and make the community closer. These events are necessary for community involvement to grow. Simply inviting a friend, neighbor, or family member to attend a frequent public event can really influence community. The same is especially true for a religious community. It is not uncommon to find a church smack in the middle of a residential neighborhood. Churches are to be welcoming of all people, so what better place for a community gathering to also be a religious education opportunity?

Perhaps the most tedious and even dangerous aspect of community involvement are moral issues. Christian education does include discussing morality just as Jesus did. Over the years, morality has become a major dilemma in church and state issues. In Christian education, such topics as abortion, euthanasia, capital punishment, and homosexuality may be taught as wrong; but the state and even society are fully supportive. Many debates, political campaigns, meetings, riots, and even smaller civil wars have been created by people expressing strong beliefs by either supporting or denying such issues. Humanity has a long way to go.

Finally, chapter 10 has detailed what the future holds for Christian education. What does Christianity have set for future goals? What would families like to see happen? How are Christian educational goals being achieved? Does Christianity have the capability to reach the entire globe? What will this new millennium bring? Mission statements and visions are wonderful to have in place wherever Christian education can be found, but are educators doing enough to make those statements real? What obstacles are hindering the learning process? Who is making the decisions and dedication to ensure Christian education for generations to come?

To answer the previous questions, Christians must take on dedication, participation, service, and faith. The dedication of Jesus's followers and the participation of the community together can make a huge difference. The increasing need for Christian education to be strengthened and reinforced is what keeps Christianity going. Focusing on not only the local needs, but also the needs of those across the world who desire to learn needs to be met. By striving to achieve the ultimate goal of extending Jesus's mission to all His followers, Christians ensure that the future will be the brightest and strongest it can possibly be. Keeping the Christian faith strong and burning within Christian hearts is all the encouragement needed to reach the mission goal.

A long journey is said to begin with one step. Perhaps a first step could be self-examination. Mother Teresa rather eloquently said,

> Open your hearts to the love God instills in them. God loves you tenderly. What He gives you is not to be kept under lock and key, but to be shared. The more you save, the less you will be able to give. The less you have, the more you will know how to share. Let us ask God, when it

comes time to ask Him for something, to help us to be generous.[378]

Many people often viewed Mother Teresa's life to be a true inspiration for what giving yourself to the well-being of others was truly all about. Although she never wanted or would willingly receive credit for any of her works, she never stopped serving until her dying day. Inspiration like that is not found every day, but those who do continue on with the Christian mission each and every day of their lives are showing more dedication and promise than they may realize. Like Mother Teresa, it may not be about the reward or credit, but more about seeing Christ in other people when the world may not see them at all. The education of the Christian faith began strong, faced many obstacles, suffered many losses/triumphs, and still continues going forward today. What a rewarding feeling that is for all Christianity!

---

[378] Jose Luiz Gonzalez-Balado, *Mother Teresa in My Own Words* (New York: Gramercy Books, 1997), 18.

AUTHOR'S NOTE

I hope you have found my research, knowledge, and exploration of Christian education to be helpful and insightful. The possibilities out there are endless in how, what, when, with whom, or where Christian education may travel next. So to all my readers, I end with this thought: May all those who *ask* for Christian education be *given* the best education. May all those who *seek* for Christian education *find* the teachers, educators, knowledge, and strength to meet their needs. And may all those who *knock* on the Christian education door have that door *opened* wide to a world of possibilities, promises, communities, missions, and service forevermore.

REFERENCES

Backman, Milton V. *Christian Churches of America: Origins and Beliefs*. Provo: Brigham Young University Press, 1976.

Berger, Eugenia Hepworth. *Parents As Partners in Education: The School and Home Working Together*. Columbus: Merrill Publishing Company, 1987.

Berry, Carmen Renee. *The Unauthorized Guide to Choosing a Church*. Grand Rapids: Brazos Press, 2003.

Bingham, Jane. *Atlas of World Faiths: Christianity*. West Mankato: Smart Apple Media, 2008.

Castle, E. B. *Moral Education in Christian Times*. London: Unwin Brothers Limited, 1958.

Certificate of Youth Ministries Program. *Foundations for Ministry Leadership*. July 2006.

Certificate of Youth Ministries Program. *Skills for Christian Leadership*. July 2005.

Clark, Lynn. *The Parent App: Understanding Families in the Digital Age*. New York: Oxford University Press, 2013.

Covey, Sean. *The 7 Habits of Highly Effective Teens,* New York: Fireside Rockefeller Center, 1998.

Cox, Edwin. *Sixth Form Religion: A Report Sponsored by the Christian Education Movement*. London: Billing and Sons Limited, 1967.

Curran, Charles E. *A New Look at Christian Morality*. Notre Dame: Fides Publishers Inc., 1968.

Dawson, Christopher. *The Historic Reality of Christian Culture: A Way to the Renewal of Human Life*. New York: Harper & Brothers Publishers, 1960.

Dean, Kendra, and Ron Foster. *The Godbearing Life: The Art of Soul Tending for Youth Ministry*. Nashville: The Upper Room Books, 1998.

Eavey, C. B. *History of Christian Education*. Chicago: Moody Press, 1964.

English, Fenwick W., Larry E. Frase, and Joanne M. Arhar. *Leading into the 21ˢᵗ Century*. Newbury Park: Corwin Press Inc., 1992.

Estep Jr., James Riley, Jonathan Hyungsoo Kim, Alvin Wallace Kuest, Mark Amos Maddix, and Michael Douglas Barton. *CE: The Heritage of Christian Education*. Joplin: College Press Publishing Company, 2003.

Farmer, W. R., C. F. D. Moule, and R. R. Niebuhr. *Christian History and Interpretation: Studies Presented to John Knox*. Cambridge: University Press, 1967.

Futuyma, Douglas. *Evolutionary Biology*. Boston: Beacon Press, 1996.

Gaddy, Barbara B., T. William Hall, and Robert J. Marzano. *School Wars: Resolving Our Conflicts over Religion and Values*. San Francisco: Jossey-Bass Publishers, 1996.

Gonzalez-Balado, Jose Luiz. *Mother Teresa in My Own Words*. New York: Gramercy Books, 1997.

Hill, Peter C., and Ralph W. Hood. *Measures of Religiosity*. Birmingham: Religious Education Press, 1999.

Hodge, A. A. *Popular Lectures on Theological Themes*. Philadelphia: Presbyterian Board of Education, 1887.

Howland, Courtney W. *Religious Fundamentalisms and the Human Rights of Women*. New York: St. Martin's Press, 1990.

Irvin, Dale T., and Scott W. Sunquist. *History of the World Christian Movement*. Maryknoll: Orbis Books, 1970.

Jersild, Paul T., and Dale A. Johnson. *Moral Issues and Christian Response*. New York: Holt, Rinehart, and Winston Inc., 1988.

Keyes, G. L. *Christian Faith and the Interpretation of History*. Lincoln: University of Nebraska Press, 1966.

Kouzes, James, and Barry Posner. *The Leadership Challenge*. San Francisco: Jossey-Bass, 2002.

Latourette, Kenneth Scott. *A History of Christianity*. New York: Harper and Brothers Publishers, 1953.

Levin, Henry M. *Privatizing Education: Can the Marketplace Deliver Choice, Efficiency, Equity, and Social Cohesion.* Cambridge: Westview Press, 2001.

Lieberman, Myron. *Public Education: An Autopsy.* Cambridge: Harvard University Press, 1993.

Matzke, Nicholas J., and Paul R. Gross. *Analyzing Critical Analysis: The Fallback Antievolutionist Strategy.* Boston: Beacon Press, 2006.

McNeill, John Thomas, Matthew Spinka, and Harold R. Willoughby. *Environmental Factors in Christian History.* London: Kennikat Press, 1939.

Meyers, David G. *Psychology.* 5th ed. New York: Worth Publishers, 1998.

Noddings, Nel. *Education and Democracy in the 21st Century.* New York: Teachers College Press, 2013.

Pazmino, Robert W. *God Our Teacher: Theological Basics of Christian Education.* Grand Rapids: Baker Academic, 2001.

Pearson, Joanne, Richard H. Roberts, and Geoffrey Samuel. Nature Religion Today: Paganism in the Modern World. Edinburgh: Edinburgh University Press, 1998.

Queen, Edward L., Stephen R. Prothero, and Gardiner H. Shattuck. Encyclopedia of American Religious History. New York: InfoBase Publishing, 2012.

Rawson, Beryl. *A Companion to Families in the Greek and Roman Worlds.* Chichester: Wiley-Blackwell Publication, 2011.

Rhodes, John. "An American Tradition: The Religious Persecution of Native Americans." *Montana Law Review* 52, 1991.

Schultz, Kevin M., and Paul Harvey. "Everywhere and Nowhere: Recent Trends in American Religious History and Historiography." *Journal of the American Academy of Religion* 78, no. 1 (March 2010).

Seymour, Jack L., and Donald E. Miller. *Theological Approaches to Christian Education.* Nashville: Abingdon Press, 1990.

The Holy Bible. New International Version. Grand Rapids: Zondervan Publishing. 2002.

Tichy, Noel M. *The Cycle of Leadership: How Great Leaders Teach their Companies to Win*. New York: HarperCollins Publishers, 2002.

Tooley, James. *The Global Education Industry: Lessons from Private Education in Developing Countries*. London: Institute of Economic Affairs, 1999.

Torr, James D. *How Does Religion Influence Politics?* Farmington Hills: Greenhaven Press, 2006.

Treadgold, Donald W. *A History of Christianity*. New York: Athens Printing Company, 1979.

Walvoord, John, and Roy B. Zuck. *The Bible Knowledge Commentary: An Exposition of the Scriptures*. Wheaton: Victor Books, 1993.

Webb, Jeffrey B. *The Complete Idiot's Guide to Christianity*. New York: Penguin Group Inc., 2004.

Wilhoit, James C., and John M. Dettoni. *Nurture That Is Christian: Developmental Perspectives on Christian Education*. Wheaton: Victor Books Inc., 1995.

Wilson, Marlene. *How to Mobilize Church Volunteers*. Minneapolis: Augsburg Publishing House, 1983.

Wood, Herbert G. *Christianity and the Nature of History*. Cambridge: University Press, 1934.

Zook, Noah, and Samuel L. Yoder. Berne, Indiana, Old Order Amish Settlement. Berne: Amish Newsletter, 2009.

ABOUT THE AUTHOR

Dr. Clara J. Ushman is a religious educator, author, and spiritual enthusiast; she's also a huge animal lover. She comes from a background of growing up in a split-religion family, thus beginning her journey into the Christian education dynamic. Learning from two different Christian faiths was an early inspiration to explore the many aspects included under the Christian education umbrella. Throughout years of study and experience, Dr. Ushman continues to learn, develop, and encourage Christians of all faith backgrounds to maintain our everyday hard work for future generations to carry out Christ's ministry.

www.ingramcontent.com/pod-product-compliance
Lightning Source LLC
Chambersburg PA
CBHW051508120626
46551CB00012B/820